D1744901

Supercharge MFC

GUI Customization with Pseudo-Multiple Inheritance

Jeffrey Scott Galbraith

R&D Books
Lawrence, Kansas 66046

R&D Books
Miller Freeman, Inc.
1601 W. 23rd Street, Suite 200
Lawrence, KS 66046
USA

Cover art created by Robert Ward.

Distributed in the U.S. and Canada by:
Publishers Group West
P.O. Box 8843
Emeryville, CA 94662
ISBN: 0-87930-569-X

 Miller Freeman
A United News & Media publication

The mediocre teacher tells.
The good teacher explains.
The superior teacher demonstrates.
The great teacher inspires.
– William Ward

This book is dedicated to
my family; especially to my wife,
for whom without her perseverance,
sacrifice, and most of all,
endless patience,
this book would have remained
a dream.

Table of Contents

Introduction

Welcome

Welcome to *Supercharge MFC – GUI Customization with Pseudo-Multiple Inheritance*. Although the title of this book suggests certain aspects that will be covered in the forthcoming chapters, the main thrust of the book really goes much further than this. Here, let me explain. In working with the MFC classes, I noticed a certain deficiency that has made MFC difficult and a royal pain to work with at times. I am sure you have enjoyed the same wonderful experiences. One of my main gripes is having two similar classes in MFC and needing to extend both. Take, for example, `CTreeCtrl` and `CTreeView`. Normally, you would create your extension classes, perhaps calling them `CTreeCtrlEx` and `CTreeViewEx`. You proceed to work on one of them until you have what you want, then copy the same code to the other class extension. This type of programming goes against the very nature of reuse in Object-Oriented programming. If you have ever had to deal with this, I am sure that later, when you updated one, you forgot to update the other. Ouch! That can sure hurt in more ways than one. In fact, perhaps it could even cost you your job. Unlikely, but not improbable.

So, you might ask, just what exactly can we do about this problem? Is there a solution? The answer is a resounding yes! The true answer is pretty simple — *subclassing*. A lot of programmers use subclassing in Windows, but few take it to the depths needed to extract the full power of its usefulness. All right, some of you know subclassing, but some of you are asking yourself, "What the heck is he talking about?" Briefly, *subclassing* is a technique that allows an application to intercept and process messages sent or posted to a particular window before the window has a chance to process them. This allows you to change the default behavior of a window. OK, some of you knew that, but did you know that through subclassing techniques you could write a subclass procedure that works with both `CTreeCtrl` and `CTreeView`? Well, I see that some more hands have gone down in my virtual audience. Hopefully, I have peaked the interest of more than a few of you. Trust me, this is good stuff.

This book you are now holding in your hands has an MFC subclassing extension in it, with all the source and neat examples on the accompanying CD. I am going to show you what it's all about, but that comes in section two of this book. The other two sections also have their merit. The first section is what I call *Building Blocks,* the second section is *Subclassers,* and the third is *Extensions.* Each section builds upon the previous section. The concept for this book was to create a framework extension that complements MFC, supports it when it limps, and goes to areas where MFC fears to tread. That's a tall order, but this book is an accumulation of several years of hard and dedicated work to extend the Windows UI using MFC. Your use of the code in this book will provide you definite benefits by giving you some interesting and powerful features not found in regular Windows products. The chapters in this book contain innovative ways of getting the desired results. By studying the code associated with each of the chapters, you should be able to come to an understanding of how easy it is to extend not only MFC, but other class libraries as well.

The class library that will be presented is by no means complete. However, the same can be said for MFC. In fact, I know of no class libraries that can be called complete — not while technologies change as fast as they do today. The doors are left open to extend both libraries, but you will find that what I present will be much easier to extend. In fact, there are over 15 classes and 40 independent functions that make up the foundation of this extension framework. It's been created with extensibility in mind which will make it just that much easier to work with for your future, as well as existing, projects.

I also hope that you, the reader of this book, will get just as excited about the new methodology presented here in this book as I am. The class library presented herein breathes new life into MFC. Using advanced subclassing and other techniques (like pseudo-multiple-inheritance), this new class library allows you to intercept messages before MFC sees them. You can then act upon that message, or let it pass through to MFC. Alternatively, you can act on it and still let MFC react to it, or act upon it after MFC. The choice is yours. You will learn through the sample programs when to let MFC take control and do the dirty work and when you should process the message. In the end, you'll also learn new ways of accomplishing things that some people have told me outright were impossible. Well, a challenge is a challenge and I am always one to pick up the gauntlet.

Who Should Read This Book

The primary target audience of this book is intended to be intermediate to advanced MFC programmers. This means you should already be familiar with writing Windows code with C++ and have an understanding of how MFC works. This book is not a tutorial on MFC, nor does it explain certain MFC aspects or architecture. If you're a programmer who falls into this category, and would like to be able to extend MFC that one step further, then this book is for you.

What You Need to Use This Book

You, of course, will need a PC, preferably a 486 100MHz or higher. You will also need Microsoft's Visual C++ 5.0/6.0, Windows 95/98 or Windows NT 4.0/2000. You will also need a CD-ROM drive if you would like to be able to access the CD that accompanies this book. If you install all of the code and samples on the CD, you will need about 100 Mb of hard drive space available. You will also need the latest controls from Microsoft. To be able to use all of the features presented, you will need the latest common control for your operating system. For best results, you should have the latest version of Internet Explorer so that you have the latest technologies installed. On the CD, you will also find a helpful API presented in Microsoft's HTML Help format. If you have installed Windows 98, Windows 2000 (NT 5.0), or Internet Explorer 4.01 (or greater), then you already have the necessary files to run this file. If not, then you can pick up the files needed from Microsoft's website.

Legal Considerations, Copyrights, and Trademarks

There are no warranties, expressed or implied, about the programming code or samples contained in this book (or on the CD-ROM), that they are free from errors, or will meet your particular requirements. Do not use this code where you feel coding errors could result in injury to a person or loss of property. Any use of the materials contained herein is entirely at your own risk and is meant to be educational only. The author and publisher disclaim any and all liability for direct or consequential damages resulting in your use of the information provided in this book and any accompanying materials.

The programming code in this book and accompanying materials is copyrighted. Permission is granted, by the author, for you to use, copy, and distribute this code and software for any purpose as long as it has substantially increased the value of your product and does not consist of more than fifty percent of your application. You may not distribute or sell this code and/or software as a single entity, for financial gain. In other words, you may not sell this source by itself, either in code or in compiled form without explicit written permission by the author. The code and software contained in this book is for personal use, either by an individual or corporation. It may not be incorporated into a product where customers or end users will be able to programmatically access the code without explicit written permission by the author. You also may not use this code or software to compete against this book or any distribution of the code in this book. In other words, you may not publish, in any form, the code or software in this book without explicit written permission from the author. In addition, you will make your best attempt to notify the author (see Contacting the Author) of any bug fixes or additions you have made to the code so that this book can be updated from time to time. Also, you may not claim the code or software as your own and must leave any copyright notices intact in each individual file.

Please respect any third party copyrights, trademarks, or other protected materials accompanying this book. All copyrights and trademarks mentioned in this book belong to their respective holders.

Contacting the Author

The author can be reached by e-mail at xendra@bigfoot.com or on my website at http://www.xendra.com.

About the Code and Samples

Everything in this book has been written and tested on Windows 95 and Windows NT 4.0, with Visual C++ 5.0 and Visual C++ 6.0. No other platforms or compilers have been thoroughly tested with the code and samples included with this book.

You will find an HTML Help file named XSEL.CHM on the CD. This is a very useful reference when you do not have the book around. This help file will be periodically updated and can be downloaded from the author's website.

The R&D Books' Web Site

If you would like to learn more about R&D Books, please visit their website at http://www.rdbooks.com.

Errors

Every attempt has been made to ensure this book is accurate. If there is part of the book that is difficult to understand, or if you find a genuine error, please check the errata sheet for this book at http://www.xendra.com website.

If the answer to your problem still cannot be found, then please take the time to let us know the problem. We'll do our best to correct the problem and add it to the errata sheet for others to see. You can submit error corrections at http://www.xendra.com/books/errors.htm. You will be able to find the latest errata at http://www.xendra.com/books/errata.htm.

What's Covered — A Chapter by Chapter Overview

Chapter 1: Getting Started

In the Getting Started chapter, I'll walk you through some important strategies in extending MFC. I'll discuss the goal we want to accomplish and give some conclusions of how we'll meet that goal. I'll also present the styles used to design the code in this book. Then, we'll begin to create the foundation for the software that will be implemented in later chapters.

Chapter 2: The DIB API

MFC is a thin wrapper around the Windows 32-bit SDK. Sometimes, to extend MFC, we have to write some API functions and then wrap them as well. This chapter explores the creation of a DIB API. In the following chapter, we'll wrap this API into a class. This code becomes one of our leading foundations for what we want to accomplish with this extension framework.

Chapter 3: Extending the `CBitmap` Class

This chapter extends the MFC `CBitmap` class with the derived `CXSBitmap` class. We'll learn how to perform transparent bitmap painting, automatic tiling, serialization, and a whole lot more. This class also encapsulates the DIB API presented in the previous chapter.

Chapter 4: Super Subclassing

If you have ever tried multiple inheritance with MFC, you know how difficult it is. In fact, in most cases, it just can't be done. This has given programmers little choice when it comes to extending MFC functionality. Wouldn't you like to write a class that can be used with multiple MFC objects without deriving every time for each MFC class? For instance, say you want to extend `CTreeCtrl`, but you also want the same functionality for `CTreeView`? In the past, that meant deriving two separate classes, one for `CTreeCtrl` and one for `CTreeView`, with identical code. Maintaining two sets of identical code presents its own problems. The `CXSSubWndCtrl` in this chapter shows you how to circumvent this problem by writing code that can be used with multiple MFC and Windows objects through subclassing. The `CXSSubWndCtrl` will become our backbone processing for all windows handling. The methodology used here is significantly easier than that of MFC, but strangely enough, it works hand-in-hand with MFC. If you want MFC to do the work, let the message pass through; otherwise, handle it. You can also choose to handle the message and still have MFC process it. If you're thinking, "Oh right, I've subclassed before...", all I can say is, "You ain't seen nothin' yet!"

Chapter 5: Handling Your Own Message Reflection

To use `CXSSubWndCtrl` as the backbone of our message processing, we need a way to handle message notification. Strangely enough, although Windows looks object-oriented, it is not. Windows does not understand the concept of having a C++ class wrap controls. Windows' methodology is to have a main message handler for each main window. Therefore, when a child window receives user input, that control sends a message to the parent. In C++, we don't need messages sent to the parent when our wrapper can handle the message itself. Some way needs to be created to have the message sent back to the C++ wrapper. This process is called *message reflection*. MFC implements message reflection, but it gets complicated and, in some cases, difficult to use. This chapter creates a class handler for message reflection that is simplistic in nature, but powerful and practical for our purposes.

Chapter 6: Roll Your Own Message Handler

Now that we have a subclass control and a class for handling message reflection, we want to create a class that makes programming even easier where Windows messages are concerned. In Chapter 5, we learned how to create a subclass handler. Yet, each time you use this class, you will have to write your own window procedure. This chapter creates a generic message handler that can be used with any Windows window. All member functions based on messages are made virtual. If you want to handle a particular message, just add the proper virtual function to your derived class. There's no need to mess around with complicated message maps the way MFC does.

Chapter 7: Creating a Background Control

A background control is a handler that controls the way the background is displayed to the user. Typically, the background control is attached to a visible HWND. It then displays a different background depending on whether the HWND has focus/activation or loses focus/activation. This chapter builds on the previous chapters to build the CXSBgCtrl class. It's your first glimpse of how easy it is to use and the power of our MFC extension code created in the previous chapters.

Chapter 8: Creating a Caption Control

Have you ever wanted to give your captions a different look? How about a bright red caption when displaying an error window? Or how about that Office 95 look-and-feel with a color gradient in the caption area? Hey, how about some bitmapped image in the caption area? The CXSCaption class presented in this chapter will answer all these questions and provide this functionality.

Appendix A — Sample: API and Class Reference

This appendix (included as an HTML file on the CD-ROM) provides a quick reference guide to all the code discussed in this book. Here we show a sample of the materials you'll find there as well as a complete listing of the classes.

Appendix B: Bibliography

In this appendix, you will find references to information used that helped me in creating the software for this book. These include articles, books, and Knowledge Base items. You may want to look up some information yourself if you need further information on a subject.

Section I

Building Blocks

Chapter 1

Getting Started

About the Source

The source included in this book comprises a complete and functional MFC framework extension library. This chapter explains how to set up your environment so you can start using the library right away. I'll talk about some of the conventions I used to create the source and explain some of the miscellaneous functions that we'll use in the chapters ahead.

Conventions

My wife and I have a web site at `http://www.xendra.com` for Xendra Software. You will see that all of the API source functions are prefixed with `XS`, which stands for Xendra Software. All classes are prefixed with `CXS`, where the `C` stands for class. This notation is generally an MFC standard.

For the API functions, the structure of a function name is `XS<Ownership>_<FunctionName>`. For example, the function that creates a palette from a DIB (Device Independent Bitmap) is named `XSDib_CreatePalette`. This structure makes the source function calls very readable and identifies ownership. Ownership is the function of type (e.g. `XSDib_CreatePalette` is owned by the DIB API). In the C++ classes, a virtual function begins with Do, as in DoPaint. If the function is in response to a Windows message, the member function name begins with On, as in OnEraseBkgnd. All On<Name> functions are also virtual. This makes the code more readable and helps programmers to determine the proper virtual function overrides when deriving their own classes.

There are a few other things I do to help make the code more readable. Macro names, set up by the #define statement, are usually all uppercase. If macro names are mixed case, they have a mac prefix (i.e., mac<Name>). For instance, the DIB API uses the macro macDibHeaderMarker to verify whether the DIB has the bitmap marker..

As is customary with MFC, class member variables follow the structure m_<{type}Name>. However, variables that have global scope follow the structure g_<{type}Name>. Global variables that are static to the file in which they live follow the structure gs_<{type}Name>.

There are a few other nomenclatures, but you now have a sense of what I do and why I do it. Some of the styles I use are unique, while others are borrowed from MFC. I have worked with many programmers over the years and almost every programmer I have met uses an individual style. Coding styles can be like fingerprints and can leave an impression on those who inherit your code. I used to be a bit of an evangelist when it came to styles, but I have relaxed my views. Now, I consider consistency much more important. In the end, the compiler doesn't care how you style your code and ultimately, the program still compiles.

Last but not least, I have tried to add good documentation to the code so that it is easier to follow and easier to understand what is being accomplished.

Compile Time Directives

There are several macros used in the compilation of XSEL (the Xendra Software Extension Library for MFC). It is important to understand how these are used in order to get the full benefit of the source files. So, let's say we get started.

Inline Macros

These types of definitions are pretty much standard in the industry. As you may know, because of the way inline functions are compiled into your target (EXE, DLL, or other), you cannot step into them when debugging through your source code. So, we make sure that inline functions are not inline when _DEBUG is defined. For the purpose of this book, I have stayed away from inline files, as this makes it easier to read. However, further updates to this library, available at http://www.xendra.com, will include inline functions.

```
// ------------------------------------------------------------
// Inline definitions
#ifdef _DEBUG
    #define XS_INLINE
#else
    #define XS_INLINE __inline
#endif // _DEBUG
```

Export and Import Macros

When you write a DLL for Windows, it can be shared between one or more other targets, including other DLLs. However, to use the code buried within, you must make sure to export the wanted functionality, whether it is classes, functions, or data. To use that functionality, you have to make sure you import it properly so it can be accessed.

The two macros used for proper exporting and importing are _XSDLL and _XSIMPORT. Whenever the XSEL source is in a DLL, use the _XSDLL macro. If you are wring an executable or DLL that will be accessing the XSEL source from a DLL, then make sure you have _XSIMPORT defined for those projects.

```
// ------------------------------------------------------------
// Import/Export definitions
#ifdef _XSDLL
    #ifdef _XSIMPORT
        #define XSCLASS     __declspec(dllimport)
        #define XSFUNC      __declspec(dllimport) WINAPI
        #define XSDATA      __declspec(dllimport)
    #else // _XSIMPORT
        #define XSCLASS     __declspec(dllexport)
        #define XSFUNC      __declspec(dllexport) WINAPI
        #define XSDATA      __declspec(dllexport)
    #endif // _XSIMPORT
#else // _XSDLL
```

```
        #define XSCLASS
        #define XSFUNC           WINAPI
        #define XSDATA
#endif // _XSDLL
```

Automatic Library Linking

If you make sure that the directory that contains the XSEL libraries is in your Library path, you can have the proper libraries link to you application automatically. The whole auto-link structure is wrapped by the macro _XSINTERNAL. This macro is only used when building the XSEL source libraries so that they don't link to themselves. The rest is pretty much self-explanatory, but for the sake of completeness, here is a quick rundown. The macro _DEBUG determines if a debug version of the library is linked. The macro UNICODE links in the proper Unicode variant of the library. The macro _XSDLL will make sure the proper import library is linked into your target. If _XSDLL is not defined, your project will automatically be linked to the static libraries.

```
#ifndef _XSINTERNAL
    #ifdef _DEBUG
        #ifdef _UNICODE
            #ifdef _XSDLL
                #pragma comment(lib,"XSD100ud.lib")
            #else
                #pragma comment(lib,"XS100ud.lib")
            #endif // _XSDLL
        #else // _UNICODE
            #ifdef _XSDLL
                #pragma comment(lib,"XSD100d.lib")
            #else
                #pragma comment(lib,"XS100d.lib")
            #endif // _XSDLL
        #endif // _UNICODE
    #else // _DEBUG
        #ifdef _UNICODE
            #ifdef _XSDLL
```

```
                    #pragma comment(lib,"XSD100u.lib")
              #else
                    #pragma comment(lib,"XS100u.lib")
              #endif // _XSDLL
         #else // _UNICODE
         #ifdef _XSDLL
                    #pragma comment(lib,"XSD100.lib")
              #else
                    #pragma comment(lib,"XS100.lib")
              #endif // _XSDLL
         #endif // _UNICODE
    #endif // _DEBUG
#endif // _XSINTERNAL
```

Using Precompiled Headers and XSMAIN.H

As is typical with any MFC program, you will most likely be using precompiled headers. Precompiled headers make incremental compilations very quick. To make working with XSEL quicker in this regard, all of the necessary header files are included in XSMAIN.H. All you have to do is make sure that XSMAIN.H is included properly in your main precompiled header file. Typically, with MFC, this is stdafx.h.

However, if you are extending XSEL by increasing the functionality, this can be quite a pain to use. Every time you make a change, you would be incurring a full recompile. To make this easier, the XSEL header #includes are wrapped with #ifndef _XSINTERNAL. This makes sure that the XSEL header files in XSMAIN.H are not used to build the source files. Instead, each source file has it's own necessary headers #included.

Miscellaneous Functions and Classes

The first functions we're going to look at are in XSERROR.H. The two functions in this file are used to set and get a static variable that contains the current error from the DIB API. In the future, this will be expanded to include the full XSEL library.

Setting and Getting Error Conditions

Sometimes returning TRUE for success or FALSE for failure in a function is not enough. We need some other mechanism to give us more details on exactly why a process failed. The following XSERROR handling gives us more details when an error is encountered.

XSERROR.H

```
// -------------------------------------------------------------------
// Errors
enum
{
    XSERR_MIN_ERROR = 0,    // All error #s >= this value
                            // XSERR_NOERROR = 0,
                            // No errors encountered
    XSERR_INVALIDFORMAT,    // Invalid format
    XSERR_HANDLENULL,       // Passed handle was NULL
    XSERR_MEMORY,           // Not enough memory!
    XSERR_READ,             // Error reading file!
    XSERR_LOCK,             // Error on a GlobalLock()!
    XSERR_OPEN,             // Error opening a file!
    XSERR_WRITE,            // Error writing a DIB file!
    XSERR_CREATEPAL,        // Error creating palette.
    XSERR_CREATEBITMAP,     // Error creating bitmap
    XSERR_FILENOTFOUND,     // Error opening file
    XSERR_INVALIDHANDLE,    // Invalid handle
    XSERR_GETOBJECT,        // Could not get object info
    XSERR_GETBITS,          // Error getting bits
    XSERR_GETDC,            // Can't get needed DC
    XSERR_PAINT,            // Error in painting
    XSERR_MAX_ERROR         // All error #s < this value
};
```

```
// -------------------------------------------------------------
// Error setting and getting routines
void XSFUNC XSError_Set(int nError = XSERR_NOERROR);
int  XSFUNC XSError_Get();
```

XSERROR.CPP

Because the gs_nXSError_Num variable is static (local to the file in which it lives), you cannot access it directly; instead, you must access it by using the XSError_Get function. Each function in the DIB API source uses the XSError_Set function to set the current error. When a function does not have a return value, or returns less than adequate information (e.g., TRUE or FALSE), you can get more information about the type of error by calling the XSError_Get function yourself.

```
#include "stdafx.h"
#include "XSError.h"

static int gs_nXSError_Num = XSERR_NOERROR;


// -------------------------------------------------------------
// Error reporting functions
// -------------------------------------------------------------


void XSFUNC
XSError_Set(int nError)
{
    ASSERT(nError >= XSERR_DIB_MIN && nError < XSERR_MAX_ERROR);
    gs_nXSError_Num = nError;
}


int XSFUNC
XSError_Get()
{
    return gs_nXSError_Num;
}
```

Extending CRect

I have found it very convenient to have several classes derived from CRect. One of these classes is CXSRect, which helps convert to and from client coordinates and screen coordinates. From CXSRect, I derive three other classes to automatically return different dimensions. One class automatically returns the client coordinates, one returns the screen coordinates, and one returns the client coordinates of the caption bar. This latter class is used in an upcoming chapter on painting the caption bar. These three derived classes all take a reference to a CWnd in the constructor to ensure that a NULL pointer is not passed. After you pass a reference to CXSRect, it will keep a pointer to the CWnd so you can call other conversions on it.

XSRect.h

```
// -------------------------------------------------------------
// Mini-class to act as a base class for CXSClientRect,
// CXSWindowRect, and CXSCaptionRect
class XSCLASS
CXSRect : public CRect
{
public:
    CXSRect();

    CXSRect& ToWindow();
    CXSRect& ToWindow(const CWnd& wnd);
    CXSRect& ToClient();
    CXSRect& ToClient(const CWnd& wnd);

protected:
    const CWnd* m_pWnd;

protected:
    // create from serialization only
    DECLARE_DYNCREATE(CXSRect);
};
```

```
// -------------------------------------------------------------
// Mini-class to get the rectangle of a window in client coords
class XSCLASS
CXSClientRect : public CXSRect
{
public:
    // use reference to deny NULL ptr
    CXSClientRect(const CWnd& wnd);

protected:
    // create from serialization only
    DECLARE_DYNCREATE(CXSClientRect);
};


// -------------------------------------------------------------
// Mini-class to get the rectangle of a window in screen coords
class XSCLASS
CXSWindowRect : public CXSRect
{
public:
    // use reference to deny NULL ptr
    CXSWindowRect(const CWnd& wnd);

protected:
    // create from serialization only
    DECLARE_DYNCREATE(CXSWindowRect);
};


// -------------------------------------------------------------
// Mini-class to get the caption rectangle of a window in
// window coordinates.  This is the area of the title bar inside
// the window frame.
class XSCLASS
CXSCaptionRect : public CXSRect
```

I

1

```
{
public:
    // use reference to deny NULL ptr
    CXSCaptionRect(const CWnd& wnd);

protected:
    // create from serialization only
    DECLARE_DYNCREATE(CXSCaptionRect);
};
```

XSRect.cpp

```
#include "stdafx.h"
#include "XSRect.h"

IMPLEMENT_DYNAMIC(CXSRect, CObject);
IMPLEMENT_DYNAMIC(CXSClientRect, CXSRect);
IMPLEMENT_DYNAMIC(CXSWindowRect, CXSRect);
IMPLEMENT_DYNAMIC(CXSCaptionRect, CXSRect);
```

CXSRect Class

The main class derived from CRect is CXSRect. CXSRect has an empty constructor. It becomes the base class for CXSClientRect, CXSWindowRect, and CXSCaptionRect. It also provides the functionality for conveniently converting to and from client and screen coordinates.

```
// -----------------------------------------------------------
// Function  :
//   CXSRect::CXSRect
// Purpose   :
//   To act as a base class for CXSClientRect, CXSWindowRect,
//   and CXSCaptionRect
// -----------------------------------------------------------
CXSRect::CXSRect()
{
    m_pWnd = NULL;
}
```

CXSRect::ToWindow

The base class CXSRect provides functionality for converting to and from client and screen coordinates. You probably wouldn't use these member functions directly from this class. Instead, you will probably use them from one of the derived classes.

There are two overloaded ToWindow functions. One takes no parameters, while the other takes a reference to a CWnd. The function that takes the passed reference stores the CWnd in a pointer. The function that takes no parameters then uses the stored pointer for later use. In both cases, the screen coordinates are retrieved by calling the Windows API function ClientToScreen.

```
// ------------------------------------------------------------
// Function :
//   CXSRect::ToWindow
// Purpose  :
//   Converts the current RECT dimensions to Screen coordinates
//   based on the stored m_pWnd.
// Parameters:
//   None
// Returns  :
//   Reference to this
// ------------------------------------------------------------
CXSRect&
CXSRect::ToWindow()
{
    ASSERT(m_pWnd);
    ASSERT(::IsWindow(*m_pWnd));

    m_pWnd->ClientToScreen(this);
    return *this;
}


// ------------------------------------------------------------
// Function :
//   CXSRect::ToWindow
```

```
// Purpose   :
//  Converts the current RECT dimensions to Screen coordinates.
// Parameters:
//  CWnd wnd - The CWnd to use as a base in converting to
//  screen coords
// Returns   :
//   Reference to this
// ------------------------------------------------------------
CXSRect&
CXSRect::ToWindow(const CWnd& wnd)
{
    ASSERT(::IsWindow(wnd));

    wnd.ClientToScreen(this);
    return *this;
}
```

CXSRect::ToClient

There are also two overloaded ToClient functions. One takes no parameters, while the other takes a reference to a CWnd. The function that takes the passed reference stores the CWnd in a pointer. The function that takes no parameters then uses the stored pointer for later use. In both cases, the client coordinates are retrieved by calling ScreenToClient.

```
// ------------------------------------------------------------
// Function  :
//  CXSRect::ToClient
// Purpose   :
//  Converts the current RECT dimensions to client coordinates.
//  based on the stored m_pWnd.
// Parameters:
//  None
// Returns   :
//  Reference to this
// ------------------------------------------------------------
CXSRect&
```

```
CXSRect::ToClient()
{
    ASSERT(m_pWnd);
    ASSERT(::IsWindow(*m_pWnd));

    m_pWnd->ScreenToClient(this);
    return *this;
}


// ------------------------------------------------------------
// Function  :
//   CXSRect::ToClient
// Purpose   :
//   Converts the current RECT dimensions to client coordinates.
// Parameters:
//   CWnd wnd - The CWnd to use as a base in converting to
//   client coordinates
// Returns   :
//   Reference to this
// ------------------------------------------------------------
CXSRect&
CXSRect::ToClient(const CWnd& wnd)
{
    ASSERT(::IsWindow(wnd));

    wnd.ScreenToClient(this);
    return *this;
}
```

CXSClientRect **Class**

The CXSClientRect class is derived from CXSRect and is quite simple. CXSClientRect takes a CWnd reference as a parameter to the constructor to prevent a NULL from being passed. Then, CXSClientRect calls the appropriate window function to get the client coordinates of the passed CWnd.

The conventional way of getting the client coordinates of a window would be

```
CRect rect;
m_pWnd->GetClientRect(&rect);
```

With `CXSClientRect`, the new way would be

```
CXSRect rect = CXSClientRect(*m_pWnd);
```

or

```
CXSClientRect rcClient(*m_pWnd);
```

There isn't much difference between the conventional and new methods, except the convenience that `CXSClientRect` provides. However, as we go along, you'll start to see just how convenient this is and how quickly you can derive classes to return the `RECT` you may need for a particular use.

```
// ------------------------------------------------------------
// Function  :
//   CXSClientRect::CXSClientRect
// Purpose   :
//   To return the client coordinates of the passed CWnd
// Parameters:
//   CWnd wnd - The CWnd for which to get client coordinates
// Returns   :
//   Nothing
// Comments  :
//   Typical usage of this class would be in the following
//   format:
//       CXSRect rect = CXSClientRect(*pWnd);
// ------------------------------------------------------------
CXSClientRect::CXSClientRect(const CWnd& wnd)
{
    ASSERT(::IsWindow(wnd));

    m_pWnd = &wnd;
```

```
    // Compute rectangle
    wnd.GetClientRect(this);  // client rect
}
```

CXSWindowRect **Class**

The CXSWindowRect class is derived from CXSRect and is quite simple. CXSWindowRect takes a CWnd reference as a parameter to the constructor to prevent a NULL from being passed. Then, CXSWindowRect calls the appropriate window function to get the screen coordinates of the passed CWnd.

The conventional way of getting the screen coordinates of a window would be

```
CRect rect;
m_pWnd->GetWindowRect(&rect);
With CXSWindowRect, the new way would be
CXSRect rect = CXSWindowRect(*m_pWnd);
or
CXSWindowRect rcClient(*m_pWnd);
```

There isn't much difference between the conventional and new methods, except the convenience that CXSWindowRect provides. However, as we go along, you'll start to see just how convenient this is and how quickly you can derive classes to return the RECT you may need for a particular use.

```
// ----------------------------------------------------------------
// Function :
//  CXSWindowRect::CXSWindowRect
// Purpose  :
//  To return the screen coordinates of the passed CWnd
// Parameters:
//  CWnd wnd - The CWnd for which to get screen coordinates
// Returns  :
//  Nothing
// Comments :
//  Typical usage of this class would be in the following
//  format:
```

```
//       CXSRect rect = CXSWindowRect(*pWnd);
// --------------------------------------------------------
CXSWindowRect::CXSWindowRect(const CWnd& wnd)
{
    ASSERT(::IsWindow(wnd));


    m_pWnd = &wnd;


    // Compute rectangle
    wnd.GetWindowRect(this);   // window rect
}
```

CXSCaptionRect **Class**

The CXSCaptionRect class is very useful for the necessary functionality to work in the CXSCaption class. Whenever the window size changes, the CXS-Caption class needs the new size of the caption area recomputed in order to do its work. We'll talk more about the CXSCaption class in an upcoming chapter.

The CXSCaptionRect class first gets the style of the passed CWnd. Using the style, CXSCaptionRect will assert if the CWnd does not have a caption (WS_CAPTION) attached to it. If there is a caption, CXSCaptionRect then uses the style to determine what type of frame surrounds the window. Then, using the GetSystemMetrics API function, we retrieve the CSize of the frame. The constructor then gets the CWnd size in window, or screen, coordinates. The constructor uses this method because client coordinates do not include any of the nonclient areas, which include the frame and caption areas.

Next, the CXSCaptionRect class constructor converts the coordinates to a sort of pseudo-client coordinates. Client coordinates always use (0,0) as the top-left in its coordinate system. Once we have the caption area in a pseudo-client coordinate system, the class constructor functionality is complete.

```
// --------------------------------------------------------
// Function  :
//   CXSCaptionRect::CXSCaptionRect
// Purpose   :
```

```
//  To return the client coordinates of the caption bar of the
//  passed CWnd
// Parameters:
//  CWnd wnd - The CWnd for which to get caption bar
//  coordinates
// Returns   :
//  Nothing
// Comments  :
//  Typical usage of this class would be in the following
//  format:
//      CXSRect rect = CXSCaptionRect(*pWnd);
// ----------------------------------------------------------
CXSCaptionRect::CXSCaptionRect(const CWnd& wnd)
{
    ASSERT(::IsWindow(wnd));

    m_pWnd = &wnd;

    // Get size of frame around window
    DWORD dwStyle = wnd.GetStyle();
    ASSERT(dwStyle & WS_CAPTION);
    CSize szFrame = (dwStyle & WS_THICKFRAME) -
        CSize(::GetSystemMetrics(SM_CXSIZEFRAME),
            ::GetSystemMetrics(SM_CYSIZEFRAME)) :
        CSize(::GetSystemMetrics(SM_CXFIXEDFRAME),
            ::GetSystemMetrics(SM_CYFIXEDFRAME));

    // Compute rectangle
    // ----------------------------------------------------------
    // window rect in screen coordinates
    wnd.GetWindowRect(this);

    // shift origin to (0,0) - makes client coordinates
    *this -= CPoint(left, top);
```

I

1

```
   left  += szFrame.cx;
   right -= szFrame.cx;
   top   += szFrame.cy;

   // height of caption minus gray shadow border
   bottom = top + ::GetSystemMetrics(SM_CYCAPTION)
       - ::GetSystemMetrics(SM_CYBORDER);
}
```

The Miscellaneous API Functions

A number of utility-type functions will be needed for the upcoming chapters. These functions are placed into a single file because of their generic nature. Since they are not discussed until later in the book, their context may not be easily apparent. Yet, each one can be used for more than its intended purpose in this library.

XSMisc.h

```
// Additional color definitions
#define COLOR_WHITE (RGB(255,255,255))
#define COLOR_BLACK (RGB(0,0,0))

BOOL XSFUNC XSPaint_Rect(CDC* pDC, int x, int y, int w, int h,
          COLORREF color);
BOOL XSFUNC XSPaint_Rect(CDC* pDC, CRect rect, COLORREF color);

BOOL XSFUNC XSPaint_Gradient(CDC* pDC, const CRect& rcRect,
          COLORREF crColor, int nGradFills = 1);

BOOL XSFUNC XSCaption_SetText(HWND hwnd, LPCTSTR lpText,
          BOOL bRedraw = TRUE);
```

XSMisc.cpp

The necessary header files to be included for this source file are as follows.

```
#include "stdafx.h"
#include "XSError.h"
#include "XSMisc.h"
#include "XSPalApi.h"
#include "XSPalette.h"
#include "XSDibApi.h"
#include "XSBitmap.h"
```

We haven't yet begun to discuss some of these files, so your patience is requested. When you develop software, it is done in three-dimensional terms. You can bounce around from source file to source file adding here and there. Trying to document this process in a book would, in my opinion, become very disorienting to the reader. In a book, we have to use a two-dimensional view of how the software is created. This method still isn't perfect, but we have to make do with the medium we use. So, keep an open mind as you read through and I'll try to keep everything tied together so it is easily understood.

XSPaint_Rect

I have found that I always need to paint RECT areas with different colors. This little function has certainly made my life easier in terms of reuse. I made this an API function, rather than putting it into a class, only because the appropriate place it belongs is in a CDC extension class. This book does not have such a class, so at this time it will remain an API function.

The main function takes parameters in terms of x, y, width, and height. A corresponding function takes the CRect. Each function also takes a pointer to a CDC and a COLORREF. The function creates a brush from the passed COLORREF and paints the intended Rect with the brush.

```
// -----------------------------------------------------------------
// Function :
//   XSPaint_Rect
// Purpose  :
//   Paint a RECT within a DC the passed color
// Parameters:
//   CDC* pDC - The frame (or window) that is to have
```

```
//  int x - the left side of the RECT
//  int y - the top of the RECT
//  int w - the width of the rect
//  int h - the height of the RECT
//  COLORREF color - the color to paint with
// Returns   :
// TRUE on success, FALSE on failure
// -------------------------------------------------------
BOOL XSFUNC
XSPaint_Rect(CDC* pDC, int x, int y, int w, int h, COLORREF
color)
{
    BOOL bResult = FALSE;

    // Create the brush and select it into the DC
    CBrush brush(color);
    CBrush* pOldBrush = pDC->SelectObject(&brush);

    // Paint according to the passed dimensions
    bResult = pDC->PatBlt(x, y, w, h, PATCOPY);

    // Set the old brush back
    pDC->SelectObject(pOldBrush);

    return bResult;
}
```

XSPaint_Gradient

The intent of this function is to paint a rectangular area, much like the XSPaint_Rect function, but to have the requested color become gradient towards black. Have you ever seen an application with a gradient caption? Perhaps an installation program that creates a gradient background? If you've ever wondered how that was done, then wonder no more. This function does exactly what you would expect.

The function is passed a color to use for the gradient. It paints from right to left, with the specified color on the right merging to black on the left. You pass the function the number of gradient iterations to use. However, if you pass the number one as the number of iteraions, it will paint a solid color. It starts by dividing the painting area into six areas. The last sixth is painted the solid color passed to the function. From then on, the rest it painted in gradients.

The original algorithm for this function was created by Paul Dilascia and was originally published in Microsoft Systems Journal.

```
// -------------------------------------------------------------
// Function  :
//   XSPaint_Gradient
// Purpose   :
//   Draws a gradient from right to left of the color to black
// Parameters:
//   CDC* pDC - The DC to paint into
//   CRect& rcRect - The RECT to paint
//   COLORREF crColor - The color to use
//   int nGradFills - The number of gradients to use
// Returns   :
//   TRUE on success, FALSE on failure
// -------------------------------------------------------------
BOOL XSFUNC
XSPaint_Gradient(CDC* pDC, CRect& rcRect, COLORREF crColor,
                 int nGradFills)
{
    ASSERT(pDC);
    ASSERT(nGradFills >= 1);

    BOOL bResult = FALSE;

    // Do this if we're doing a single color
    if (1 == nGradFills)
    {
        if (::XSPaint_Rect(pDC, 0, 0, rcRect.Width(),
            rcRect.Height(), crColor))
            bResult = TRUE;
```

```
    }
else
{
    // Get Red, Green, and Blue color values
    int r = GetRValue(crColor);
    int g = GetGValue(crColor);
    int b = GetBValue(crColor);

    // start 5/6 of the way right
    int x = 5 * rcRect.right / 6;

    // width of area to shade
    int w = x - rcRect.left;

    // height of area to shade
    int h = rcRect.Height();

    // width of one shade band
    int xDelta= max(w / nGradFills, 1);

    // Paint far right 1/6 of the caption the background color
    ::XSPaint_Rect(pDC, x, 0, rcRect.right - x, h, crColor);

    // Compute new color brush for each band from
    // x to x + xDelta.
    // Excel uses a linear algorithm from black to normal:
    //
    //   color = crColor * r
    //
    // where r is the ratio x/w, which ranges from 0
    // (x = 0, left) to 1 (x = w, right). This results in a
    // mostly black title bar, since we humans don't
    // distinguish dark colors as well as light ones. So
    // instead, I use the formula:
```

I

1

```
//
//  color = crColor * [1-(1-r)^2]
//
// which still equals black when r = 0 and crColor when
// r = 1, but spends more time near crColor. For
// example, when r = .5, the multiplier is
// [1 - (1 - .5) ^ 2] = .75, closer to 1 than .5.
// I leave the algebra to the reader to verify that the
// above formula is equivalent to
//
// color = crColor - (crColor * (w - x) * (w - x)) / (w * w)

// paint bands right to left
while (x > xDelta)
{
    // next band
    x -= xDelta;

    // w minus x squared
    int wmx2 = (w - x) * (w - x);

    // w squared
    int w2  = w * w;

    // Paint it
    ::XSPaint_Rect(pDC, x, 0, xDelta, h,
        RGB(r - (r * wmx2) / w2,
            g - (g * wmx2) / w2,
            b - (b * wmx2) / w2));
}

// Paint whatever is left black
::XSPaint_Rect(pDC, 0, 0, x, h, COLOR_BLACK);
```

```
        bResult = TRUE;
    }


    return bResult;
}
```

XSCaption_SetText

When you have a window with a caption area, Windows maintains a buffer for the text that goes into that caption. By setting the text, Windows automatically assumes that you want to update the caption area as well. Sometimes this is not the preferred behavior. There are occasions when you want to update the internal buffer but you don't want Windows to draw it, or at least draw it at that moment. This next function stops the caption area from being updated when the internal text buffer is changed by temporarily turning off the WS_VISIBLE flag, calling the default handler, and then turning the WS_VISIBLE flag back on. The routine that sets the internal buffer checks to see if the window is visible. If it is not visible, it skips the caption update, but updates the buffer.

```
// --------------------------------------------------------------
// Function  :
//   XSCaption_SetText
// Purpose   :
//   Changes the text of the passed HWND
// Parameters:
//   HWND hwnd - The frame (or window) that is to have its text
//        changed
//   LPCTSTR lpText - The text to change to
//   BOOL bRedraw - TRUE to redraw the text
//                  FALSE to not repaint immediately
// Returns   :
//   TRUE on success, FALSE on failure
// --------------------------------------------------------------
BOOL XSFUNC
XSCaption_SetText(HWND hwnd, LPCTSTR lpText, BOOL bRedraw)
{
    // Turn off WS_VISIBLE if necessary to avoid painting
```

```
DWORD dwStyle = ::GetWindowLong(hwnd, GWL_STYLE);

// If this HWND has no caption, then return
if (!(dwStyle & WS_CAPTION))
    return FALSE;

if (!bRedraw)
{
    if (dwStyle & WS_VISIBLE)
        ::SetWindowLong(hwnd, GWL_STYLE,
        (dwStyle & ~WS_VISIBLE));
}

// Call DefWindowProc directly to set internal window text
DefWindowProc(hwnd, WM_SETTEXT, 0, (LPARAM)lpText);

if (!bRedraw)
{
    if (dwStyle & WS_VISIBLE)
        ::SetWindowLong(hwnd, GWL_STYLE, dwStyle);
}

return TRUE;
}
```

Summary

This chapter has examined a number of utility functions that will be needed in the upcoming chapters. Since they are used often, and by different classes, they have been placed into the XSMisc source file.

Now, without further ado, it's time to get on with the more exciting chapters and to start having a bit of fun.

Chapter 2

The DIB API

Introduction

Graphics are the fundamental backbone of the user interface in Windows. Besides your typical GDI (Graphical Device Interface) functions for line, ellipse, polygon, pie, and rectangles, there are also functions for working with images. In Windows, there are two types of native images: the Device Dependent Bitmap (DDB) and the Device Independent Bitmap (DIB). While the DDB is always kept in memory and usually referenced by the handle HBITMAP, a DIB is usually used for storing the image to a file as a bitmap (.bmp file). The GDI is optimized for handling a DDB much faster than a DIB on its internal canvas. However, many newer video cards and their associated drivers are now providing much better DIB support. The critical difference in speed when handling the two types of images is not as much as it used to be.

One of the main problems with the Windows SDK and MFC is the lack of good imaging functions for DIBs. For instance, there is no function to save DIBs to a file. There are now more functions than when we used to program for Windows 3.1. Some of those functions still lack the desired functionality, but this problem is slowly being corrected. In the meantime,

Microsoft Technical Support with their Knowledge Base, as well as a host of other good programmers, has freely published different techniques for DIB handling. There are also a number of good software toolkits available. Either of these types of resources will help if you need technical assistance. If you don't feel the need for technical assistance, the functions we're about to explore should get your meter going.

While the XS DIB API contains a number of useful functions, it is far from complete. In fact, I do not know of any DIB-type library that could call itself complete. You can always add more and more functionality. With images, it never seems to end.

The Windows DIB

Since we're going to be programming with bitmap images in this chapter, I thought it would be prudent to have a small review on the containment of a Windows DIB.

The Microsoft DIB file can contain images that are 1-, 4-, 8-, 24-, or 36-bits per pixel. The 1-, 4-, and 8-bit images all have color maps while the 24- and 32-bit images are direct color. Each file contains a file header, a bitmap header, a color map (unless the image is 24- or 36-bit direct color) and the image. The image may also be compressed using an RLE (Run Length Encoded) format.

All DIB files contain a common file header.

Table 2.1   **The** BITMAPFILEHEADER **File Header**

Offset	Size	Name	Description
0	2	bfType	ASCII "BM"
2	4	bfSize	Size in bytes of the file
6	2	bfReserved1	Zero
8	2	bfReserved2	Zero
10	4	bfOffBits	Byte offset in file where image begins

The bfOffBits field contains the distance in bytes from the beginning of the file to the beginning of the image data bits. This makes it easier to skip over the image header information.

Following the file header is the bitmap header and, possibly, the optional color table. The bitmap information contains the bitmap header and the start of the color table.

Table 2.2 **The** `BITMAPINFO/BITMAPINFOHEADER` **Image Header**

Offset	Size	Name	Description
14	4	biSize	Size of this header, 40 bytes
18	4	biWidth	Image width in pixels
22	4	biHeight	Image height in pixels
26	2	biPlanes	Number of image planes, must be 1
28	2	biBitCount	Bits per pixel (1, 4, 8, 24, or 32)
30	4	biCompression	Compression type
34	4	biSizeImage	Size in bytes of compressed image, or zero
38	4	biXPelsPerMeter	Horizontal resolution, in pixels/meter
42	4	biYPelsPerMeter	Vertical resolution, in pixels/meter
46	4	biClrUsed	Number of colors used
50	4	biClrImportant	Number of important colors
54	4*N	bmiColors	Color map

Images using 1-, 4-, or 8-bits per pixel must have a color map. The color map sizes are normally 2, 16, and 256 colors, respectively, but may be smaller if the image does need the full set of colors. If the `biClrUsed` field is nonzero, it contains the actual number of colors used in the image, which is also the number of entries in the color map. If the field is zero, the color map is the full size. For 24- and 32-bit images, there is no color map. The image is stored with direct RGB color.

Since it is possible that the device used to display the image may not have all the available colors needed by the bitmap, entries in the color map should have the most important colors first. Notice I said, "should" as this is not always adhered to when paint utilities manipulate bitmaps. The `biClrImportant` field, if nonzero, indicates how many of the initial colors are important for good image reproduction.

Following the BITMAPINFOHEADER is table of color map entries for 1-, 4-, and 8-bits per pixel bitmaps.

Table 2.3 The RGBQUAD **Color Map Entry**

Offset	Name	Description
0	RgbBlue	Blue color value
1	RgbGreen	Green color value
2	RgbRed	Red color value
3	RgbReserved	Zero

The bitmap data follows the color table. The data may be uncompressed, or for 4- and 8-bit images, it may use an RLE compression type. Bits are logically (and physically, without compression) stored one row at a time. Each row is padded to a 4-byte (DWORD) boundary with zero bytes. Rows are stored in order from the bottom of the image to the top — in other words, upside down. This can sometimes be rather confusing for some program-mers. Fortunately, or at least I hope, this DIB API will take some of the pain away when you have a need to work with DIBs.

XSDIBAPI.H

Macros Used in the DIB API

When we work with DIBs, we need a memory handle to help identify the memory type with which we are working. For DDBs, Windows uses the memory handle HBITMAP. We can create a similar memory handle called HDIB by using the DECLARE_HANDLE Windows macro.

```
// ------------------------------------------------------
// DIB Definition
DECLARE_HANDLE(HDIB);
The other macros we need help us when working with DIBs and cut
down on repetitive code.
// ------------------------------------------------------
// DIB Macros
```

```
#define macDibHeaderMarker      ((WORD) ('M' << 8) | 'B')
#define macIsWinDib(lpbi)       ((*(LPDWORD)(lpbi)) == \
                                 sizeof(BITMAPINFOHEADER))
#define macDibWidthBytes(bits)  (((bits) + 31) / 32 * 4)
```

Function Declarations

For functions that take and return either a DIB or a DDB, the original passed memory handle object, a DIB or a DDB, is left intact and not modified in any way. It is up to you to release this memory if you no longer have a need for it.

```
// ----------------------------------------------------------
// Create a new DIB based on passed parameters
HDIB       XSFUNC XSDib_Create(DWORD dwWidth, DWORD dwHeight,
              WORD wBitCount);
HDIB       XSFUNC XSDib_Template(BITMAPINFOHEADER& bi,
              HBITMAP hBitmap);


// ----------------------------------------------------------
// Load a DDB/DIB from a Resource
HBITMAP    XSFUNC XSBmp_Load(HINSTANCE hInst, UINT nID);


// ----------------------------------------------------------
// Load and Save DIBs from/to a File
HDIB       XSFUNC XSDib_Load(CString strFileName);
HDIB       XSFUNC XSDib_ReadFile(CFile& file,
              DWORD dwOffset = 0L);
WORD       XSFUNC XSDib_Save(HDIB hDib, CString strFileName);
WORD       XSFUNC XSDib_WriteFile(HDIB hDib, CFile& file);


// ----------------------------------------------------------
// Destroy DIB Memory
void       XSFUNC XSDib_Destroy(HDIB hDib);


// ----------------------------------------------------------
```

```
// DIB Utility Functions
LONG        XSFUNC XSDib_Width(LPVOID lpDib);
LONG        XSFUNC XSDib_Width(HDIB hDib);
LONG        XSFUNC XSDib_Height(LPVOID lpDib);
LONG        XSFUNC XSDib_Height(HDIB hDib);
WORD        XSFUNC XSDib_PaletteSize(LPVOID lpDib);
WORD        XSFUNC XSDib_PaletteSize(HDIB hDib);
WORD        XSFUNC XSDib_NumColors(LPVOID lpDib);
WORD        XSFUNC XSDib_NumColors(HDIB hDib);
LPVOID      XSFUNC XSDib_FindBits(LPVOID lpDib);
LPVOID      XSFUNC XSDib_FindBits(HDIB hDib);
DWORD       XSFUNC XSDib_CalcPadding(DWORD dwBitsPerPixel,
                      DWORD dwPixels);
DWORD       XSFUNC XSDib_CalcBytesPerLine(DWORD dwBitsPerPixel,
                      DWORD dwWidth);
DWORD       XSFUNC XSDib_LastByte(DWORD dwBitsPerPixel,
                      DWORD dwPixels);


// -------------------------------------------------------------
// DIB Palette Functions
HPALETTE    XSFUNC XSDib_CreatePalette(HDIB hDib);


// -------------------------------------------------------------
// DIB/DDB Conversion Functions
HDIB        XSFUNC XSBmp_ToDib(HBITMAP hBitmap, HPALETTE hPal);
HBITMAP     XSFUNC XSDib_ToBmp(HDIB hDib, HPALETTE hPal);
HDIB        XSFUNC XSBmp_ChangeFormat(HBITMAP hBitmap,
                      WORD wBitCount, DWORD dwCompression,
                      HPALETTE hPal);
HDIB        XSFUNC XSDib_ChangeFormat(HDIB hDib, WORD wBitCount,
                      DWORD dwCompression);


// -------------------------------------------------------------
// DIB Painting Functions
BOOL        XSFUNC XSDib_Paint(HDC hDC, CRect rcDim, HDIB hDib,
```

```
                    CRect rcDib, HPALETTE hPal);


// ------------------------------------------------------------
// DIB Operation Functions
HDIB        XSFUNC XSDib_Rotate(HDIB hDibSrc,
                    BOOL bClockwise = TRUE);
```

XSDIBAPI.CPP

The DIB API presented here is a good starting point for needing DIB functionality. This API will continue to grow beyond the scope of this book. You should look for changes and additions to this source, as well as the rest of the XSEL source, continuously. Refer to the section "Contacting the Author" in the Introduction.

XSDib_Create

This function allocates the memory needed to store a DIB based on the desired width, height, and bit count. It then fills in the BITMAPINFOHEADER with appropriate default values.

```
// ------------------------------------------------------------
// XSDib_Create
//  Parameters:
//      DWORD dwWidth   - Width for new bitmap, in pixels
//      DWORD dwHeight  - Height for new bitmap
//      WORD  wBitCount - Bit Count for new DIB (1, 4, 8, 24,
//                        or 36)
//  Return Value:
//      HDIB            - Handle to new DIB
//  Description:
//      This function allocates memory for and initializes a
//      new DIB by filling in the BITMAPINFOHEADER, allocating
//      memory for the color table, and allocating memory for
//      the bitmap bits.  As with all HDIBs, the header, color
//      table and bits are all in one contiguous memory block.
//      This function is similar to the CreateBitmap() Windows
//      API.
// ------------------------------------------------------------
```

```
HDIB XSFUNC
XSDib_Create(DWORD dwWidth, DWORD dwHeight, WORD wBitCount)
{
    BITMAPINFOHEADER bi;        // Bitmap header
    LPBITMAPINFOHEADER lpbi;    // Pointer to BITMAPINFOHEADER
    DWORD dwLen;                // Size of memory block
    HDIB hDib;                  // Handle for new DIB
    DWORD dwBytesPerLine;       // Number of bytes per scanline

    // Make sure bits per pixel is valid
    if (wBitCount <= 1)
        wBitCount = 1;
    else if (wBitCount <= 4)
        wBitCount = 4;
    else if (wBitCount <= 8)
        wBitCount = 8;
    else if (wBitCount <= 24)
        wBitCount = 24;
    else if (wBitCount <= 36)
        wBitCount = 36;
    else
        wBitCount = 4;  // Set default value to 4
                        // if parameter is bogus

    // Initialize BITMAPINFOHEADER
    bi.biSize = sizeof(BITMAPINFOHEADER);
    bi.biWidth = dwWidth;       // Fill in width from parameter
    bi.biHeight = dwHeight;     // Fill in height from parameter
    bi.biPlanes = 1;            // Must be 1
    bi.biBitCount = wBitCount;  // From parameter
    bi.biCompression = BI_RGB;
    bi.biSizeImage = 0;         // 0's here mean "default"
    bi.biXPelsPerMeter = 0;
    bi.biYPelsPerMeter = 0;
```

```
bi.biClrUsed = 0;
bi.biClrImportant = 0;

// Calculate size of memory block required to store the
// DIB. This block should be big enough to hold the
// BITMAPINFOHEADER, the color table, and the bits
dwBytesPerLine = macDibWidthBytes(wBitCount * dwWidth);
dwLen = bi.biSize + ::XSDib_PaletteSize(&bi) +
    (dwBytesPerLine * dwHeight);

// Allocate memory block to store our bitmap
if (!(hDib = (HDIB)::GlobalAlloc(GHND, dwLen)))
{
    ::XSError_Set(XSERR_MEMORY);
    return NULL;
}

// Lock memory and get pointer to it
lpbi = (LPBITMAPINFOHEADER)::GlobalLock(hDib);

// Use our bitmap info structure to fill in first part of
// our DIB with the BITMAPINFOHEADER
*lpbi = bi;

// Since we don't know what the color table and bits
// should contain, just leave these blank.  Unlock
// the DIB and return the HDIB.
::GlobalUnlock(hDib);

// Set error to no error
::XSError_Set(XSERR_NOERROR);

// Return handle to the DIB
return hDib;
}
```

I

2

XSDib_Template

This function is much like the XSDib_Create function except that it creates a new DIB based on the values of the passed BITMAPINFOHEADER and HBITMAP. As the name implies, it uses the passed information as a template to create the new DIB.

```
// -----------------------------------------------------------
// XSDib_Template
//  Parameters:
//      BITMAPINFOHEADER - bitmap info header structure
//      HBITMAP          - handle to the bitmap
//  Return Value:
//      HDIB             - handle to memory block
//  Description:
//      This routine takes a BITMAPINOHEADER, and returns a
//      handle to global memory, which can contain a DIB with
//      that header.  It also initializes the header portion of
//      the global memory.  GetDIBits() is used to determine
//      the amount of room for the DIB's bits.  The total amount
//      of memory needed = sizeof(BITMAPINFOHEADER)
//      + size of color table + size of bits.
// -----------------------------------------------------------
HDIB XSFUNC
XSDib_Template(BITMAPINFOHEADER& bi, HBITMAP hBitmap)
{
    DWORD              dwLen;
    HDIB               hDib;
    HDC                hDC;
    LPBITMAPINFOHEADER lpbi;
    HDIB               hDibTemp;

    // Figure out the size needed to hold the BITMAPINFO
    // structure (which includes the BITMAPINFOHEADER and
    // the color table).
    dwLen = bi.biSize + ::XSDib_PaletteSize(&bi);
    hDib  = (HDIB)::GlobalAlloc(GHND, dwLen);
```

I

2

```
// Check that DIB handle is valid
if (!hDib)
{
    ::XSError_Set(XSERR_HANDLENULL);
    return NULL;
}


// Set up the BITMAPINFOHEADER in the newly allocated
// global memory, then call GetDIBits() with
// lpBits = NULL to have it fill in the biSizeImage
// field for us.
lpbi  = (LPBITMAPINFOHEADER)::GlobalLock(hDib);
*lpbi = bi;

hDC   = ::GetDC(NULL);
::GetDIBits(hDC, hBitmap, 0, (WORD) bi.biHeight, NULL,
    (LPBITMAPINFO)lpbi, DIB_RGB_COLORS);
::ReleaseDC(NULL, hDC);

// If the driver did not fill in the biSizeImage field,
// fill it in -- NOTE: there is a bug in some drivers!
if (lpbi->biSizeImage == 0)
    lpbi->biSizeImage = macDibWidthBytes((DWORD)lpbi->biWidth
    * lpbi->biBitCount) * lpbi->biHeight;

// Get the size of the memory block we need
dwLen = lpbi->biSize + ::XSDib_PaletteSize(&bi)
    + lpbi->biSizeImage;

// Unlock the memory block
::GlobalUnlock(hDib);


// ReAlloc the buffer big enough to hold all the bits
```

```
    if (hDibTemp = (HDIB)::GlobalReAlloc(hDib, dwLen, 0))
    {
        ::XSError_Set(XSERR_MEMORY);
        return hDibTemp;
    }
    else
    {
        ::XSError_Set(XSERR_NOERROR);

        // Else free the memory block and return failure
        ::GlobalFree(hDib);
        return NULL;
    }
}
```

XSBmp_Load

This function reads a bitmap resource from the specified HINSTANCE, while maintaining the included color palette. In the past, you would use the function LoadBitmap to do this. However, LoadBitmap does not read the color table of the bitmap. Instead, it remaps the bitmap's colors using the system palette. If there were many colors in the bitmap then you would notice a distinctive difference when the bitmap is displayed. You would see a bit of what I call "a negative effect". To get rid of this, you would have had to use FindResource/LockResource and manually load the bitmap.

For 32-bit Windows, we can now use the LoadImage function. If you ever get the time, study the documentation of this function carefully. It has many characteristics that can make it quite useful. Even for loading DIBs from a file. However, as of this writing, the LoadImage function does not read DIBs under Windows NT. Therefore, we will not be using it to do anything other than reading a bitmap from a resource file.

```
// ----------------------------------------------------------------
// XSBmp_Load
//   Parameters:
//       HINSTANCE hInst - Specifies the HINSTANCE to load a DDB
//       UINT nID - ID for the resource to load
//   Return Value:
```

```
//      HBITMAP - the handle to the loaded bitmap, NULL on
//         failure
// Description:
//      Loads the specified BMP from the resources of the
//      specified HINSTANCE
// -------------------------------------------------------------
HBITMAP XSFUNC
XSBmp_Load(HINSTANCE hInst, UINT nID)
{
    HBITMAP hBitmap = NULL;


    hBitmap = (HBITMAP)::LoadImage(hInst, MAKEINTRESOURCE(nID),
        IMAGE_BITMAP, 0, 0, LR_CREATEDIBSECTION);

    // Set error number
    if (!hBitmap)
        ::XSError_Set(XSERR_CREATEBITMAP);
    else
        ::XSError_Set(XSERR_NOERROR);


    return hBitmap;
}
```

XSDib_Load

Use this function when you have the full path and name of a DIB that you want to load from a file. Typically, these files have a `.bmp` extension. This function's only real functionality is to open the file for reading. It then passes the `CFile` handle to the `XSDib_ReadFile` function.

```
// -------------------------------------------------------------
// XSDib_Load
// Parameters:
//      CString strFileName - Specifies the DIB file
// Return Value:
//      HDIB of the loaded DIB or NULL on failure
// Description:
```

```
//       Loads the specified DIB from a file, allocates memory
//       for it, and reads the disk file into the memory.
// -------------------------------------------------------------
HDIB XSFUNC
XSDib_Load(CString strFileName)
{
#ifdef _USRDLL
    // if this code is in a user DLL, we need to set up the MFC
    // state if we use MFC in this function
    AFX_MANAGE_STATE(AfxGetStaticModuleState());
#endif

    HDIB hDib = NULL;     // Handle to new DIB
    CFile file;           // File handling class
    CFileException e;     // File exception catcher

    // Set the cursor to a hourglass, in case the loading
    // operation takes more than a sec, the user will know
    // what's going on.
    CWaitCursor wait;

    if (!file.Open(strFileName,
        CFile::modeRead|CFile::shareDenyNone, &e))
    {
#ifdef _DEBUG
        afxDump << "File (" << strFileName <<
            ") could not be opened: " << e.m_cause << "\n";
#endif
        ::XSError_Set(XSERR_OPEN);
        return NULL;
    }
    else
    {
        hDib = ::XSDib_ReadFile(file, 0L);
```

```
        file.Close();

        // Set error to no error
        ::XSError_Set(XSERR_NOERROR);

        return hDib;
    }
}
```

XSDib_ReadFile

This function provides the main functionality for reading a DIB file. You must pass it a reference to a CFile that has already been opened for reading. I created this function with serialization in mind. The second parameter to this function is an offset of the location at which to start reading within the file. When you read a DIB file, this will always be 0. However, if you have serialized your DIB into a compound document, this parameter is the offset of DIB's start location. If you are using a compound document for storage and are reading it in, you can get the DIB offset using the following: CArchive::GetFile()->GetPosition().

```
// --------------------------------------------------------------
// XSDib_ReadFile
//   Parameters:
//       CFile& file - Reference to an already open CFile object
//          that has opened a DIB (*.BMP) file for reading.
//       DWORD dwOffset - The offset from the beginning of the
//          file to where the reading begins.
//   Return Value:
//       HDIB on success or NULL on failure.
//   Description:
//       Reads in the specified DIB file into a global chunk of
//       memory.
//       BITMAPFILEHEADER is stripped off of the DIB.  Everything
//       from the end of the BITMAPFILEHEADER structure on is
//       returned in the global memory handle.
// --------------------------------------------------------------
```

```
HDIB XSFUNC
XSDib_ReadFile(CFile& file, DWORD dwOffset)
{
#ifdef _USRDLL
    // if this code is in a user DLL, we need to set up the MFC
    // state if we use MFC in this function
    AFX_MANAGE_STATE(AfxGetStaticModuleState());
#endif

    BITMAPFILEHEADER bmfHeader;
    HDIB hDib;
    UINT nNumColors;                // Number of colors in DIB
    HDIB hDibtmp;                   // Used for GlobalRealloc()
    LPBITMAPINFOHEADER lpbi;
    DWORD offBits;

    // Allocate memory for header & color table. We'll enlarge
    // this memory as needed.
    hDib = (HDIB)::GlobalAlloc(GHND,
        (DWORD)(sizeof(BITMAPINFOHEADER) + 256 * sizeof(RGBQUAD)));
    if (!hDib)
    {
        ::XSError_Set(XSERR_MEMORY);
        return NULL;
    }

    lpbi = (LPBITMAPINFOHEADER)::GlobalLock((HGLOBAL)hDib);
    if (!lpbi)
    {
        ::GlobalFree(hDib);
        ::XSError_Set(XSERR_LOCK);
        return NULL;
    }
```

```
// read the BITMAPFILEHEADER from the file
if (sizeof(BITMAPFILEHEADER) !=
    file.Read((LPVOID)&bmfHeader, sizeof(BITMAPFILEHEADER)))
{
    ::XSError_Set(XSERR_OPEN);
    goto ErrExit;
}

// Verify BITMAP type
if (bmfHeader.bfType != macDibHeaderMarker)
{
    ::XSError_Set(XSERR_INVALIDFORMAT);
    goto ErrExit;
}

// read the BITMAPINFOHEADER from the file
if (sizeof(BITMAPINFOHEADER) !=
    file.Read((LPVOID)lpbi, sizeof(BITMAPINFOHEADER)))
{
    ::XSError_Set(XSERR_READ);
    goto ErrExit;
}

// Check to see that it's a Windows DIB -- an OS/2 DIB
// would cause strange problems with the rest of the
// DIB API since the fields in the header are different
// and the color table entries are smaller.
//
// If it's not a Windows DIB (e.g. if biSize is wrong),
// return NULL.
if (lpbi->biSize == sizeof(BITMAPCOREHEADER))
{
    ::XSError_Set(XSERR_INVALIDFORMAT);
    goto ErrExit;
```

```
    }

    // Now determine the size of the color table and read it.
    // Since the bitmap bits are offset in the file by
    // bfOffBits, we need to do some special processing here
    // to make sure the bits directly follow the color table
    // (because that's the format we are susposed to pass back)
    if (!(nNumColors = (UINT)lpbi->biClrUsed))
    {
        // No color table for 24-bit, default size otherwise
        if (lpbi->biBitCount != 24)
        {
            // Standard size table
            nNumColors = 1 << lpbi->biBitCount;
        }
    }


    // Fill in some default values if they are zero
    if (lpbi->biClrUsed == 0)
        lpbi->biClrUsed = nNumColors;


    if (lpbi->biSizeImage == 0)
    {
        lpbi->biSizeImage = (((((lpbi->biWidth *
            (DWORD)lpbi->biBitCount) + 31) & ~31) >> 3) *
            lpbi->biHeight;
    }

    // Get a proper-sized buffer for header,
    // color table and bits
    ::GlobalUnlock(hDib);
    hDibtmp = (HDIB)::GlobalReAlloc(hDib, lpbi->biSize +
        nNumColors * sizeof(RGBQUAD) + lpbi->biSizeImage, 0);
```

```
    if (!hDibtmp) // can't resize buffer for loading
    {
        ::XSError_Set(XSERR_MEMORY);
        goto ErrExitNoUnlock;
    }
    else
        hDib = hDibtmp;

    lpbi = (LPBITMAPINFOHEADER)::GlobalLock((HGLOBAL)hDib);

    // Read the color table
    file.Read((LPVOID)((LPSTR)(lpbi) + lpbi->biSize),
        nNumColors * sizeof(RGBQUAD));

    // Offset to the bits from start of DIB header
    offBits = lpbi->biSize + nNumColors * sizeof(RGBQUAD);

    // If the bfOffBits field is non-zero, then the bits might
    // *not* be directly following the color table in the file.
    // Use the value in bfOffBits to seek the bits.
    if (bmfHeader.bfOffBits != OL)
        file.Seek(dwOffset + bmfHeader.bfOffBits, SEEK_SET);

    if (file.Read((LPVOID)((LPBYTE)lpbi + offBits),
        lpbi->biSizeImage))
        goto OKExit;

ErrExit:
    ::GlobalUnlock(hDib);
ErrExitNoUnlock:
    ::GlobalFree(hDib);
    return NULL;

OKExit:
```

```
    ::GlobalUnlock(hDib);

    // Set error to no error
    ::XSError_Set(XSERR_NOERROR);

    return hDib;
}
```

XSDib_Save

This function is used to write a DIB to a file. You pass the DIB to write and the filename of the new DIB file to the function. It creates the file, truncating any existing file, and calls XSDib_WriteFile to do the actual saving into the file. If you call this function, your own code should first check to see if the file exists before it is overwritten. If it does exist, you may want to prompt the user and ask if it is okay to overwrite the existing file.

```
// ----------------------------------------------------------------
// XSDib_Save
//   Parameters:
//       HDIB hDib - Handle to the DIB to save to a file
//       CString strFileName - File name of the DIB to save to
//   Return Value:
//       XSERR_NOERROR - if successful
//       XSERR_HANDLENULL - the hDib handle was NULL
//       XSERR_OPEN - Unable to open file
//       XSERR_LOCK - Unable to lock memory
//       XSERR_INVALIDFORMAT - Invalid DIB format
//   Description:
//       Saves the specified DIB into the specified file name on
//       disk. No error checking is done, so if the file already
//       exists, it will be over written.
// ----------------------------------------------------------------
WORD XSFUNC
XSDib_Save(HDIB hDib, CString strFileName)
{
#ifdef _USRDLL
```

```
    // if this code is in a user DLL, we need to set up the MFC
    // state if we use MFC in this function
    AFX_MANAGE_STATE(AfxGetStaticModuleState());
#endif

    ::XSError_Set(XSERR_NOERROR);

    CFile file;
    CFileException e;

    if (!hDib)
    {
        ::XSError_Set(XSERR_HANDLENULL);
        return XSERR_HANDLENULL;
    }

    if (!file.Open(strFileName,
        CFile::modeCreate|CFile::modeWrite|CFile::shareExclusive,
        &e))
    {
#ifdef _DEBUG
        afxDump << "File (" << strFileName <<
            ") could not be created: " << e.m_cause << "\n";
#endif
        ::XSError_Set(XSERR_OPEN);
        return XSERR_OPEN;
    }

    WORD wResult = ::XSDib_WriteFile(hDib, file);
    file.Close();

    return wResult;
}
```

I

2

XSDib_WriteFile

This function provides the main functionality for writing a DIB to a file. Again, I created this function with serialization in mind. By passing in a reference to a CFile to an already opened file, you could serialize your DIB with other objects. If you want to use MFC's CArchive class in your document's Serialize member function, you would make your call as follows, where ar is the reference to the Carchive.

```
if (XSERR_NOERROR !=::XSDib_WriteFile(hDib, *(ar.GetFile())))
    AfxThrowArchiveException(CArchiveException::generic);
```

If you just wanted to write to a *.bmp file, it would be better to call the XSDib_Save function.

```
// ------------------------------------------------------------
// XSDib_WriteFile
//   Parameters:
//       HDIB hDib - Handle to the DIB to save to a file
//       CFile& file - Reference to an already open CFile object
//        that has opened a DIB (*.BMP) file for writing.
//   Return Value:
//       XSERR_NOERROR - if successful
//       XSERR_HANDLENULL - the hDib handle was NULL
//       XSERR_OPEN - Unable to open file
//       XSERR_LOCK - Unable to lock memory
//       XSERR_INVALIDFORMAT - Invalid DIB format
//   Description:
//       Saves the specified DIB into already opened file handle
// ------------------------------------------------------------
WORD XSFUNC
XSDib_WriteFile(HDIB hDib, CFile& file)
{
#ifdef _USRDLL
    // if this code is in a user DLL, we need to set up the MFC
    // state if we use MFC in this function
    AFX_MANAGE_STATE(AfxGetStaticModuleState());
#endif
```

I

2

```
BITMAPFILEHEADER bmfHdr;    // Header for Bitmap file
LPBITMAPINFOHEADER lpBI;    // Pointer to DIB info structure
DWORD dwDIBSize;

if (!hDib)
{
    ::XSError_Set(XSERR_HANDLENULL);
    return XSERR_HANDLENULL;
}


// Get a pointer to the DIB memory, the first of which
// contains a BITMAPINFO structure
lpBI = (LPBITMAPINFOHEADER)::GlobalLock((HGLOBAL)hDib);
if (!lpBI)
{
    ::XSError_Set(XSERR_LOCK);
    return XSERR_LOCK;
}


// Check to see if we're dealing with an OS/2 DIB.  If so,
// don't save it because our functions aren't written to
// deal with these DIBs.
if (lpBI->biSize != sizeof(BITMAPINFOHEADER))
{
    ::GlobalUnlock(hDib);
    ::XSError_Set(XSERR_INVALIDFORMAT);
    return XSERR_INVALIDFORMAT;
}


//Fill in the fields of the file header

// Fill in file type
// (first 2 bytes must be "BM" for a bitmap)
```

```
bmfHdr.bfType = macDibHeaderMarker;  // "BM"

// Calculating the size of the DIB is a bit tricky (if we
// want to do it right).  The easiest way to do this is to
// call GlobalSize() on our global handle, but since the
// size of our global memory may have been padded a few
// bytes, we may end up writing out a few too many bytes
// to the file (which may cause problems with some apps)
//
// So, instead let's calculate the size manually.
//
// To do this, find size of header plus size of color
// table.  Since the first DWORD in both BITMAPINFOHEADER
// and BITMAPCOREHEADER contains the size of the structure,
// let's use this.

// Partial Calculation
dwDIBSize = *(LPDWORD)lpBI + ::XSDib_PaletteSize(lpBI);

// Now calculate the size of the image
if ((lpBI->biCompression == BI_RLE8) ||
    (lpBI->biCompression == BI_RLE4))
{
    // It's an RLE bitmap, we can't calculate size, so
    // trust the biSizeImage field
    dwDIBSize += lpBI->biSizeImage;
}
else
{
    DWORD dwBmBitsSize;  // Size of Bitmap Bits only

    // It's not RLE, so size is
    // Width (DWORD aligned) * Height
    dwBmBitsSize = macDibWidthBytes((lpBI->biWidth) *
```

```
             ((DWORD)lpBI->biBitCount)) * lpBI->biHeight;

        dwDIBSize += dwBmBitsSize;

        // Now, since we have calculated the correct size, why
        // don't we fill in the biSizeImage field (this will
        // fix any .BMP files which  have this field incorrect).
        lpBI->biSizeImage = dwBmBitsSize;
    }

    // Calculate the file size by adding the DIB size
    // to sizeof(BITMAPFILEHEADER)
    bmfHdr.bfSize = dwDIBSize + sizeof(BITMAPFILEHEADER);
    bmfHdr.bfReserved1 = 0;
    bmfHdr.bfReserved2 = 0;

    // Now, calculate the offset the actual bitmap bits will
    // be in the file -- It's the Bitmap file header plus the
    // DIB header, plus the size of the color table.
    bmfHdr.bfOffBits = (DWORD)sizeof(BITMAPFILEHEADER) +
        lpBI->biSize + ::XSDib_PaletteSize(lpBI);

    try
    {
        // Write the file header
        file.Write(&bmfHdr, sizeof(BITMAPFILEHEADER));

        // Write the DIB header and the bits
        file.Write(lpBI, dwDIBSize);
    }
    catch (CFileException* e)
    {
#ifdef _DEBUG
        afxDump << "Could not write to file (" <<
```

```
            file.GetFilePath() << "): " << e->m_cause << "\n";
#endif
        e->Delete();
        ::GlobalUnlock(hDib);
        ::XSError_Set(XSERR_WRITE);
        return XSERR_WRITE; // error in the write

    }

    ::GlobalUnlock(hDib);

    ::XSError_Set(XSERR_NOERROR);
    return XSERR_NOERROR; // Success code

}
```

XSDib_Destroy

As with all memory allocations, we must take care to clean up when we are done. Pass the memory handle for your DIB to this function to complete the process.

```
// -----------------------------------------------------------------
// XSDib_Destroy
//   Parameters:
//       HDIB hDib - The handle to the DIB to be freed
//   Return Value:
//       None
//   Description:
//       Frees memory associated with a DIB
// -----------------------------------------------------------------
void XSFUNC
XSDib_Destroy(HDIB hDib)
{
    if (hDib)
    {
        ::GlobalFree(hDib);
        hDib = NULL;
```

I

2

```
        }

        ::XSError_Set(XSERR_NOERROR);

}
```

XSDib_Width

The XSDib_Width function is a utility function that comes in two flavors. In the first version, you can pass a pointer to your DIB. In the second version, you can pass the DIB memory handle to your DIB. Of course, the first version is going to be much faster, but the second version is there to do the dirty work for you when you need it.

Following the XSDib_Width function is a number of other utility functions that are built upon this same premise. The first version takes a pointer, the second takes a DIB memory handle and, ultimately, calls the first version.

Use the XSDib_Width function when you need to get at the width of the DIB.

```
// --------------------------------------------------------------
// XSDib_Width
//   Parameters:
//       LPVOID lpDib - pointer to a packed DIB memory block
//   Return Value:
//       LONG - the width of the DIB, -1 on error
//   Description:
//       Returns the width of the DIB
// --------------------------------------------------------------
LONG XSFUNC
XSDib_Width(LPVOID lpDib)
{
    ASSERT(lpDib);

    return ((LPBITMAPINFOHEADER)lpDib)->biWidth;
}


// --------------------------------------------------------------
// XSDib_Width
```

```
//   Parameters:
//       HDIB hDib - The handle to a DIB
//   Return Value:
//       LONG - the width of the DIB, -1 on error
//   Description:
//       Returns the width of the DIB
// -------------------------------------------------------------
LONG XSFUNC
XSDib_Width(HDIB hDib)
{
    ASSERT(hDib);

    LPVOID lpDIBHdr = NULL;  // Pointer to BITMAPINFOHEADER

    ::XSError_Set(XSERR_NOERROR);

    // Lock the memory block
    lpDIBHdr  = ::GlobalLock((HGLOBAL)hDib);
    if (!lpDIBHdr)
    {
        ::XSError_Set(XSERR_LOCK);
        return -1;
    }

    // Call the function
    LONG lWidth = ::XSDib_Width(lpDIBHdr);

    // Unlock the memory block
    ::GlobalUnlock(hDib);

    return lWidth;
}
```

XSDib_Height

Use the XSDib_Height function when you need the height, in pixels, of the DIB. Again, there are two version of this function. The first takes a memory pointer and the second takes a DIB memory handle.

```
// -----------------------------------------------------------------
// XSDib_Height
//  Parameters:
//       LPVOID lpDib - pointer to a packed DIB memory block
//  Return Value:
//       LONG - the height of the DIB, -1 on error
//  Description:
//       Returns the height of the DIB
// -----------------------------------------------------------------
LONG XSFUNC
XSDib_Height(LPVOID lpDib)
{
    ASSERT(lpDib);

    return ((LPBITMAPINFOHEADER)lpDib)->biHeight;
}


// -----------------------------------------------------------------
// XSDib_Height
//  Parameters:
//       HDIB hDib - The handle to a DIB
//  Return Value:
//       LONG - the height of the DIB, -1 on error
//  Description:
//       Returns the height of the DIB
// -----------------------------------------------------------------
LONG XSFUNC
XSDib_Height(HDIB hDib)
{
    ASSERT(hDib);
```

```
    LPVOID lpDIBHdr = NULL;  // Pointer to BITMAPINFOHEADER

    ::XSError_Set(XSERR_NOERROR);

    // Lock the memory block
    lpDIBHdr  = ::GlobalLock((HGLOBAL)hDib);
    if (!lpDIBHdr)
    {
        ::XSError_Set(XSERR_LOCK);
        return -1;
    }

    // Call the function
    LONG lHeight = ::XSDib_Height(lpDIBHdr);

    // Unlock the memory block
    ::GlobalUnlock(hDib);

    return lHeight;
}
```

XSDib_PaletteSize

The XSDib_PaletteSize function is used to return the size of the palette
associated with the DIB. It calculates the size of the palette by multiplying
the number of colors in use by the DIB by the size of an RGBQUAD. An
RGBQUAD is the structure used to maintain color map entries in the DIB and is
discussed earlier in this chapter.

```
// ------------------------------------------------------------------
// XSDib_PaletteSize
//  Parameters:
//      LPVOID lpDib - pointer to a packed DIB memory block
//  Return Value:
//      WORD - the size of the associated palette, -1 on error
//  Description:
```

```
//      Returns the size of the palette
//      This function gets the size required to store the
//      DIB's palette by multiplying the number of colors by
//      the size of an RGBQUAD
// ----------------------------------------------------------
WORD XSFUNC
XSDib_PaletteSize(LPVOID lpDib)
{
    ASSERT(lpDib);

    ::XSError_Set(XSERR_NOERROR);

    // Calculate the size required by the palette
    if (macIsWinDib(lpDib))
        return (::XSDib_NumColors(lpDib) * sizeof(RGBQUAD));
    else
    {
        ::XSError_Set(XSERR_INVALIDFORMAT);
        return -1;
    }
}


// ----------------------------------------------------------
// XSDib_PaletteSize
// Parameters:
//      HDIB hDib - The handle to a DIB
// Return Value:
//      WORD - the size of the associated palette, -1 on error
// Description:
//      Returns the size of the palette
//      This function gets the size required to store the
//      DIB's palette by multiplying the number of colors by
//      the size of an RGBQUAD
// ----------------------------------------------------------
```

I

2

```
WORD XSFUNC
XSDib_PaletteSize(HDIB hDib)
{
    ASSERT(hDib);

    LPVOID lpDIBHdr = NULL;  // Pointer to BITMAPINFOHEADER

    ::XSError_Set(XSERR_NOERROR);

    // Lock the memory block
    lpDIBHdr  = ::GlobalLock((HGLOBAL)hDib);
    if (!lpDIBHdr)
    {
        ::XSError_Set(XSERR_LOCK);
        return -1;
    }

    // Call the function
    WORD wPalSize = ::XSDib_PaletteSize(lpDIBHdr);

    // Unlock the memory block
    ::GlobalUnlock(hDib);

    return wPalSize;
}
```

XSDib_NumColors

The XSDib_NumColors function returns the number of colors in the DIB's color table. This very basic routine makes some assumptions on the number of colors based on the DIB's bit count. This routine is enough to get you what you need, but when you write your DIBs to a file, they may be a bit bigger than is necessary.

It's conceivable that although a DIB may contain 256 colors that it may not use all of those entries or that some of them may even be duplicates. You can reduce the color table and optimize it by using a quantization rou-

XSDib_CalcBytesPerLine

XSDib_CalcBytesPerLine isery similar to the XSDib_CalcPadding function. The XSDib_CalcBytesPerLine function calculates the number of bytes needed per scan line given the desired width of a DIB. Again, you will probably never call this function directly, but it is used by this DIB API.

```
// -------------------------------------------------------------
// XSDib_CalcBytesPerLine
//  Parameters:
//        DWORD - count of BPP (Bits Per Pixel)
//        DWORD - source width
//  Return Value:
//        DWORD - needed bytes per line, DWORD aligned
//  Description:
//        Calculate the bytes per line required to align on
//        DWORDs since DIB scan lines are aligned on DWORD
//        boundaries.
// -------------------------------------------------------------
DWORD XSFUNC
XSDib_CalcBytesPerLine(DWORD dwBitsPerPixel, DWORD dwWidth)
{
    DWORD dwBits, dwPadBits;

    dwBits    = dwBitsPerPixel * dwWidth;

    if ((dwBits % 32) == 0)
    {
        // Already DWORD aligned, no padding needed
        return (dwBits / 8);
    }
    else
        dwPadBits = 32 - (dwBits % 32);

    return (dwBits / 8 + dwPadBits / 8 + (((dwPadBits % 8) > 0) - 1 : 0));
}
```

XSDib_LastByte

The XSDib_LastByte function returns the byte of the last pixel based on the number of bits per pixel and the number of pixels (like a width or height). This is another function that you will probably never call directly, unless you get into extreme image manipulation on your own.

```
// ------------------------------------------------------------
// XSDib_LastByte
// Parameters:
//        DWORD - count of BPP (Bits Per Pixel)
//        DWORD - the number of pixels in this scanline
// Return Value:
//        DWORD - the byte offset of the last pixel
// Description:
//        Returns the byte of the last pixel based on number of
//        pixels and BPP.
// ------------------------------------------------------------
DWORD XSFUNC
XSDib_LastByte(DWORD dwBitsPerPixel, DWORD dwPixels)
{
    DWORD dwBits, extraBits, numBytes;

    dwBits = dwBitsPerPixel * dwPixels;
        numBytes  = dwBits / 8;

        extraBits = dwBits - numBytes * 8;
        if((extraBits % 8) > 0)
                numBytes++;

    return (numBytes);
}
```

XSDib_CreatePalette

Use the XSDib_CreatePalette function to create a palette based on the passed DIB memory handle. This function returns an HPALETTE memory

handle. You are responsible for calling ::DestroyObject() on the palette
handle once you are done with it.

```
// -----------------------------------------------------------
// XSDib_CreatePalette
//   Parameters:
//       hDib - handle to a DIB
//   Return Value:
//       HPALETTE - handle to new palette, NULL on error
//   Description:
//       Returns a handle to an HPALETTE created from the
//       associated DIB.
//       This function creates a palette from a DIB by allocating
//       memory for the logical palette, reading and storing the
//       colors from the DIB's color table into the logical
//       palette, creating a palette from this logical palette,
//       and then returning the palette's handle. This allows the
//       DIB to be displayed using the best possible colors
//       (important for DIBs with 256 or more colors).
// -----------------------------------------------------------
HPALETTE XSFUNC
XSDib_CreatePalette(HDIB hDib)
{
    ASSERT(hDib);

    // pointer to a logical palette
    LPLOGPALETTE lpPal = NULL;

    // handle to a logical palette
    HANDLE hLogPal = NULL;

    // handle to a palette
    HPALETTE hPal = NULL;

    // loop index, number of colors in color table
```

```
int i, wNumColors;

// pointer to packed-DIB
LPVOID lpbi = NULL;

// pointer to BITMAPINFO structure (Win3.0)
LPBITMAPINFO lpbmi = NULL;

// flag which signifies whether this is a Win3.0 DIB
BOOL bWinStyleDib;

// if handle to DIB is invalid, return a half tone palette
if (!hDib)
{
    HDC hDC = ::GetDC(NULL);
    hPal = ::CreateHalftonePalette(hDC);
    ::ReleaseDC(NULL, hDC);
    ::XSError_Set(XSERR_HANDLENULL);
    return hPal;
}

// lock DIB memory block and get a pointer to it
lpbi = ::GlobalLock((HGLOBAL)hDib);
ASSERT(lpbi);  // sanity check
if (!lpbi)
{
    ::XSError_Set(XSERR_LOCK);
    return NULL;
}

// get pointer to BITMAPINFO (Win 3.0)
lpbmi = (LPBITMAPINFO)lpbi;

// get the number of colors in the DIB
```

```
wNumColors = ::XSDib_NumColors(lpbi);

// is this a Win 3.0 DIB-
bWinStyleDib = macIsWinDib(lpbi);

// We're not handling OS/2 bitmap
if (!bWinStyleDib)
    return FALSE;

if (wNumColors)
{
    // allocate memory block for logical palette
    hLogPal = ::GlobalAlloc(GHND, sizeof(LOGPALETTE) +
        sizeof(PALETTEENTRY) * wNumColors);

    // if not enough memory, clean up and return NULL
    if (!hLogPal)
    {
        ::GlobalUnlock(hDib);
        ::XSError_Set(XSERR_MEMORY);
        return NULL;
    }

    // lock memory block and get pointer to it
    lpPal = (LPLOGPALETTE)::GlobalLock((HGLOBAL)hLogPal);
    if (!lpPal)
    {
        ::GlobalUnlock(hDib);
        ::XSError_Set(XSERR_LOCK);
        return NULL;
    }

    // set version and number of palette entries
    lpPal->palVersion = PALVERSION;
```

```
            lpPal->palNumEntries = wNumColors;

            // store RGB triples into palette
            for (i = 0; i < wNumColors; i++)
            {
                lpPal->palPalEntry[i].peRed =
                    lpbmi->bmiColors[i].rgbRed;
                lpPal->palPalEntry[i].peGreen =
                    lpbmi->bmiColors[i].rgbGreen;
                lpPal->palPalEntry[i].peBlue =
                    lpbmi->bmiColors[i].rgbBlue;
                lpPal->palPalEntry[i].peFlags = 0;
            }

            // create the palette and get handle to it
            hPal = ::CreatePalette(lpPal);

            // if error getting handle to palette, clean up and
            // return NULL
            if (!hPal)
            {
                ::GlobalUnlock(hLogPal);
                ::GlobalFree(hLogPal);
                ::XSError_Set(XSERR_CREATEPAL);
                return NULL;
            }
        }
    else
    {
        HDC hDC = ::GetDC(NULL);
        hPal = ::CreateHalftonePalette(hDC);
        ::ReleaseDC(NULL, hDC);
    }
```

```
    // clean up
    if (hLogPal)
    {
        ::GlobalUnlock(hLogPal);
        ::GlobalFree(hLogPal);
    }

    ::GlobalUnlock(hDib);

    ::XSError_Set(XSERR_NOERROR);

    // return handle to DIB's palette
    return hPal;
}
```

XSBmp_ToDib

The function XSBmp_ToDib is one of two conversion routines that convert to or from a DIB. This function converts a DDB to a DIB.

```
// -------------------------------------------------------------
// XSBmp_ToDib
// Parameters:
//     HBITMAP - handle to a Bitmap that the DIB is to be
//      created from
//     HPALETTE - palette to use in creation of DIB
// Return Value:
//     HDIB - handle of the DIB created from the Bitmap, NULL
//      on error
// Description:
//     Returns an HDIB created from an HBITMAP.
//     This function creates a DIB from a bitmap using the
//     specified palette.
// -------------------------------------------------------------
HDIB XSFUNC
XSBmp_ToDib(HBITMAP hBitmap, HPALETTE hPal)
```

```
{
    ASSERT(hBitmap);

    BITMAP bm;                 // bitmap structure
    BITMAPINFOHEADER bi;       // bitmap header
    LPBITMAPINFOHEADER lpbi;   // pointer to BITMAPINFOHEADER
    DWORD dwLen;               // size of memory block
    HDIB hDib, h;              // handle to DIB, temp handle
    HDC hDC;                   // handle to DC
    WORD biBits;               // bits per pixel
    UINT wLineLen;
    DWORD dwSize;
    DWORD wColSize;

    // check if bitmap handle is valid
    if (!hBitmap)
    {
        ::XSError_Set(XSERR_HANDLENULL);
        return NULL;
    }

    // fill in BITMAP structure, return NULL if it didn't work
    if (!::GetObject(hBitmap, sizeof(bm), &bm))
    {
        ::XSError_Set(XSERR_GETOBJECT);
        return NULL;
    }

    // if no palette is specified, use default palette
    if (hPal == NULL)
        hPal = (HPALETTE)::GetStockObject(DEFAULT_PALETTE);

    // calculate bits per pixel
    biBits = bm.bmPlanes * bm.bmBitsPixel;
```

```
wLineLen = ( bm.bmWidth * biBits + 31 ) / 32 * 4;
wColSize = sizeof(RGBQUAD) * (( biBits <= 8 ) -
    1 << biBits : 0 );
dwSize = sizeof( BITMAPINFOHEADER ) + wColSize +
    (DWORD)(UINT)wLineLen * (DWORD)(UINT)bm.bmHeight;

// make sure bits per pixel is valid
if (biBits <= 1)
    biBits = 1;
else if (biBits <= 4)
    biBits = 4;
else if (biBits <= 8)
    biBits = 8;
else // if greater than 8-bit, force to 24-bit
    biBits = 24;

// initialize BITMAPINFOHEADER
bi.biSize = sizeof(BITMAPINFOHEADER);
bi.biWidth = bm.bmWidth;
bi.biHeight = bm.bmHeight;
bi.biPlanes = 1;
bi.biBitCount = biBits;
bi.biCompression = BI_RGB;
bi.biSizeImage = dwSize - sizeof(BITMAPINFOHEADER) - wCol-
Size;
bi.biXPelsPerMeter = 0;
bi.biYPelsPerMeter = 0;
bi.biClrUsed = ( biBits <= 8 ) - 1 << biBits : 0;
bi.biClrImportant = 0;

// calculate size of memory block required to store BITMAPINFO
dwLen = bi.biSize + ::XSDib_PaletteSize(&bi);

// get a DC
```

```
hDC = ::GetDC(NULL);

// select and realize our palette
hPal = ::SelectPalette(hDC, hPal, FALSE);
::RealizePalette(hDC);

// alloc memory block to store our bitmap
hDib = (HDIB)::GlobalAlloc(GHND, dwLen);

// if we couldn't get memory block
if (!hDib)
{
    // clean up and return NULL
    ::SelectPalette(hDC, hPal, TRUE);
    ::RealizePalette(hDC);
    ::ReleaseDC(NULL, hDC);

    ::XSError_Set(XSERR_MEMORY);
    return NULL;
}

// lock memory and get pointer to it
lpbi = (LPBITMAPINFOHEADER)::GlobalLock((HGLOBAL)hDib);
if (!lpbi)
{
    // clean up and return NULL
    ::SelectPalette(hDC, hPal, TRUE);
    ::RealizePalette(hDC);
    ::ReleaseDC(NULL, hDC);

    ::XSError_Set(XSERR_LOCK);
    return NULL;
}
```

```
// use our bitmap info. to fill BITMAPINFOHEADER
*lpbi = bi;


// call GetDIBits with a NULL lpBits param, so it will
// calculate the biSizeImage field for us
::GetDIBits(hDC, hBitmap, 0, (WORD)bi.biHeight, NULL,
    (LPBITMAPINFO)lpbi, DIB_RGB_COLORS);


// get the info. returned by GetDIBits and unlock
// memory block
bi = *lpbi;
bi.biClrUsed = ( biBits <= 8 ) - 1 << biBits : 0;
::GlobalUnlock(hDib);


// if the driver did not fill in the biSizeImage field,
// make one up
if (bi.biSizeImage == 0)
    bi.biSizeImage =
    macDibWidthBytes((DWORD)bm.bmWidth * biBits) * bm.bmHeight;


// realloc the buffer big enough to hold all the bits
dwLen = bi.biSize + ::XSDib_PaletteSize(&bi) +
    bi.biSizeImage;
if (h = (HDIB)::GlobalReAlloc(hDib, dwLen, 0))
    hDib = h;
else
{
    // clean up and return NULL
    ::GlobalFree(hDib);
    hDib = NULL;

    ::SelectPalette(hDC, hPal, TRUE);
    ::RealizePalette(hDC);
    ::ReleaseDC(NULL, hDC);
```

```
        ::XSError_Set(XSERR_MEMORY);
    return NULL;
}

// lock memory block and get pointer to it
lpbi = (LPBITMAPINFOHEADER)::GlobalLock((HGLOBAL)hDib);
if (!lpbi)
{
    // clean up and return NULL
    ::GlobalFree(hDib);
    hDib = NULL;

    ::SelectPalette(hDC, hPal, TRUE);
    ::RealizePalette(hDC);
    ::ReleaseDC(NULL, hDC);

    ::XSError_Set(XSERR_MEMORY);
    return NULL;
}

// call GetDIBits with a NON-NULL lpBits param, and
// actualy get the bits this time
if (::GetDIBits(hDC, hBitmap, 0, (WORD)bi.biHeight,
    (LPSTR)lpbi + (WORD)lpbi->biSize +
    ::XSDib_PaletteSize(lpbi), (LPBITMAPINFO)lpbi,
    DIB_RGB_COLORS) == 0)
{
    // clean up and return NULL
    ::GlobalUnlock(hDib);
    hDib = NULL;

    ::SelectPalette(hDC, hPal, TRUE);
    ::RealizePalette(hDC);
```

```
        ::ReleaseDC(NULL, hDC);

        ::XSError_Set(XSERR_GETBITS);
        return NULL;
    }

    bi = *lpbi;

    // clean up
    ::GlobalUnlock(hDib);
    ::SelectPalette(hDC, hPal, TRUE);
    ::RealizePalette(hDC);
    ::ReleaseDC(NULL, hDC);

    ::XSError_Set(XSERR_NOERROR);

    // return handle to the DIB
    return hDib;
}
```

XSDib_ToBmp

This is the second of two conversion routines that convert to or from a DIB. Use XSDib_ToBmp to convert a DIB to a DDB.

```
// -------------------------------------------------------------
// XSDib_ToBmp
//  Parameters:
//      HDIB - handle to a DIB that the Bitmap (DDB) is to be
//        created from
//      HPALETTE - palette to use in creation of bitmap (DDB)
//  Return Value:
//      HBITMAP - handle of the Bitmap created from the DIB,
//        NULL on error
//  Description:
//      Returns an HBITMAP created from an HDIB.
```

```
//      This function creates a bitmap from a DIB using the
//      specified palette. If no palette is specified, one is
//      created, used for the conversion, and then deleted.
//
//      The bitmap returned from this function is always a
//      bitmap compatible with the screen (e.g. same
//      bits/pixel and color planes) rather than a bitmap
//      with the same attributes as the DIB.
//
//      This behavior is by design, and occurs because this
//      function calls ::CreateDIBitmap to do its work, and
//      ::CreateDIBitmap always creates a bitmap compatible with
//      the hDC parameter passed in (because it in turn calls
//      ::CreateCompatibleBitmap).
//
//      So for instance, if your DIB is a monochrome DIB and
//      you call this function, you will not get back a
//      monochrome HBITMAP -- you will get an HBITMAP
//      compatible with the screen DC, but with only 2 colors
//      used in the bitmap.
//
//      If your application requires a monochrome HBITMAP
//      returned for a monochrome DIB, use the function
//      ::SetDIBits().
// --------------------------------------------------------------
HBITMAP XSFUNC
XSDib_ToBmp(HDIB hDib, HPALETTE hPal)
{
    ASSERT(hDib);

    LPVOID lpDIBHdr = NULL;  // pointer to DIB header
    LPVOID lpDIBBits = NULL; // pointer to DIB bits
    HBITMAP hBitmap = NULL;  // handle to DDB
    HDC hDC = NULL;          // handle to DC
```

```
HPALETTE hOldPal = NULL; // handle to a palette
BOOL bPalCreated = FALSE;


::XSError_Set(XSERR_NOERROR);


// if invalid handle, return NULL
if (!hDib)
{
    ::XSError_Set(XSERR_HANDLENULL);
    return NULL;
}


// lock memory block and get a pointer to it
lpDIBHdr = ::GlobalLock((HGLOBAL)hDib);
if (!lpDIBHdr)
{
    ::XSError_Set(XSERR_LOCK);
    return NULL;
}


// get a pointer to the DIB bits
lpDIBBits = ::XSDib_FindBits(lpDIBHdr);
if (!lpDIBBits)
    return NULL;


// get a DC
hDC = ::GetDC(NULL);
if (!hDC)
{
    // clean up and return NULL
    ::GlobalUnlock(hDib);

    ::XSError_Set(XSERR_GETDC);
    return NULL;
```

I

2

```
}

// select and realize palette
if (!hPal)
{
    hPal = ::XSDib_CreatePalette(hDib);
    bPalCreated = TRUE;
}
hOldPal = ::SelectPalette(hDC, hPal, FALSE);
::RealizePalette(hDC);

// create bitmap from DIB info. and bits
hBitmap = ::CreateDIBitmap(hDC, (LPBITMAPINFOHEADER)lpDIBHdr,
    CBM_INIT, lpDIBBits, (LPBITMAPINFO)lpDIBHdr,
    DIB_RGB_COLORS);
if (!hBitmap)
{
    if (hOldPal)
        ::SelectPalette(hDC, hOldPal, FALSE);
    ::DeleteObject(hPal);
    ::XSError_Set(XSERR_CREATEBITMAP);
    return NULL;
}

// restore previous palette
if (hOldPal)
    ::SelectPalette(hDC, hOldPal, FALSE);

// if we created the palette then we clean it up
if (bPalCreated && hPal)
    ::DeleteObject(hPal);

// clean up
::ReleaseDC(NULL, hDC);
```

```
      ::GlobalUnlock(hDib);

      // return handle to the bitmap
      return hBitmap;
}
```

XSDib_Paint

The XSDib_Paint function paints a DIB to the passed device context. You must also pass a CRect that contains the coordinate values of the location at which to paint. If the CRect is the same dimensions as the DIB, the function uses ::SetDIBitsToDevice; otherwise, it uses ::StretchDIBits.

```
// ----------------------------------------------------------
// XSDib_Paint
//  Parameters:
//      HDC hDC - DC to do output to
//      CRect rcDim - rectangle on DC to do output to
//      HDIB hDib - handle to global memory with a DIB spec in
//       it followed by the DIB bits
//      CRect rcDib - rectangle of DIB to output into DC
//  Return Value:
//      BOOL - TRUE if DIB was drawn, FALSE otherwise
//  Description:
//      Painting routine for a DIB.  Calls StretchDIBits() or
//      SetDIBitsToDevice() to paint the DIB.  The DIB is
//      output to the specified DC, at the coordinates given
//      in lpDCRect.  The area of the DIB to be output is
//      given by lpDIBRect.
//
//      This function always selects the palette as
//      background. Before calling this function, be sure your
//      palette is selected to desired priority (foreground
//      or background).
// ----------------------------------------------------------
BOOL XSFUNC
XSDib_Paint(HDC hDC, CRect rcDim, HDIB hDib, CRect rcDib,
```

```
                    HPALETTE hPal)
{
#ifdef _USRDLL
    // if this code is in a user DLL, we need to set up the MFC
    // state if we use MFC in this function
    AFX_MANAGE_STATE(AfxGetStaticModuleState());
#endif


    ASSERT(hDib);


    LPVOID lpDIBHdr = NULL;  // pointer to DIB header
    LPVOID lpDIBBits = NULL; // pointer to DIB bits
    BOOL bSuccess = FALSE;   // Success/fail flag
    HPALETTE hOldPal = NULL; // Previous palette


    // Check for valid DIB handle
    if (!hDib)
    {
        ::XSError_Set(XSERR_HANDLENULL);
        return FALSE;
    }


    // Lock the DIB, and get a pointer to the beginning
    // of the bit buffer
    lpDIBHdr  = ::GlobalLock((HGLOBAL)hDib);
    if (!lpDIBHdr)
    {
        ::XSError_Set(XSERR_LOCK);
        return FALSE;
    }


    lpDIBBits = ::XSDib_FindBits(lpDIBHdr);
    if (!lpDIBBits)
        return FALSE;
```

```
// Select and realize our palette as background
if (hPal)
{
    hOldPal = ::SelectPalette(hDC, hPal, TRUE);
    ::RealizePalette(hDC);
}


// Make sure to use the stretching mode best for color
// pictures
::SetStretchBltMode(hDC, COLORONCOLOR);


// Determine whether to call StretchDIBits() or
// SetDIBitsToDevice()
if ((rcDim.Width()  == rcDib.Width()) &&
    (rcDim.Height() == rcDib.Height()))
{
    bSuccess = ::SetDIBitsToDevice(hDC, rcDim.left, rcDim.top,
        rcDim.Width(), rcDim.Height(), rcDib.left,
        (int)::XSDib_Height(lpDIBHdr) - rcDib.top -
        rcDib.Height(), 0, ::XSDib_Height(lpDIBHdr),
        lpDIBBits, (LPBITMAPINFO)lpDIBHdr, DIB_RGB_COLORS);
}
else
{
    bSuccess = ::StretchDIBits(hDC, rcDim.left, rcDim.top,
        rcDim.Width(), rcDim.Height(), rcDib.left, rcDib.top,
        rcDib.Width(), rcDib.Height(), lpDIBBits,
        (LPBITMAPINFO)lpDIBHdr, DIB_RGB_COLORS, SRCCOPY);
}


if (bSuccess)
    ::XSError_Set(XSERR_NOERROR);
else
```

```
                ::XSError_Set(XSERR_PAINT);

        // Unlock the memory block
        ::GlobalUnlock(hDib);

        // Reselect old palette
        if (hOldPal)
            ::SelectPalette(hDC, hOldPal, FALSE);

        // Return with success/fail flag
        return bSuccess;
}
```

XSBmp_ChangeFormat

The XSBmp_ChangeFormat function is used to convert a DDB to a DIB with different bits per pixel (BPP) than the original DDB. For instance, use this function to convert an 8-bit BPP DDB to a 24-bit BPP DIB.

```
// -------------------------------------------------------------
// XSBmp_ChangeFormat
//  Parameters:
//        HBITMAP - handle to a bitmap
//        WORD - desired bits per pixel (BPP)
//          - May be 0 if you pass BI_RLE4 or BI_RLE8
//        DWORD - desired compression format
//          BI_RLE4 - Use with 4-bit BPP
//          BI_RLE8 - Use with 8-bit BPP
//          BI_RGB - Use with 1, 4, 8, 16, or 32-bit BPP
//        HPALETTE - handle to palette
//  Return Value:
//        HDIB - handle to the new DIB if successful, else NULL
//  Description:
//        This function will convert a bitmap to the specified
//        bits per pixel and compression format. The bitmap and
//        it's palette will remain after calling this function.
```

```
// -------------------------------------------------------------
HDIB XSFUNC
XSBmp_ChangeFormat(HBITMAP hBitmap, WORD wBitCount,
    DWORD dwCompression, HPALETTE hPal)
{
    HDC                 hDC;            // Screen DC
    HDIB                hNewDIB=NULL;   // Handle to new DIB
    BITMAP              bm;             // BITMAP data structure
    BITMAPINFOHEADER    bi;             // Bitmap info. header
    LPBITMAPINFOHEADER lpbi;            // Pointer to bitmap header
    HPALETTE            hOldPal=NULL;   // Handle to palette
    WORD                NewBPP;         // New bits per pixel
    DWORD               NewComp;        // New compression format

    // Check for a valid bitmap handle
    if (!hBitmap)
    {
        ::XSError_Set(XSERR_HANDLENULL);
        return NULL;
    }

    // Validate wBitCount and dwCompression
    // They must match correctly (i.e., BI_RLE4 and 4 BPP or
    // BI_RLE8 and 8BPP, etc.) or we return failure
    if (wBitCount == 0)
    {
        NewComp = dwCompression;
        if (NewComp == BI_RLE4)
            NewBPP = 4;
        else if (NewComp == BI_RLE8)
            NewBPP = 8;
        else // Not enough info
        {
            ::XSError_Set(XSERR_INVALIDFORMAT);
```

```
                return NULL;
        }
    }
    else if (wBitCount == 1 && dwCompression == BI_RGB)
    {
        NewBPP = wBitCount;
        NewComp = BI_RGB;
    }
    else if (wBitCount == 4)
    {
        NewBPP = wBitCount;
        if (dwCompression == BI_RGB || dwCompression == BI_RLE4)
            NewComp = dwCompression;
        else
        {
            ::XSError_Set(XSERR_INVALIDFORMAT);
            return NULL;
        }
    }
    else if (wBitCount == 8)
    {
        NewBPP = wBitCount;
        if (dwCompression == BI_RGB || dwCompression == BI_RLE8)
            NewComp = dwCompression;
        else
        {
            ::XSError_Set(XSERR_INVALIDFORMAT);
            return NULL;
        }
    }
    else if ((wBitCount == 24 || wBitCount == 36)
        && dwCompression == BI_RGB)
    {
        NewBPP = wBitCount;
```

```
        NewComp = BI_RGB;
}
else
{
    ::XSError_Set(XSERR_INVALIDFORMAT);
    return NULL;
}


// Get info about the bitmap
::GetObject(hBitmap, sizeof(BITMAP), &bm);

// Fill in the BITMAPINFOHEADER appropriately
bi.biSize              = sizeof(BITMAPINFOHEADER);
bi.biWidth             = bm.bmWidth;
bi.biHeight            = bm.bmHeight;
bi.biPlanes            = 1;
bi.biBitCount          = NewBPP;
bi.biCompression       = NewComp;
bi.biSizeImage         = 0;
bi.biXPelsPerMeter     = 0;
bi.biYPelsPerMeter     = 0;
bi.biClrUsed           = 0;
bi.biClrImportant      = 0;


// Go allocate room for the new DIB
hNewDIB = ::XSDib_Template(bi, hBitmap);
if (!hNewDIB)
    return NULL;


// Get a pointer to the new DIB
lpbi = (LPBITMAPINFOHEADER)::GlobalLock(hNewDIB);
if (!lpbi)
{
    ::XSError_Set(XSERR_LOCK);
```

```
        return NULL;
    }


    // If we have a palette, get a DC and select/realize it
    if (hPal)
    {
        hDC  = ::GetDC(NULL);
        hOldPal = ::SelectPalette(hDC, hPal, FALSE);
        ::RealizePalette(hDC);
    }


    // Call GetDIBits and get the new DIB bits
    if (!GetDIBits(hDC, hBitmap, 0, (WORD) lpbi->biHeight,
        (LPSTR)lpbi + (WORD)lpbi->biSize
        + ::XSDib_PaletteSize(lpbi),
        (LPBITMAPINFO)lpbi, DIB_RGB_COLORS))
    {
        ::GlobalUnlock(hNewDIB);
        ::GlobalFree(hNewDIB);
        hNewDIB = NULL;
    }


    // Clean up and return
    if (hOldPal)
    {
        ::SelectPalette(hDC, hOldPal, TRUE);
        ::RealizePalette(hDC);
        ::ReleaseDC(NULL, hDC);
    }


    if (hNewDIB)
    {
        // Unlock the new DIB's memory block
        ::GlobalUnlock(hNewDIB);
```

```
      }

      ::XSError_Set(XSERR_NOERROR);
      return hNewDIB;
}
```

XSDib_ChangeFormat

Use the XSDib_ChangeFormat function to change a DIB with one type of BPP to another. For instance, you can use this function to change an 8-bit BPP DIB to a 24-bit BPP DIB.

```
// -------------------------------------------------------------
// XSDib_ChangeFormat
//   Parameters:
//        HDIB - handle to packed-DIB in memory
//        WORD - desired bits per pixel
//        DWORD - desired compression format
//          BI_RLE4 - Use with 4-bit BPP
//          BI_RLE8 - Use with 8-bit BPP
//          BI_RGB - Use with 1, 4, 8, 16, or 32-bit BPP
//   Return Value:
//        HDIB - handle to the new DIB if successful, else NULL
//   Description:
//        Formats a DIB to a new BPP.
//        This function will convert the bits per pixel and/or the
//        compression format of the specified DIB. Note: If the
//        conversion was unsuccessful, we return NULL. The
//        original DIB is left alone. Don't use code like the
//        following:
//
//        hMyDIB = XSDib_ChangeFormat(hMyDIB, 8, BI_RLE4);
//
//        The conversion will fail, but hMyDIB will now be NULL
//        and the original DIB will now hang around in memory. We
//        could have returned the old DIB, but we wanted to allow
```

```
//      the programmer to check whether this conversion
//      succeeded or failed.
// ------------------------------------------------------------
HDIB XSFUNC
XSDib_ChangeFormat(HDIB hDib, WORD wBitCount, DWORD dwCompression)
{
    HDC                 hDC;              // Handle to DC
    HBITMAP             hBitmap;          // Handle to bitmap
    BITMAP              bm;               // BITMAP data structure
    BITMAPINFOHEADER    bi;               // Bitmap info header
    LPBITMAPINFOHEADER  lpbi;             // Pointer to bitmap info
    HDIB                hNewDIB = NULL;   // Handle to new DIB
    HPALETTE            hPal, hOldPal;    // Handle to palette, prev pal
    WORD                DIBBPP, NewBPP;   // DIB bits per pixel, new bpp
    DWORD               DIBComp, NewComp; // DIB compression, new
                                          // compression


    // Check for a valid DIB handle
    if (!hDib)
    {
        ::XSError_Set(XSERR_HANDLENULL);
        return NULL;
    }


    // Get the old DIB's bits per pixel and compression format
    lpbi = (LPBITMAPINFOHEADER)::GlobalLock(hDib);
    DIBBPP = ((LPBITMAPINFOHEADER)lpbi)->biBitCount;
    DIBComp = ((LPBITMAPINFOHEADER)lpbi)->biCompression;
    ::GlobalUnlock(hDib);


    // Validate wBitCount and dwCompression
    // They must match correctly (i.e., BI_RLE4 and 4 BPP or
    // BI_RLE8 and 8BPP, etc.) or we return failure
    if (wBitCount == 0)
```

```
{
    NewBPP = DIBBPP;
    if ((dwCompression == BI_RLE4 && NewBPP == 4) ||
        (dwCompression == BI_RLE8 && NewBPP == 8) ||
        (dwCompression == BI_RGB))
        NewComp = dwCompression;
    else
    {
        ::XSError_Set(XSERR_INVALIDFORMAT);
        return NULL;
    }
}
else if (wBitCount == 1 && dwCompression == BI_RGB)
{

    NewBPP = wBitCount;
    NewComp = BI_RGB;
}
else if (wBitCount == 4)
{

    NewBPP = wBitCount;
    if (dwCompression == BI_RGB || dwCompression == BI_RLE4)
        NewComp = dwCompression;
    else
    {
        ::XSError_Set(XSERR_INVALIDFORMAT);
        return NULL;
    }
}
else if (wBitCount == 8)
{
    NewBPP = wBitCount;
    if (dwCompression == BI_RGB || dwCompression == BI_RLE8)
        NewComp = dwCompression;
    else
```

```
        {
            ::XSError_Set(XSERR_NOERROR);
            return NULL;
        }
    }
    else if ((wBitCount == 24 || wBitCount == 36 )
        && dwCompression == BI_RGB)
    {

        NewBPP = wBitCount;
        NewComp = BI_RGB;
    }
    else
    {

        ::XSError_Set(XSERR_INVALIDFORMAT);
        return NULL;
    }


    // Save the old DIB's palette
    hPal = ::XSDib_CreatePalette(hDib);
    if (!hPal)
    {

        ::XSError_Set(XSERR_CREATEPAL);
        return NULL;
    }


    // Convert old DIB to a bitmap
    hBitmap = ::XSDib_ToBmp(hDib, hPal);
    if (!hBitmap)
    {

        ::DeleteObject(hPal);
        ::XSError_Set(XSERR_CREATEBITMAP);
        return NULL;
    }
```

```
// Get info about the bitmap
::GetObject(hBitmap, sizeof(BITMAP), &bm);

// Fill in the BITMAPINFOHEADER appropriately
bi.biSize            = sizeof(BITMAPINFOHEADER);
bi.biWidth           = bm.bmWidth;
bi.biHeight          = bm.bmHeight;
bi.biPlanes          = 1;
bi.biBitCount        = NewBPP;
bi.biCompression     = NewComp;
bi.biSizeImage       = 0;
bi.biXPelsPerMeter   = 0;
bi.biYPelsPerMeter   = 0;
bi.biClrUsed         = 0;
bi.biClrImportant    = 0;

// Go allocate room for the new DIB
hNewDIB = ::XSDib_Template(bi, hBitmap);
if (!hNewDIB)
    return NULL;

// Get a pointer to the new DIB
lpbi = (LPBITMAPINFOHEADER)::GlobalLock(hNewDIB);
if (!lpbi)
{
    ::XSError_Set(XSERR_NOERROR);
    return NULL;
}

// Get a DC and select/realize our palette in it
hDC   = ::GetDC(NULL);
hOldPal = ::SelectPalette(hDC, hPal, FALSE);
::RealizePalette(hDC);
```

```
// Call GetDIBits and get the new DIB bits
if (!::GetDIBits(hDC, hBitmap, 0, (WORD) lpbi->biHeight,
    (LPSTR)lpbi + (WORD)lpbi->biSize
    + ::XSDib_PaletteSize(lpbi),
    (LPBITMAPINFO)lpbi, DIB_RGB_COLORS))
{

    ::GlobalUnlock(hNewDIB);
    ::GlobalFree(hNewDIB);
    hNewDIB = NULL;
}


// Clean up and return
::SelectPalette(hDC, hOldPal, TRUE);
::RealizePalette(hDC);
::ReleaseDC(NULL, hDC);

// Unlock the new DIB's memory block
if (hNewDIB)
    ::GlobalUnlock(hNewDIB);

::DeleteObject(hBitmap);
::DeleteObject(hPal);


::XSError_Set(XSERR_NOERROR);
return hNewDIB;

}
```

XSDib_Rotate

The XSDib_Rotate function is a complicated function that takes a DIB and rotates it, either clockwise or counter-clockwise. The framework exposed in this book really doesn't need this function. I added it because I wanted to show that the capabilities of a true DIB API are endless. Besides, it was fun to write. Unfortunately, as I mentioned earlier, there's a lot more I wanted to add to this API, but just didn't have the time allotted to get it in.

```
// -------------------------------------------------------------
// XSDib_Rotate
// Parameters:
//      HDIB - handle to a DIB
//      BOOL - TRUE to rotate clockwise, FALSE for
//      counter-clockwise
// Return Value:
//      HDIB - handle to the new DIB if successful, else NULL
// Description:
//      This function will rotate the passed DIB in 90 degree
//      increments and return the handle to the new DIB.
// -------------------------------------------------------------
HDIB XSFUNC
XSDib_Rotate(HDIB hDibSrc, BOOL bClockwise)
{
#ifdef _USRDLL
    // if this code is in a user DLL, we need to set up the MFC
    // state if we use MFC in this function
    AFX_MANAGE_STATE(AfxGetStaticModuleState());
#endif

    DWORD       dwSrcWidth;     // DIB src width
    DWORD       dwSrcHeight;    // DIB src height
    DWORD       dwPadWidth;     // Needed padding width
    DWORD       x, y, z;
    WORD        i;
    WORD        wBitCount;      // DIB src BPP
    WORD        wNumColors;     // DIB src number of colors
    BYTE        lpSrcByte;
    BYTE        lpDestByte;
    LPSTR       lpSrcBits;
    LPSTR       lpDestBits;
    LPSTR       lpSrc;
    LPSTR       lpDest;
    LPSTR       lpTmp;
    HDIB        hDibDest;       // Destination DIB (rotated)
    LPRGBQUAD   lpSrcColor;     // Pointer to src color table
```

```
LPRGBQUAD    lpDestColor;    // Pointer to dest color table

ASSERT(hDibSrc);

CWaitCursor wait;

// Get pointer to source DIB and it's bits
lpSrc     = (LPSTR)::GlobalLock(hDibSrc);
lpSrcBits = (LPSTR)::XSDib_FindBits(lpSrc);

// Get some useful info about our source DIB
dwSrcWidth  = ((LPBITMAPINFOHEADER)lpSrc)->biWidth;
dwSrcHeight = ((LPBITMAPINFOHEADER)lpSrc)->biHeight;
wBitCount   = ((LPBITMAPINFOHEADER)lpSrc)->biBitCount;
wNumColors  = ::XSDib_NumColors(lpSrc);

// Create a new dib that will contain the rotated bits
hDibDest = ::XSDib_Create(dwSrcHeight, dwSrcWidth, wBitCount);
if (!hDibDest)
{
    ::GlobalUnlock(hDibSrc);
    return NULL;
}

lpDest     = (LPSTR)::GlobalLock(hDibDest);
lpDestBits = (LPSTR)::XSDib_FindBits(lpDest);

// Copy source DIB's color table to destination DIB
lpSrcColor  = (LPRGBQUAD)(lpSrc + (sizeof(BITMAPINFOHEADER)));
lpDestColor = (LPRGBQUAD)(lpDest + (sizeof(BITMAPINFOHEADER)));
for (i = 0; i < wNumColors; i++)
{
    *lpDestColor++ = *lpSrcColor++;
}

// Calculate the padding required to align on DWORDs
// since DIB scanlines are aligned on DWORD boundaries
// Padding for the height is required since rotating by
// 90 degrees turns our source height into the destination's
// width, which would need to be DWORD aligned too
```

```
dwPadWidth  = ::XSDib_CalcPadding(wBitCount, dwSrcWidth);

// Copy the source bits to the destination while rotating each scanline
DWORD dwScanline = ::XSDib_CalcBytesPerLine(wBitCount, dwSrcHeight);
switch (wBitCount)
{
    case 1: // monochrome DIBs
    {
        BYTE BitMask = 0x80;
        long destPos;
        BYTE destBit;
        memset((void *)lpDestBits, 0, (size_t)(dwScanline * dwSrcWidth));

        if (bClockwise)
        {
            // Clockwise
            for (y = 0; y < dwSrcHeight; y++)
            {
                destPos = (y % 8);
                destBit = (unsigned char)(BitMask >> destPos);
                for (x = 0; x < dwSrcWidth; x++)
                {
                    // Mask off the bit we want from the src
                    if (*lpSrcBits & (BitMask >> (x % 8)))
                    {
                        // Get the destination byte
                        lpTmp = lpDestBits + ((dwSrcWidth - x - 1) *
                            dwScanline);

                        // Set the destination bit
                        *lpTmp |= (BitMask >> destPos);
                    }

                    if (((x + 1) % 8) == 0)
                    {
                        // Point to next source byte
                        lpSrcBits++;
                    }
                }
```

```
                        // Skip bytes in the source to pad to a DWORD
                        lpSrcBits += dwPadWidth;

                        if (((y + 1) % 8) == 0)
                        {
                            // Point to next column in the destination
                            lpDestBits++;
                        }
                    }
                }
                else
                {
                    // Counter-clockwise
                    lpDestBits += (::XSDib_LastByte(wBitCount,
                        dwSrcHeight) - 1);

                    for (y = 0; y < dwSrcHeight; y++)
                    {
                        destPos = ((dwSrcHeight - y - 1) % 8);
                        destBit = (unsigned char)(BitMask >> destPos);

                        for (x = 0; x < dwSrcWidth; x++)
                        {
                            // Shift src bit to dest bit's position
                            if (*lpSrcBits & (BitMask >> (x % 8)))
                            {
                                // Get the destination byte
                                lpTmp = lpDestBits +
                                    (x * dwScanline);

                                // Set the destination bit
                                *lpTmp |= (BitMask >> destPos);
                            }

                            if (((x + 1) % 8) == 0)
                            {
                                // Point to next source byte
                                lpSrcBits++;
                            }
                        }
                    }
```

I

2

```
                    // Skip bytes in the source to pad
                    // to a DWORD
                    lpSrcBits += dwPadWidth;

                    if (destPos == 0)
                    {
                        // Point to next column in the
                        // destination
                        lpDestBits--;
                    }
                }
            }
        }
    break;

    case 4: // 16-color DIBs
    {
        BYTE LoMask    = 0x0F;
        BYTE HiMask    = 0xF0;
        BOOL bLoNibble = FALSE;

        if (bClockwise)
        {
            // Clockwise
            for (y = 0; y < dwSrcHeight; y++)
            {
                for (x = 0; x < dwSrcWidth; x++)
                {
                    // Get the source byte
                    lpSrcByte = *lpSrcBits;

                    // Mask off the nibble we want
                    if (x % 2)
                    {
                        if (bLoNibble)
                            lpSrcByte &= LoMask;
                        else
                            lpSrcByte = (unsigned char)
                            ((lpSrcByte << wBitCount) & HiMask);
```

```
        }
        else
        {
            if (bLoNibble)
                lpSrcByte = (unsigned char)
                ((lpSrcByte >> wBitCount) & LoMask);
            else
                lpSrcByte &= HiMask;
        }

        // Get the destination byte
        lpTmp = lpDestBits +
            ((dwSrcWidth - x - 1) * dwScanline);
        lpDestByte = *lpTmp;

        // Mask off the unneeded nibble
        if (bLoNibble)
            lpDestByte &= HiMask;
        else
            lpDestByte = 0x00;

        // Set the dest nibble
        *lpTmp = (char)(lpSrcByte | lpDestByte);

        if (x % 2)
        {
            // Point to next source byte
            lpSrcBits++;
        }
    }

    // Skip bytes in the source to pad
    // to a DWORD
    lpSrcBits += dwPadWidth;

    if (y % 2)
    {
        // Point to next column in the destination
        lpDestBits++;
    }
```

```
                    // Toggle LoNibble flag
                    bLoNibble = !bLoNibble;
              }
        }
        else
        {
              // Counter-clockwise
              lpDestBits += (::XSDib_LastByte(wBitCount,
                    dwSrcHeight) - 1);
              if((dwSrcHeight % 2) == 0)
                    bLoNibble = TRUE;

              for (y = 0; y < dwSrcHeight; y++)
              {
                    for (x = 0; x < dwSrcWidth; x++)
                    {
                          // Get the source byte
                          lpSrcByte = *lpSrcBits;

                          // Mask off the nibble we want
                          if (x % 2)
                          {
                                if (bLoNibble)
                                      lpSrcByte &= LoMask;    // 2
                                else
                                      lpSrcByte = (unsigned char)
                                          ((lpSrcByte << wBitCount)
                                          & HiMask);          // 4
                          }
                          else
                          {
                                if (bLoNibble)                // 3
                                      lpSrcByte = (unsigned char)
                                          ((lpSrcByte >> wBitCount)
                                          & LoMask);
                                else
                                      lpSrcByte &= HiMask;    // 1
                          }
```

I

2

```
                        // Get the destination byte
                        lpTmp = lpDestBits + (x * dwScanline);
                        lpDestByte = *lpTmp;

                        // Mask off the unneeded nibble
                        if (bLoNibble)
                            lpDestByte = 0x00;
                        else
                            lpDestByte &= LoMask;

                        // Set the dest nibble
                        *lpTmp = (char)(lpSrcByte | lpDestByte);

                        if (x % 2)
                        {
                            // Point to next source byte
                            lpSrcBits++;
                        }
                    }

                    // Skip bytes in the source to pad
                    // to a DWORD
                    lpSrcBits += dwPadWidth;

                    if ((dwSrcHeight - y) % 2)
                    {
                        // Point to next column in the destination
                        lpDestBits--;
                    }

                    // Toggle LoNibble flag
                    bLoNibble = !bLoNibble;
                }
            }
        }
        break;

        case 8: // 256-color DIBs
        {
            if (bClockwise)
```

```
    {
        // clockwise
        for (y = 0; y < dwSrcHeight; y++)
        {
            for (x = 0; x < dwSrcWidth; x++)
            {
                // Get the source byte
                lpSrcByte = *lpSrcBits++;

                // Set the destination byte
                lpTmp  = lpDestBits +
                    ((dwSrcWidth - x - 1) * dwScanline);
                *lpTmp = lpSrcByte;
            }

            // Skip bytes in the source
            // to pad to a DWORD.
            lpSrcBits += dwPadWidth;

            // Next column in the destination.
            // Only for 90 degree rotations.
            lpDestBits++;
        }
    }
    else
    {
        // counter clockwise
        lpDestBits += (::XSDib_LastByte(wBitCount,
            dwSrcHeight) - 1);
        for (y = 0; y < dwSrcHeight; y++)
        {
            for (x = 0; x < dwSrcWidth; x++)
            {
                // Get the source byte
                lpSrcByte = *lpSrcBits++;

                // Set the destination byte
                lpTmp  = lpDestBits + (x * dwScanline);
                *lpTmp = lpSrcByte;
            }
```

```
                    // Skip bytes in the source to pad
                    // to a DWORD.
                    lpSrcBits += dwPadWidth;

                    // Next column in the destination.
                    // Only for 90 degree rotations.
                    lpDestBits--;
                }
            }
        }
        break;

        case 16:
        case 24:
        case 32:
        {
            if (bClockwise)
            {
                for (y = 0; y < dwSrcHeight; y++)
                {
                    for (x = 0; x < dwSrcWidth; x++)
                    {
                        // Get the source byte
                        // lpSrcByte = *lpSrcBits++;

                        // Set the destination byte
                        lpTmp  = lpDestBits +
                            ((dwSrcWidth - x - 1) * dwScanline);
                        for (z = 0; z < 3; z++)
                        {
                            lpSrcByte = *lpSrcBits++;
                            *lpTmp++ = lpSrcByte;
                        }
                    }

                    // Skip bytes in the source to pad to a DWORD.
                    lpSrcBits += dwPadWidth;

                    // Next column in the destination.
```

```
                            // Only for 90 degree rotations.
                            lpDestBits += 3;
                        }
                }
                else
                {
                    lpDestBits += (::XSDib_LastByte(wBitCount,
                        dwSrcHeight) - 3);
                    for (y = 0; y < dwSrcHeight; y++)
                    {
                        for (x = 0; x < dwSrcWidth; x++)
                        {
                            lpTmp = lpDestBits + (x * dwScanline);
                            for (z=0; z<3; z++)
                            {
                                lpSrcByte = *lpSrcBits++;
                                *lpTmp++ = lpSrcByte;
                            }
                        }

                        lpSrcBits += dwPadWidth;
                        lpDestBits -= 3;
                    }
                }
            break;

            default: // Unsupported format
                ::GlobalUnlock(hDibSrc);
                ::GlobalUnlock(hDibDest);
                ::XSDib_Destroy(hDibDest);
                ::AfxMessageBox(_T("Rotate: Error, unsupported bit format."),
                    MB_OK);
                ::XSError_Set(XSERR_INVALIDFORMAT);
                return FALSE;
    }

    // When we get here, a rotated DIB is available.
    ::GlobalUnlock(hDibSrc);
    ::GlobalUnlock(hDibDest);
```

```
    ::XSError_Set(XSERR_NOERROR);

    return hDibDest;
}
```

Summary

In this chapter, we discussed the code for the DIB API. This API is by no means complete. In fact, an imaging API can never be said to be complete. Many routines can be added to manipulate the bits and give different effects. You would certainly need to add a lot more than these routines if you wanted to write a program that competed against a program like Adobe PhotoShop™ or PaintShop Pro™. This API is the minimum you need in order to start adding your own routines that require imaging routines. However, the basic functionality exposed here is enough to get through the rest of the chapters in this book and into some of the more fun programming we'll be playing with soon.

Chapter 3

Extending the `CBitmap` Class

Introduction

Now that we've completed the DIB API from the previous chapter, let's make it just a little easier to work with by encapsulating some of the DIB API code in a class. MFC already has a `CBitmap` class for working with bitmaps. The best thing we can do is leverage the technology already in this class and extend it with our own additions.

Some of the items on our short list of what we want to accomplish with this derived class are serialization and painting. The serialization is important to MFC and, therefore, derived classes. MFC, unfortunately, did not provide serialization in the `CBitmap` class. However, we're going to fix that with our derived class. As far as painting bitmaps, if you've ever needed to do this before, I am sure you have recognized that your code is always similar. By putting this code into our class, we're going to save ourselves time in the future. From now on, we'll only have to call the member function to get our desired results. We'll also be cutting down on potential bugs. If we do find any bugs, we only have one place to fix them. Don't you just love C++?

Based on my earlier description of the naming convention I use, the CBitmap derived class will be called CXSBitmap. Several of the functions are virtual. You will recognize them because they begin with Do.

XSBITMAP.H

You will notice in this code a forward declaration for CXSPalette.

```
// -------------------------------------------------------------------
// Forward declarations
class CXSPalette;
```

This is an empty class derived from CPalette. It was intended to have more functionality, but the limitations of this book did not allow me the time to add what I wanted. At a later date, this class will get the functionality it deserves. Check the web site URLs listed in the Introduction for updates.

Serialization Schema Number

When you work with serialization and MFC, you need to supply a schema number. Since we're already experienced MFC programmers, I won't go into detail on this. However, if you would like more information, look up CArchive::SetObjectSchema, CArchive::GetObjectScema and the IMPLEMENT_SERIAL/DECLARE_SERIAL macros from the MFC help. For our purposes, we're going to set the schema number to 1. In future releases of this software, we may increment this number if we change the way we serialize bitmaps.

```
// -------------------------------------------------------------------
// Schema Definition for Serialization
#define XS_DIB_SCHEMA                    1
```

Enumerated Painting Operations

As I mentioned earlier, there are a number of different types of painting operations we want to encapsulate with this class. The first is the normal painting operation, used to place the image at the desired location. The second is the stretching operation, used to stretch (increase or decrease) the image to the desired location with a specified width and height that's different from the original bitmap. The third operation, transparent painting, is one on which I see a lot of "How do I..." messages in the Internet news-groups. To paint an image transparently, you must select a color within the bitmap and making each pixel that contains that color transparent so that the background color shows through the transparent areas of the bitmap. This is a complicated procedure that makes use of a monochrome bit mask. In a sense, this is similar to the `MaskBlt` SDK function. Unfortunately, this function only works with Windows NT. The fourth operation is a combination of stretching the bitmap and making it transparent.

To make it easy on us, we're going to create a single function that we can call with the desired parameters and include the type of painting operation. This in turn will call the appropriate member function that gives the results we want. To tell the function the type of painting operation, I created an `enum` structure with mnemonics for each type of painting operation.

```
// ------------------------------------------------------------
// Enumerated painting operations
enum PaintType
{
    NormalPaint = 0,
    StretchPaint,
    TransparentPaint,
    TransparentStretchPaint
};
```

CXSBitmap **Class Declaration**

To complete our header file, we need our class declaration. Since this is the first class to be discussed in this book, I should point out a few things. Notice the XSCLASS moniker. This is used to export the class if this source is to be used in creating a DLL. If it's not to be in a DLL, then this moniker translates to nothing. I am also going to point out again that if a function is virtual, then it begins with Do. This has always been important to me. When I derive other classes from my own base classes, I don't have to think twice, or do the required look up, to see if the function is virtual. If I know the name, I know it's virtual property. The only time this rule is not followed is when I derive one of my base classes from another (third party) base class that didn't follow this rule.

```
class XSCLASS
CXSBitmap : public CBitmap
{
    DECLARE_SERIAL(CXSBitmap);

// Construction
public:
                        CXSBitmap();
    virtual             ~CXSBitmap();

    virtual BOOL        DoDeleteObject();

    virtual BOOL        DoAttach(HDIB hDIB, HPALETTE hPal = NULL);

// Attributes
public:
    CXSPalette          m_Palette;
    BITMAP              m_bm;

    CSize               Size();
    DWORD               Width();
    DWORD               Height();

// Operations
public:
    virtual BOOL        DoLoad(CString strFileName);
    virtual BOOL        DoLoad(HINSTANCE hInst, UINT nID);
    virtual BOOL        DoLoad(UINT nID);
    virtual BOOL        DoSave(CString strFileName);

    virtual BOOL        DoPaintNormal(CDC* pDC, CRect rcDest,
                            BOOL bTile = FALSE);
```

```
        virtual BOOL        DoPaintTransparent(CDC* pDC, CRect rcDest,
                                COLORREF crTransparentColor,
                                BOOL bTile = FALSE);
        virtual BOOL        DoPaintStretch(CDC* pDC, CRect rcDest);
        virtual BOOL        DoPaintTransparentStretch(CDC* pDC, CRect
rcDest,

                                COLORREF crTransparentColor);


        virtual BOOL        DoPaint(CDC* pDC, int x1, int y1,
                                int cx1, int cy1, CDC* srcDC,
                                int x2, int y2, int cx2, int cy2,
                                DWORD dwROP, PaintType pntType);
        virtual BOOL        DoPaint(CDC* pDC, CRect rcDest,
                                CDC* srcDC, CRect rcSrc, DWORD dwROP,
                                PaintType pntType);


        virtual void        DoSerialize(CArchive& ar);


        BOOL                Rotate(BOOL bClockwise = TRUE);
};
```

XSBitmap.cpp

Header Files

The following list contains the needed header files to include for SXBitmap.cpp.

```
#include "stdafx.h"
#include "XSError.h"
#include "XSDibApi.h"
#include "XSPalApi.h"
#include "XSPalette.h"
#include "XSBitmap.h"
```

The IMPLEMENT_SERIAL macro is needed to use serialization. You probably noticed the corresponding DECLARE_SERIAL macro in the XSBitmap.h header file.

```
IMPLEMENT_SERIAL(CXSBitmap, CBitmap, XS_DIB_SCHEMA)
```

CXSBitmap::CXSBitmap

There's not much we need to do with the CXSBitmap constructor. We keep a member variable of the BITMAP structure, so we need to initialize it so that there is no derogatory data.

```
// -----------------------------------------------------------
// Function :
//     CXSBitmap::CXSBitmap
// Purpose  :
//     Constructor, initializes memory
// -----------------------------------------------------------
CXSBitmap::CXSBitmap()
{
    memset(&m_bm, '\0', sizeof(BITMAP));
}
```

CXSBitmap::~CXSBitmap

In the destructor for CXSBitmap, we call the clean-up member function DoDeleteObject. This is almost equivalent to CBitmap::DeleteObject. However, our function is virtual and does more in its duties. We'll discuss DoDeleteObject in further detail when we get to it.

```
// -----------------------------------------------------------
// Function :
//     CXSBitmap::~CXSBitmap
// Purpose  :
//     Destructor, cleans up memory
// -----------------------------------------------------------
CXSBitmap::~CXSBitmap()
```

```
{
    // clean up
    DoDeleteObject();
}
```

CXSBitmap::DoDeleteObject

The DoDeleteObject member function does several things. First, it resets our BITMAP structure member variable. Second, it calls the DeleteObject function of our CXSPalette member variable. Lastly, it deletes our attached HBITMAP by calling the base function CBitmap::DeleteObject.

```
// -------------------------------------------------------------
// Function :
//       CXSBitmap::DoDeleteObject
// Purpose  :
//       Cleans up memory
// -------------------------------------------------------------
BOOL
CXSBitmap::DoDeleteObject()
{
    ASSERT_VALID(this);

    memset(&m_bm, 0, sizeof(BITMAP));
    m_Palette.DeleteObject();
    ::XSError_Set(XSERR_NOERROR);
    return CBitmap::DeleteObject();
}
```

CXSBitmap::DoAttach

The DoAttach member variable is very close to the CBitmap::Attach base class function. However, I'll point out again, this member function is virtual. It also does a lot more than its cousin. The CXSBitmap class was created with three goals in mind: to make bitmap painting easier, to have a way of serializing bitmaps, and to maintain an appropriate palette for the bitmap.

With DoAttach, you can pass a memory handle of type HPALETTE if you have already created a palette for your bitmap. The HPALETTE parameter defaults to NULL, so you don't need to pass it anything if you do not have a palette already created. If you choose to do this, then a palette will be created for your bitmap.

Lastly, the DoAttach member function differs in that it takes an HDIB memory handle and not an HBITMAP memory handle. The HDIB is then converted to the required HBITMAP and attached to the underlying CGdiObject (the base class for CBitmap).

```
// ----------------------------------------------------------------
// Function  :
//     CXSBitmap::DoAttach
// Purpose   :
//     Converts the passed HDIB to an HBITMAP and attaches it to
//     the underlying CGdiObject. Also, attaches the HPALETTE to
//     the CPalette associated with this object.  If the HPALETTE
//     is NULL, a halftone palette will be created.  Destroys the
//     passed HDIB when it return successfully, otherwise on
//     failure it does not destroy the passed DIB.
// Parameters:
//     HDIB hDib - The DIB to convert and attach
//     HPALETTE hPal - the associated palette
// Returns   :
//     TRUE on success, FALSE on failure
// ----------------------------------------------------------------
BOOL
CXSBitmap::DoAttach(HDIB hDib, HPALETTE hPal)
{
    ASSERT_VALID(this);
    ASSERT(hDib);  // must be valid

    HBITMAP hBitmap = NULL;
    BOOL bResult = FALSE;
    HPALETTE hPalette = hPal;

    // See if palette is valid. If not, create one to use
    if (!hPalette)
```

I

3

```cpp
    {
        hPalette = ::XSDib_CreatePalette(hDib);
        if (!hPalette)
        {
            HDC hDC = ::GetDC(NULL);
            hPalette = ::CreateHalftonePalette(hDC);
            ::ReleaseDC(NULL, hDC);
        }
    }

    // Convert DIB to a Bitmap
    hBitmap = ::XSDib_ToBmp(hDib, hPalette);

    // Kill any existing bitmap and palette
    // attached to this object
    DoDeleteObject();

    // Attach the palette
    m_Palette.Attach(hPalette);

    // Attach the new bitmap
    // Call base class as this is a DDB now
    if (hBitmap && CBitmap::Attach(hBitmap))
    {
        // Destroy the passed DIB
        ::XSDib_Destroy(hDib);

        // Calculate image size
        Size();

        bResult = TRUE;
        ::XSError_Set(XSERR_NOERROR);
    }
    else
```

```
{
    // If we couldn't Attach, clean up memory
    // Only delete the palette if we created it
    if (!hPal)
        DoDeleteObject();

    ::XSError_Set(XSERR_CREATEBITMAP);
}

return bResult;
}
```

CXSBitmap::DoLoad

There are three versions of the `DoLoad` member function. This first version requires the `HINSTANCE` of the location of the bitmap resource. This allows you to load the bitmap resource from a resource DLL or from some other file. The second parameter is the required resource ID of the bitmap resource you want to load.

Once a bitmap is loaded, it is converted to an `HDIB` memory handle and then sent to `DoAttach` to be processed.

```
// ----------------------------------------------------------------
// Function :
//    CXSBitmap::DoLoad
// Purpose  :
//    Loads a bitmap from resource of the specified HINSTANCE.
//    Uses a DIB Section to create the proper palette
// Parameters:
//    HINSTANCE hInst - where to load from
//    UINT nID - ID of the bitmap to load
// Returns  :
//    TRUE on success, FALSE on failure
// ----------------------------------------------------------------
BOOL
CXSBitmap::DoLoad(HINSTANCE hInst, UINT nID)
```

I

3

```cpp
{
    ASSERT_VALID(this);

    HBITMAP hBitmap = NULL;
    HDIB hDib = NULL;
    BOOL bResult = FALSE;

    ::XSError_Set(XSERR_CREATEBITMAP);

    // load the Bitmap from specified HINSTANCE,
    // creating a DIB Section
    hBitmap = ::XSBmp_Load(hInst, nID);
    if (hBitmap)
    {
        // make a temporary DIB
        HDIB hDib = ::XSBmp_ToDib(hBitmap, NULL);
        ASSERT(hDib);  // sanity check

        // Kill the Bitmap
        ::DeleteObject(hBitmap);

        // Attach the bitmap to the GDI object
        // Attach creates a palette for us
        if (DoAttach(hDib))
        {
            bResult = TRUE;
            ::XSError_Set(XSERR_NOERROR);
        }
    }

    return bResult;
}
```

The second version of DoLoad does not require an HINSTANCE. Instead, it uses MFC's AfxFindResourceHandle to locate the bitmap resource.

`AfxFindResourceHandle` is used to find the desired resource in a chain of MFC extension DLLs. So, all that is required is the resource ID of the bitmap file to load. Once this second version of `DoLoad` has the required information, it then calls the first version of `DoLoad` to do the work.

```
// -----------------------------------------------------------
// Function  :
//    CXSBitmap::DoLoad
// Purpose   :
//    Finds the bitmap ID and loads it
// Parameters:
//    UINT nID - ID of the bitmap to load
// Note      :
//    This function calls MFC's AfxFindResourceHandle to get
the
//    HINSTANCE of where the resource with the specified ID
//    lives.  It finds the first bitmap with the specified ID,
//    which may not be the one you want.
// Returns   :
//    TRUE on success, FALSE on failure
// -----------------------------------------------------------
BOOL
CXSBitmap::DoLoad(UINT nID)
{
    // find HINSTANCE with specified resource ID
    HINSTANCE hInstApp =
        AfxFindResourceHandle(MAKEINTRESOURCE(nID), RT_BITMAP);
    return DoLoad(hInstApp, nID);
}
```

The third version of `DoLoad` requires a filename to an external bitmap. The file is then loaded and attached to the current `CXSBitmap` object.

```
// -----------------------------------------------------------
// Function  :
//    CXSBitmap::DoLoad
// Purpose   :
```

```
//    Loads a DIB bitmap from a file
// Parameters:
//    CString strFileName - path to the DIB to load
// Returns   :
//    TRUE on success, FALSE on failure
// --------------------------------------------------------------
BOOL
CXSBitmap::DoLoad(CString strFileName)
{
    ASSERT_VALID(this);

    HDIB hDib = NULL;
    HPALETTE hPalette = NULL;
    HBITMAP hBitmap = NULL;
    BOOL bResult = FALSE;

    if (strFileName.IsEmpty())
        return FALSE;

    // load the DIB
    hDib = ::XSDib_Load(strFileName);
    if (hDib)
    {
        // attach the DIB
        if (DoAttach(hDib))
        {
            bResult = TRUE;
            ::XSError_Set(XSERR_NOERROR);
        }
    }

    return bResult;
}
```

CXSBitmap::DoSave

The `DoSave` member function takes the attached `HBITMAP` and converts it to an `HDIB`. `DoSave` then saves the new `HDIB` to the requested filename. It does not check for an existing file, but instead will overwrite any file with the existing name. You can pass a path with the filename. After the file is written, the `HDIB` memory handle is then deleted.

```
// -----------------------------------------------------------
// Function  :
//    CXSBitmap::DoSave
// Purpose   :
//    Converts the attached bitmap to a DIB and saves it to the
//    specified file.
// Parameters:
//    CString strFileName - path of file to save to
// Returns   :
//    TRUE on success, FALSE on failure
// -----------------------------------------------------------
BOOL
CXSBitmap::DoSave(CString strFileName)
{
    ASSERT_VALID(this);
    ASSERT(GetSafeHandle());

    HDIB hDib = NULL;
    BOOL bResult = FALSE;

    // convert Bitmap to DIB
    hDib = ::XSBmp_ToDib((HBITMAP)GetSafeHandle(),
        (HPALETTE)m_Palette.GetSafeHandle());
    if (hDib)
    {
        // save DIB
        WORD wResult = ::XSDib_Save(hDib, strFileName);
```

```
        // destroy DIB
        ::XSDib_Destroy(hDib);
        if (wResult == 0)
        {
            bResult = TRUE;
            ::XSError_Set(XSERR_NOERROR);
        }
    }

    return bResult;
}
```

CXSBitmap::DoSerialize

The DoSerialize member function allows you to save (or read) your bitmap to (or from) a compound document file rather than an individual bitmap (.bmp) file. All that is required is the mandatory CArchive object that is used for MFC serialization.

For writing, the underlying HBITMAP object is converted to an HDIB memory handle, which is then written to the compound document file. When the write is complete, the HDIB is deleted.

For reading, the DIB is read in-place by using the location of the file pointer. The resulting HDIB is then attached to the current CXSBitmap object.

```
// -----------------------------------------------------------
// Function :
//     CXSBitmap::DoSerialize
// Purpose  :
//     Serialize the attached bitmap as a DIB into a document
// Parameters:
//     CArchive& ar - the archive to write into/read from
// Returns  :
//     Nothing. Throws an archive exception on error of type
//     CArchiveException::generic
// -----------------------------------------------------------
void
CXSBitmap::DoSerialize(CArchive& ar)
```

```
{
    ASSERT_VALID(this);

    CBitmap::Serialize(ar);

    HDIB hDib = NULL;

    if (ar.IsStoring())
    {
        // make sure there is something to store
        ASSERT(GetSafeHandle());

        // convert Bitmap to DIB
        hDib = ::XSBmp_ToDib((HBITMAP)GetSafeHandle(),
            (HPALETTE)m_Palette.GetSafeHandle());
        if (hDib)
        {
            // write of the DIB
            if (XSERR_NOERROR !=
                ::XSDib_WriteFile(hDib, *(ar.GetFile())))
              AfxThrowArchiveException(CArchiveException::generic);

            // remove the DIB memory
            ::XSDib_Destroy(hDib);

            ::XSError_Set(XSERR_NOERROR);
        }
        else
        {
            ::XSError_Set(XSERR_WRITE);
            AfxThrowArchiveException(CArchiveException::generic);
        }
    }
    else
```

```
    {
        hDib = ::XSDib_ReadFile(*(ar.GetFile()),
            ar.GetFile()->GetPosition());
        if (hDib)
        {
            DoAttach(hDib);
            ::XSError_Set(XSERR_NOERROR);
        }
        else
        {
            ::XSError_Set(XSERR_READ);
            AfxThrowArchiveException(CArchiveException::generic);
        }
    }
}
```

CXSBitmap::Size

The Size member function is a small utility function to return the width and height of the current bitmap in a CSize class. The Size function always calls the GetBitmap base class function to fill in the BITMAP structure member variable to get the size information.

```
// -------------------------------------------------------------
// Function  :
//     CXSBitmap::Size
// Purpose   :
//     Returns the bitmap width and height in a CSize
// Parameters:
//     None
// Returns   :
//     The width and height of the bitmap in a CSize
// -------------------------------------------------------------
CSize
CXSBitmap::Size()
{
```

```
    ::XSError_Set(XSERR_NOERROR);
    GetBitmap(&m_bm);
    return CSize(m_bm.bmWidth, m_bm.bmHeight);
}
```

CXSBitmap::Width

The Width member function is dependent on the Size member function. Width returns the width of the bitmap based on the bmWidth value in the BITMAP structure member variable. If the value is 0, then the Width function calls the Size function to get the information.

It's important to note that if you manipulate the bitmap to modify the width or height, you should immediately call the Size function to reinitialize the BITMAP structure member variable. Otherwise, the values returned may be incorrect.

```
// --------------------------------------------------------
// Function :
//     CXSBitmap::Width
// Purpose  :
//     Returns the width of the bitmap
// Parameters:
//     None
// Returns  :
//     The width of the bitmap
// --------------------------------------------------------
DWORD
CXSBitmap::Width()
{
    ::XSError_Set(XSERR_NOERROR);
    if (m_bm.bmWidth == 0 )
        Size();
    return m_bm.bmWidth;
}
```

CXSBitmap::Height

The Height member function is very similar to the Width function. The same restrictions apply if you change the dimensions of the bitmap through some other manipulation technique.

```
// -----------------------------------------------------------
// Function :
//     CXSBitmap::Height
// Purpose   :
//     Returns the height of the bitmap
// Parameters:
//     None
// Returns   :
//     The height of the bitmap
// -----------------------------------------------------------
DWORD
CXSBitmap::Height()
{
    ::XSError_Set(XSERR_NOERROR);
    if (m_bm.bmHeight == 0 )
        Size();
    return m_bm.bmHeight;
}
```

CXSBitmap::DoPaintNormal

The DoPaintNormal member function is one of four functions that provide the power behind the bitmap painting operations for the CXSBitmap class.

The DoPaintNormal function does as the name implies; it paints a bitmap in a normal fashion. This means that it will paint the bitmap in the passed device context at the specified coordinates as determined by the passed CRect. A third parameter allows you have the bitmap tiled if the CRect's dimensions are larger than the bitmap.

DoPaintNormal uses the concept of double-buffering to avoid screen flicker. This means that all painting is drawn into a memory device context, rather than directly to the screen. Only when all of the painting is done to the temporary buffer is it then drawn to the screen. This gives a nice clean effect when painting to the screen, especially with bitmaps.

```
// ------------------------------------------------------------
// Function  :
//     CXSBitmap::DoPaintNormal
// Purpose   :
//     Paints the bitmap inside the CRect of the specified DC.
//     There is also an option to tile the bitmap
// Parameters:
//     CDC* pDC - pointer to the DC to write into
//     CRect rcDest - the destination rectangle
//     BOOL bTile - TRUE to tile the bitmap,
//                - FALSE to paint the bitmap normally (default)
// Returns   :
//     TRUE on success, FALSE on failure
// ------------------------------------------------------------
BOOL
CXSBitmap::DoPaintNormal(CDC* pDC, CRect rcDest, BOOL bTile)
{
    ASSERT_VALID(this);
    ASSERT(GetSafeHandle());

    CDC imageDC;  // DC for image
    CDC memDC;    // DC for assembling image
    CPoint ptSize;

    CBitmap bmpMem;
    CBitmap* pbmpMem;
    CBitmap* pbmpImage;

    int cxBitmap = Width();    // current bitmap width
    int cyBitmap = Height();   // current bitmap height
    int cxWidth = rcDest.Width();   // destination width
    int cyHeight = rcDest.Height(); // destination width
```

```
    int j;  // counter
    int i;  // counter


    ::XSError_Set(XSERR_NOERROR);


    // create an image DC for the original bitmap and select it
    imageDC.CreateCompatibleDC(pDC);
    pbmpImage = (CBitmap*)imageDC.SelectObject(this);


    if (!bTile)
    {
        ptSize.x = cxBitmap;  // Width of drawing area
        ptSize.y = cyBitmap;  // Height of drawing area
    }
    else
    {
        ptSize.x = cxWidth;   // Width of drawing area
        ptSize.y = cyHeight;  // Height of drawing area
    }


    // create a memory DC
    memDC.CreateCompatibleDC(pDC);


    // create a bitmap to draw into and select into memory DC
    bmpMem.CreateCompatibleBitmap(pDC, ptSize.x, ptSize.y);
    pbmpMem = (CBitmap*)memDC.SelectObject(&bmpMem);


    // Set the proper mapping mode
    imageDC.SetMapMode(pDC->GetMapMode());


    if (bTile)
    {
        // paint the bitmap
```

```
        for (i = rcDest.left; i < rcDest.right; i += cxBitmap)
            for (j = rcDest.top; j < rcDest.bottom; j += cyBitmap)
                memDC.BitBlt(i, j, cxBitmap, cyBitmap, &imageDC,
                    0, 0, SRCCOPY);

        DoPaint( pDC, rcDest.left, rcDest.top,
            rcDest.Width(), rcDest.Height(),
            &memDC, 0, 0, 0, 0, SRCCOPY, NormalPaint);
    }
    else
    {
        DoPaint( pDC, rcDest.left, rcDest.top,
            cxBitmap, cyBitmap, &imageDC,
            0, 0, 0, 0, SRCCOPY, NormalPaint);
    }

    // Clean up
    memDC.SelectObject(pbmpMem);
    bmpMem.DeleteObject();
    if (pbmpImage)
        imageDC.SelectObject(pbmpImage);

    return TRUE;
}
```

CXSBitmap::DoPaintTransparent

DoPaintTransparent is the equivalent of DoPaintNormal with one exception: one color within the bitmap is selected to become transparent. Each pixel in the bitmap that has the selected color will not be displayed. Instead, the color that was originally on the screen will be displayed. This is quite a complicated procedure. It involves several device contexts and bitmaps to be used at the same time. Rather than explain it here, look at the following code. It is well documented and you should be able to follow the logic needed to understand the end result.

First, though, just let me explain about the parameters for a bit. The first parameter is the device context (the CDC) of the location to paint the bitmap. The second parameter is the CRect of the location of the painting within the device context. The third parameter is the color to which the transparency effect will be applied. The fourth parameter specifies whether the bitmap will be tiled.

```
// -----------------------------------------------------------------
// Function  :
//     CXSBitmap::DoPaintTransparent
// Purpose   :
//     Paints the bitmap transparently inside the CRect of the
//     specified DC.  There is also an option to tile the bitmap
// Parameters:
//     CDC* pDC - pointer to the DC to write into
//     CRect rcDest - the destination rectangle
//     COLORREF crTransparentColor - transparent color
//     BOOL bTile - TRUE to tile the bitmap,
//                - FALSE to paint the bitmap normally (default)
// Returns   :
//     TRUE on success, FALSE on failure
// -----------------------------------------------------------------
BOOL
CXSBitmap::DoPaintTransparent(CDC* pDC, CRect rcDest,
                              COLORREF crTransparentColor,
                              BOOL bTile)
{
    ASSERT_VALID(this);
    ASSERT(GetSafeHandle());

    CDC tempDC;                // Temp DC to hold original Bitmap
    CBitmap* pbmpTemp;         // old Bitmap for Temp DC
    CPoint ptSize;
    COLORREF crColor;          // old Color
    CDC imageDC;               // Image DC
    CDC backDC;                // Back DC
```

```
CDC maskDC;          // Mask DC
CDC memDC;           // Memory DC
CBitmap bmpImage;    // drawing Bitmap for Image DC
CBitmap bmpBack;     // drawing Bitmap for Back DC
CBitmap bmpMask;     // drawing Bitmap for Mask DC
CBitmap bmpMem;      // drawing Bitmap for Memory DC
CBitmap* pbmpImage;  // old Bitmap for Image DC
CBitmap* pbmpBack;   // old Bitmap for Back DC
CBitmap* pbmpMask;   // old Bitmap for Mask DC
CBitmap* pbmpMem;    // old Bitmap for Memory DC

int cxBitmap = Width();   // bitmap width
int cyBitmap = Height();  // bitmap height

int j;  // counter
int i;  // counter

::XSError_Set(XSERR_NOERROR);

// Create an memory DC for the
// original bitmap and select it
tempDC.CreateCompatibleDC(pDC);
pbmpTemp = (CBitmap*)tempDC.SelectObject(this);

if (!bTile)
{
    ptSize.x = cxBitmap;  // Width actual drawing area
    ptSize.y = cyBitmap;  // Height actual drawing area
}
else
{
    ptSize.x = rcDest.Width();   // Width of drawing area
    ptSize.y = rcDest.Height();  // Height of drawing area
}
```

```cpp
// Create the image DC (this is the one we work with)
imageDC.CreateCompatibleDC(pDC);
bmpImage.CreateCompatibleBitmap(pDC, ptSize.x, ptSize.y);
pbmpImage = (CBitmap*)imageDC.SelectObject(&bmpImage);

if (!bTile)
{
    // Put the bitmap into the Image DC
    imageDC.BitBlt(rcDest.left, rcDest.top, ptSize.x,
        ptSize.y, &tempDC, 0, 0, SRCCOPY);
}
else
{
    // Tile the bitmap into the Image DC
    for (i = rcDest.left; i < rcDest.right; i += cxBitmap)
        for (j = rcDest.top; j < rcDest.bottom;
            j += cyBitmap)
            imageDC.BitBlt(i, j, cxBitmap, cyBitmap,
                &tempDC,
                0, 0, SRCCOPY);
}

// Create DCs to hold temporary data
backDC.CreateCompatibleDC(pDC);
maskDC.CreateCompatibleDC(pDC);
memDC.CreateCompatibleDC(pDC);

// Monochrome DCs
bmpBack.CreateBitmap(ptSize.x, ptSize.y, 1, 1, NULL);
bmpMask.CreateBitmap(ptSize.x, ptSize.y, 1, 1, NULL);

bmpMem.CreateCompatibleBitmap(pDC, ptSize.x, ptSize.y);

// Each DC must select a bitmap to store pixel data
```

```
pbmpBack = backDC.SelectObject(&bmpBack);
pbmpMask = maskDC.SelectObject(&bmpMask);
pbmpMem = memDC.SelectObject(&bmpMem);

// Set the proper mapping mode
tempDC.SetMapMode(pDC->GetMapMode());

// Set the background color of the source DC
// to the color contained in the parts of the
// bitmap that will be transparent
crColor = imageDC.SetBkColor(crTransparentColor);

// Create the mask for the bitmap by performing a BitBlt
// from the source bitmap to a monochrome bitmap
maskDC.BitBlt(0, 0, ptSize.x, ptSize.y, &imageDC,
    0, 0, SRCCOPY);

// Set the background color of the source DC back to the
// original color
imageDC.SetBkColor(crColor);

// Create the inverse of the mask
backDC.BitBlt(0, 0, ptSize.x, ptSize.y, &maskDC,
    0, 0, NOTSRCCOPY);

// Copy the background of the main DC to the destination
memDC.BitBlt(0, 0, ptSize.x, ptSize.y, pDC,
    rcDest.left, rcDest.top, SRCCOPY);

// Mask out the places where the bitmap will be placed
memDC.BitBlt(0, 0, ptSize.x, ptSize.y, &maskDC,
    0, 0, SRCAND);

// Mask out the transparent colored pixels in the bitmap
```

```
        imageDC.BitBlt(0, 0, ptSize.x, ptSize.y, &backDC,
            0, 0, SRCAND);

        // XOR the bitmap with the background on the destination DC
        memDC.BitBlt(0, 0, ptSize.x, ptSize.y, &imageDC,
            0, 0, SRCPAINT);

        // Copy the source to the screen
        DoPaint( pDC, rcDest.left, rcDest.top, ptSize.x, ptSize.y,
            &memDC, 0, 0, 0, 0, SRCCOPY, TransparentPaint);

        // Delete objects
        if (pbmpTemp)
            tempDC.SelectObject(pbmpTemp);

        imageDC.SelectObject(pbmpImage);
        bmpImage.DeleteObject();

        backDC.SelectObject(pbmpBack);
        bmpBack.DeleteObject();

        maskDC.SelectObject(pbmpMask);
        bmpMask.DeleteObject();

        memDC.SelectObject(pbmpMem);
        bmpMem.DeleteObject();

        return TRUE;
}
```

CXSBitmap::DoPaintStretch

The `DoPaintStretch` member function is the third function that provides the backbone behind the painting operations of the `CXSBitmap` class. `DoPaint-Stretch` basically wraps the `StretchBlt` SDK function. `DoPaintStretch` then provides the necessary setup for double-buffering, plus the clean up needed afterwards.

```
// -----------------------------------------------------------------
// Function  :
//     CXSBitmap::DoPaintStretch
// Purpose   :
//     Paints the bitmap inside the CRect of the specified DC,
//     stretching the bitmap to fill the CRect dimension
// Parameters:
//     CDC* pDC - pointer to the DC to write into
//     CRect rcDest - the destination rectangle
// Returns   :
//     TRUE on success, FALSE on failure
// -----------------------------------------------------------------
BOOL
CXSBitmap::DoPaintStretch(CDC* pDC, CRect rcDest)
{
    ASSERT_VALID(this);
    ASSERT(GetSafeHandle());

    CDC imageDC;    // DC for image
    CPoint ptSize;

    CBitmap* pbmpImage;                  // old Bitmap for Image DC

    ::XSError_Set(XSERR_NOERROR);

    int cxBitmap = Width();          // current bitmap width
    int cyBitmap = Height();         // current bitmap height
    int cxWidth = rcDest.Width();    // destination width
    int cyHeight = rcDest.Height();  // destination height

    // create an image DC for the original bitmap and select it
    imageDC.CreateCompatibleDC(pDC);
```

```
        pbmpImage = (CBitmap*)imageDC.SelectObject(this);


        ptSize.x = cxWidth;    // Width of drawing area
        ptSize.y = cyHeight;   // Height of drawing area


        // stretch paint the bitmap
        DoPaint( pDC, rcDest.left, rcDest.top,
            rcDest.Width(), rcDest.Height(), &imageDC, 0, 0,
            cxBitmap, cyBitmap, SRCCOPY, StretchPaint);


        // clean up
        if (pbmpImage)
            imageDC.SelectObject(pbmpImage);


        return TRUE;
}
```

CXSBitmap::DoPaintTransparentStretch

The DoPaintTransparentStretch member function is an amalgamation of the previous three painting operation functions. As the function name implies, it allows you to stretch a bitmap and then set up a transparency color. Again, rather than explaining the code twice, look at the documentation in the following code and I am sure you will understand the logic of what is being accomplished.

```
// -----------------------------------------------------------
// Function  :
//    CXSBitmap::DoPaintTransparentStretch
// Purpose   :
//    Paints the bitmap inside the CRect of the specified DC
//    using transparency and stretching
// Parameters:
//    CDC* pDC - pointer to the DC to write into
//    CRect rcDest - the destination rectangle
//    COLORREF crTransparentColor - transparent color
```

```cpp
// Returns   :
//    TRUE on success, FALSE on failure
// ---------------------------------------------------------------
BOOL
CXSBitmap::DoPaintTransparentStretch(CDC* pDC, CRect rcDest,
                                     COLORREF crTransparentColor)
{
    ASSERT_VALID(this);
    ASSERT(GetSafeHandle());

    CPoint ptSize;
    COLORREF crColor;          // old Color
    CDC stretchDC;             // DC for stretched image
    CDC imageDC;               // Image DC
    CDC backDC;                // Back DC
    CDC maskDC;                // Mask DC
    CDC memDC;                 // Memory DC
    CBitmap bmpStretch;        // drawing Bitmap for Stretch DC
    CBitmap bmpImage;          // drawing Bitmap for Image DC
    CBitmap bmpBack;           // drawing Bitmap for Back DC
    CBitmap bmpMask;           // drawing Bitmap for Mask DC
    CBitmap bmpMem;            // drawing Bitmap for Memory DC
    CBitmap* pbmpStretch;      // old Bitmap for Stretch DC
    CBitmap* pbmpImage;        // old Bitmap for Image DC
    CBitmap* pbmpBack;         // old Bitmap for Back DC
    CBitmap* pbmpMask;         // old Bitmap for Mask DC
    CBitmap* pbmpMem;          // old Bitmap for Memory DC

    ::XSError_Set(XSERR_NOERROR);

    int cxBitmap = Width();           // current bitmap width
    int cyBitmap = Height();          // current bitmap height
    int cxWidth = rcDest.Width();   // destination width
    int cyHeight = rcDest.Height(); // destination height
```

I

3

```cpp
// create an image DC for the original bitmap and select it
imageDC.CreateCompatibleDC(pDC);
pbmpImage = (CBitmap*)imageDC.SelectObject(this);

ptSize.x = cxWidth;   // Width of drawing area
ptSize.y = cyHeight;  // Height of drawing area

// stretched version of the bitmap
stretchDC.CreateCompatibleDC(pDC);
bmpStretch.CreateCompatibleBitmap(pDC, cxWidth, cyHeight);
pbmpStretch = (CBitmap*)stretchDC.SelectObject(&bmpStretch);

// See if this device is palette compatible
if ((pDC->GetDeviceCaps(RASTERCAPS) & RC_PALETTE) &&
    m_Palette.GetSafeHandle())
{
    TRACE0("CXSImage: Palette supported\n");

    stretchDC.SelectPalette(&m_Palette, FALSE);
    stretchDC.RealizePalette();
}

// stretch the bitmap
stretchDC.StretchBlt(rcDest.left, rcDest.top,
    rcDest.Width(), rcDest.Height(), &imageDC, 0, 0,
    cxBitmap, cyBitmap, SRCCOPY);

// clean up
imageDC.SelectObject(pbmpImage);

// Create the image bitmap (this is the one we work with)
bmpImage.CreateCompatibleBitmap(pDC, ptSize.x, ptSize.y);
pbmpImage = (CBitmap*)imageDC.SelectObject(&bmpImage);
```

```
// Put the bitmap into the Image DC
imageDC.BitBlt(rcDest.left, rcDest.top,
    ptSize.x, ptSize.y, &stretchDC, 0, 0, SRCCOPY);

// Create DCs to hold temporary data
backDC.CreateCompatibleDC(pDC);
maskDC.CreateCompatibleDC(pDC);
memDC.CreateCompatibleDC(pDC);

// Monochrome DCs
bmpBack.CreateBitmap(ptSize.x, ptSize.y, 1, 1, NULL);
bmpMask.CreateBitmap(ptSize.x, ptSize.y, 1, 1, NULL);

bmpMem.CreateCompatibleBitmap(pDC, ptSize.x, ptSize.y);

// Each DC must select a bitmap to store pixel data
pbmpBack = backDC.SelectObject(&bmpBack);
pbmpMask = maskDC.SelectObject(&bmpMask);
pbmpMem = memDC.SelectObject(&bmpMem);

// Set the proper mapping mode
stretchDC.SetMapMode(pDC->GetMapMode());

// Set the background color of the source DC
// to the color contained in the parts of the
// bitmap that will be transparent
crColor = imageDC.SetBkColor(crTransparentColor);

// Create the mask for the bitmap by performing
// a BitBlt from the source bitmap to a
// monochrome bitmap
maskDC.BitBlt(0, 0, ptSize.x, ptSize.y, &imageDC,
    0, 0, SRCCOPY);
```

I

3

```cpp
// Set the background color of the source DC back to the
// original color
imageDC.SetBkColor(crColor);

// Create the inverse of the mask
backDC.BitBlt(0, 0, ptSize.x, ptSize.y, &maskDC,
    0, 0, NOTSRCCOPY);

// Copy the background of the main DC to the destination
memDC.BitBlt(0, 0, ptSize.x, ptSize.y, pDC,
    rcDest.left, rcDest.top, SRCCOPY);

// Mask out the places where the bitmap will be placed
memDC.BitBlt(0, 0, ptSize.x, ptSize.y, &maskDC,
    0, 0, SRCAND);

// Mask out the transparent colored pixels in the bitmap
imageDC.BitBlt(0, 0, ptSize.x, ptSize.y, &backDC,
    0, 0, SRCAND);

// XOR the bitmap with the background on the destination DC
memDC.BitBlt(0, 0, ptSize.x, ptSize.y, &imageDC,
    0, 0, SRCPAINT);

// Copy the source to the screen
DoPaint( pDC, rcDest.left, rcDest.top, ptSize.x, ptSize.y,
    &memDC, 0, 0, 0, 0, SRCCOPY, TransparentStretchPaint);

// Delete objects
if (pbmpImage)
    imageDC.SelectObject(pbmpImage);

stretchDC.SelectObject(pbmpStretch);
```

```
    bmpStretch.DeleteObject();

    backDC.SelectObject(pbmpBack);
    bmpBack.DeleteObject();

    maskDC.SelectObject(pbmpMask);
    bmpMask.DeleteObject();

    memDC.SelectObject(pbmpMem);
    bmpMem.DeleteObject();

    return TRUE;
}
```

CXSBitmap::DoPaint

All four major painting functions found in CXSBitmap call DoPaint. This function determines how the bitmap is actually drawn to the screen once it is ready to be painted. Either BitBlt is used or StretchBlt depending on the painting operation desired. The function is virtual in case you need to change this behavior in a derived class.

There are two versions of DoPaint. The first version, which takes X and Y, plus width and height coordinates, is the original function. The second version of DoPaint calls the original version and instead uses a CRect class to place the X, Y, width and height coordinates.

```
// ---------------------------------------------------------------
// Function  :
//     CXSBitmap::DoPaint
// Purpose   :
//     Called by the painting functions to do the actual painting
//     to the specified DC
// Parameters:
//     CDC* pDC - DC to paint into
//     int x1 - left position of corner to write to
//     int y1 - top position of corner to write to
//     int cx1 - width of where we want to write to
```

```
//      int cy1 - height of where we want to write to
//      CDC* srcDC - source DC containing bitmap
//      int x2 - left position of corner to write from
//      int y2 - top position of corner to write from
//      int cx2 - width of where we want to write from
//                (Only needed for PAINT_STRETCH)
//      int cy2 - height of where we want to write from
//                (Only needed for PAINT_STRETCH)
//      DWORD dwROP - raster operation code
//      PaintType pntType - painting operation type
//                - PaintNormal
//                - PaintTransparent
//                - PaintStretch
//                - PaintTransparentStretch
// Returns  :
//      TRUE on success, FALSE on failure
// ---------------------------------------------------------------
BOOL
CXSBitmap::DoPaint(CDC* pDC, int x1, int y1, int cx1, int cy1,
                CDC* srcDC, int x2, int y2, int cx2, int cy2,
                DWORD dwROP, PaintType pntType)
{
    ASSERT_VALID(this);
    ASSERT(pDC);
    ASSERT(srcDC);


    ::XSError_Set(XSERR_NOERROR);

    // See if this device is palette compatible
    if ((pDC->GetDeviceCaps(RASTERCAPS) & RC_PALETTE) &&
        m_Palette.GetSafeHandle())
    {
        TRACE0("CXSBitmap: Palette supported\n");
```

```
        pDC->SelectPalette(&m_Palette, FALSE);
        pDC->RealizePalette();
    }


    switch (pntType)
    {
        case NormalPaint:
        case TransparentPaint:
        case TransparentStretchPaint:
            return pDC->BitBlt(x1, y1, cx1, cy1, srcDC,
                x2, y2, dwROP);

        case StretchPaint:
            return pDC->StretchBlt(x1, y1, cx1, cy1, srcDC,
                x2, y2, cx2, cy2, dwROP);

        default:
            // unsupported command
            ::XSError_Set(XSERR_INVALIDFORMAT);
            ASSERT(FALSE);
            return FALSE;
    }
}

BOOL
CXSBitmap::DoPaint(CDC* pDC, CRect rcDest, CDC* srcDC, CRect rcSrc,
                DWORD dwROP, PaintType pntType)
{
    return DoPaint(pDC, rcDest.left, rcDest.top, rcDest.Width(),
        rcDest.Height(), srcDC, rcSrc.left, rcSrc.top,
        rcSrc.Width(), rcSrc.Height(), dwROP, pntType);
}
```

CXSBitmap::Rotate

The Rotate member function is a wrapper for the XSDib_Rotate DIB API function. It's only parameter is a BOOL, for which TRUE rotates the bitmap clockwise and FALSE rotates the bitmap counter-clockwise. The rotation is in 90° increments.

```
// --------------------------------------------------------------
// Function  :
//     CXSBitmap::Rotate
// Purpose   :
//     Rotates the current bitmap attached to this object by 90
//     degrees.
// Parameters:
//     BOOL - TRUE to rotate clockwise (Default)
//          - FALSE to rotate counter-clockwise
// Returns   :
//     TRUE on success, FALSE on failure
// --------------------------------------------------------------
BOOL CXSBitmap::Rotate(BOOL bClockwise)
{
    HDIB hDibSrc;
    HDIB hDibDest;

    ASSERT_VALID(this);

    if (!GetSafeHandle())
        return FALSE;

    ::XSError_Set(XSERR_NOERROR);

    // Get a HDIB to work with from the current Bitmap
    hDibSrc = ::XSBmp_ToDib((HBITMAP)GetSafeHandle(),
        (HPALETTE)m_Palette.GetSafeHandle());
    ASSERT(hDibSrc);  // sanity check
```

```
    if (!hDibSrc)
        return FALSE;


    // Rotate the DIB
    hDibDest = ::XSDib_Rotate(hDibSrc, bClockwise);


    // Destroy the temp DIB
    XSDib_Destroy(hDibSrc);


    ASSERT(hDibDest);   // sanity check
    if (!hDibDest)
        return FALSE;


    // Now that we have the rotated bitmap as a DIB, attach
    // the new DIB as a bitmap to this object
    // (DoAttach removes previous objects and creates new
    // palette for us if we don't provide one)
    if (DoAttach(hDibDest))
        return TRUE;


    // If the attach failed, the original Bitmap is retained
    return FALSE;

}
```

Using `CXSBitmap`

The code displayed here for the sample program is not complete. I am only showing the code that interacts with the presented framework.

BMPTest is a sample program on the CD-ROM that uses the `CXSBitmap` class. The program is an MDI application that either loads a bitmap from disk or from its own resources. The menu has been modified to allow us to tile, stretch, or rotate the bitmap in the current child frame by calling the appropriate functions from the `CXSBitmap` class.

The bitmap pictures in Figures 3.1, 3.2, 3.3, and 3.4 show the capabilities of this program. The first picture is a bitmap loaded from a resource. Unfortunately, it cannot be displayed in color. Run the program to see the results for yourself.

Figure 3.1 BMPTest can display a bitmap using the CXSBitmap class.

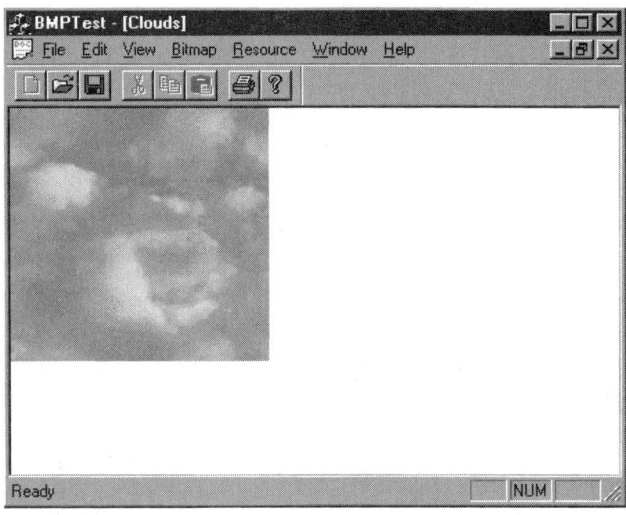

Figure 3.2 BMPTest can rotate a bitmap using the CXSBitmap **class.**

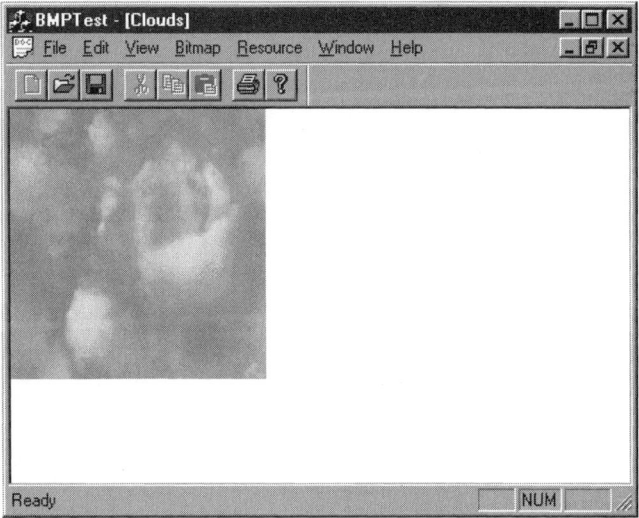

Figure 3.3 **BMPTest can stretch a bitmap using the** CXSBitmap **class.**

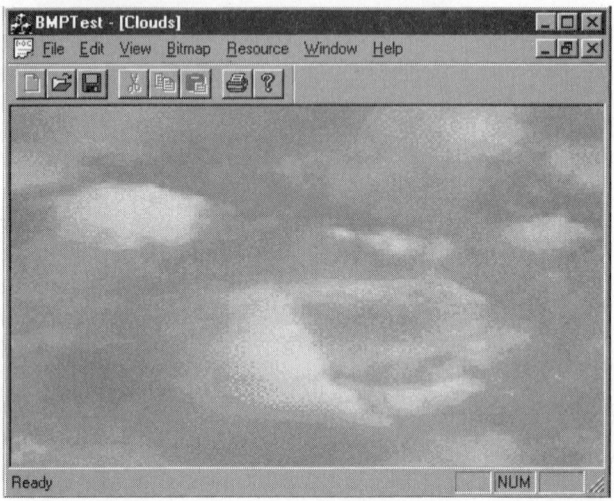

Figure 3.4 **BMPTest can tile a bitmap using the** CXSBitmap **class.**

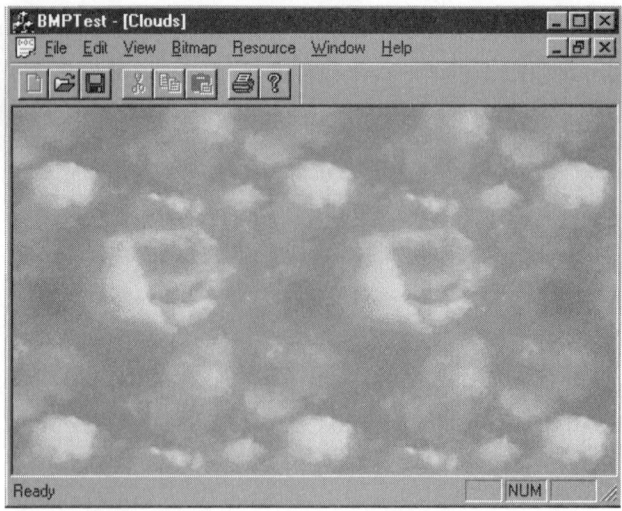

I've also cut out some unnecessary code and comments added by the App Wizard. stdafx.h is one of the source files used, but it is not displayed. stdafx.h includes the main XSEL header file, XSMAIN.H.

In the resource file, I added references for two bitmaps. One image is of the earth and the other is an image of clouds. Menu options were added to load these images from the resource file. I also added to the menu options to tile, stretch, or rotate the bitmap in the current frame.

In the code, you will see that I adjusted the source that the App Wizard created so that a child frame would not be loaded when the application is started. I did this by setting `cmdInfo.m_nShellCommand` to `CCommandLineInfo::FileNothing`.

I created the function `CreateDocFromResource` to load a bitmap resource and display it in a child frame. This involved creating a new document and then a new child frame that would be associated with the document. I added the function `SetBitmap` to the document code, which is called at the end of `CreateDocFromResource` to load the bitmap resource into the document. `SetBitmap` uses the `m_Bitmap` variable, of type `CXSBitmap`, to load the passed bitmap resource ID.

To load and save a bitmap, I had to override the `CDocument` virtual functions `OnOpenDocument` and `OnSaveDocument`. The modifications to these two functions were easy. In `OnOpenDocument`, I check to see if a bitmap image is already loaded. If so, then I clean up the memory. I proceed to do a `CXSBitmap::DoLoad` with the bitmap filename as the argument to this function. For the `OnSaveDocument`, I call `CXSBitmap::DoSave` with the name of the file. After saving the bitmap, I set the `CDocument` modified flag to `FALSE` to indicate that the document has been saved.

Now, one might argue that this might have been more appropriate for the `OnSerialize` function of `CDocument`, but I prefer to use `OnSerialize` only if there is more than one object type being written to the file. In this case, there is only a bitmapped image being read or saved to disk. In this situation, I prefer to override the `OnSaveDocument` and `OnOpenDocument` virtual functions.

In the application's view, two member variable flags are used: `m_bTile` and `m_bStretch`. These flags indicate whether the current view is to display the bitmapped image in a tiled or stretched manner. For our purposes, if both are set, the stretched view will override the tiled view. When the menu option Tile or Stretch is selected from the menu, the appropriate flag is toggled and the view is updated.

The code to handle the painting of the bitmapped image is in the view's `OnDraw` function. `OnDraw` first verifies that there is a valid bitmap to draw, then it gets the `RECT` area of the client window. If the `m_bStretch` flag is set, `OnDraw` calls the `CXSBitmap::DoPaintStretch` function to display the bitmapped image stretched to the size of the client window. If the `m_bStretch` flag is not set, OnDraw calls CXSBitmap::DoPaintNormal and passes the m_bTile flag as one of the parameters. If the m_bTile flag is set, OnDraw tiles the bitmapped image to the size of the client window; otherwise, OnDraw paints the bitmapped image normally.

```
///////////////////////////////////////////////////////////////
// BMPTest.h : main header file for the BMPTEST application

#include "resource.h"          // main symbols

// CBMPTestApp:

class CBMPTestApp : public CWinApp
{
public:
    CBMPTestApp();

// Overrides
    // ClassWizard generated virtual function overrides
    //{{AFX_VIRTUAL(CBMPTestApp)
    public:
    virtual BOOL InitInstance();
    //}}AFX_VIRTUAL

// Implementation
    BOOL CreateDocFromResource(UINT nID, CString strDocName);

    //{{AFX_MSG(CBMPTestApp)
    afx_msg void OnAppAbout();
    afx_msg void OnResourceClouds();
    afx_msg void OnUpdateResourceClouds(CCmdUI* pCmdUI);
    afx_msg void OnResourceEarth();
    afx_msg void OnUpdateResourceEarth(CCmdUI* pCmdUI);
    //}}AFX_MSG
    DECLARE_MESSAGE_MAP()
};

#endif
```

I

3

```
/////////////////////////////////////////////////////////////
// BMPTest.cpp : Defines the class behaviors for the application.

#include "stdafx.h"
#include "BMPTest.h"

#include "MainFrm.h"
#include "ChildFrm.h"
#include "BMPTestDoc.h"
#include "BMPTestView.h"


// CBMPTestApp

BEGIN_MESSAGE_MAP(CBMPTestApp, CWinApp)
    //{{AFX_MSG_MAP(CBMPTestApp)
    ON_COMMAND(ID_APP_ABOUT, OnAppAbout)
    ON_COMMAND(ID_RESOURCE_CLOUDS, OnResourceClouds)
    ON_UPDATE_COMMAND_UI(ID_RESOURCE_CLOUDS, OnUpdateResourceClouds)
    ON_COMMAND(ID_RESOURCE_EARTH, OnResourceEarth)
    ON_UPDATE_COMMAND_UI(ID_RESOURCE_EARTH, OnUpdateResourceEarth)
    //}}AFX_MSG_MAP
    // Standard file based document commands
//    ON_COMMAND(ID_FILE_NEW, CWinApp::OnFileNew)
    ON_COMMAND(ID_FILE_OPEN, CWinApp::OnFileOpen)
    // Standard print setup command
    ON_COMMAND(ID_FILE_PRINT_SETUP, CWinApp::OnFilePrintSetup)
END_MESSAGE_MAP()

// CBMPTestApp construction

CBMPTestApp::CBMPTestApp()
{
    // TODO: add construction code here,
    // Place all significant initialization in InitInstance
}
```

```
// The one and only CBMPTestApp object

CBMPTestApp theApp;

// CBMPTestApp initialization

BOOL CBMPTestApp::InitInstance()
{
    AfxEnableControlContainer();

    // Standard initialization
    // If you are not using these features and wish to reduce
    // the size of your final executable, you should remove from
    // the following the specific initialization routines you do
    // not need.

#ifdef _AFXDLL
    // Call this when using MFC in a shared DLL
    Enable3dControls();
#else
    // Call this when linking to MFC statically
    Enable3dControlsStatic();
#endif

    // Change the registry key under which our settings are stored.
    // You should modify this string to be something appropriate
    // such as the name of your company or organization.
    SetRegistryKey(_T("Xendra Software\\Samples"));

    // Load standard INI file options (including MRU)
    LoadStdProfileSettings();

    // Register the application's document templates.
    // Document templates serve as the connection between
    // documents, frame windows and views.

    CMultiDocTemplate* pDocTemplate;
```

I

3

```
    pDocTemplate = new CMultiDocTemplate(
        IDR_BMPTYPE,
        RUNTIME_CLASS(CBMPTestDoc),
        RUNTIME_CLASS(CChildFrame), // custom MDI child frame
        RUNTIME_CLASS(CBMPTestView));
    AddDocTemplate(pDocTemplate);

    // create main MDI Frame window
    CMainFrame* pMainFrame = new CMainFrame;
    if (!pMainFrame->LoadFrame(IDR_MAINFRAME))
        return FALSE;
    m_pMainWnd = pMainFrame;

    // Enable drag/drop open
    m_pMainWnd->DragAcceptFiles();

    // Enable DDE Execute open
    EnableShellOpen();
    RegisterShellFileTypes(TRUE);

    // Parse command line for standard shell commands,
    // DDE, file open
    CCommandLineInfo cmdInfo;
    cmdInfo.m_nShellCommand = CCommandLineInfo::FileNothing;
    ParseCommandLine(cmdInfo);

    // Dispatch commands specified on the command line
    if (!ProcessShellCommand(cmdInfo))
        return FALSE;

    // The main window has been initialized, so show and
    // update it.
    pMainFrame->ShowWindow(m_nCmdShow);
    pMainFrame->UpdateWindow();

    return TRUE;
}
```

```
//////////////////////////////////////////////////////////////
// CBMPTestApp commands

void CBMPTestApp::OnResourceClouds()
{
    CreateDocFromResource(IDB_CLOUDS, _T("Clouds"));
}

void CBMPTestApp::OnUpdateResourceClouds(CCmdUI* pCmdUI)
{
    pCmdUI->Enable();
}

void CBMPTestApp::OnResourceEarth()
{
    CreateDocFromResource(IDB_EARTH_BIG, _T("Earth"));
}

void CBMPTestApp::OnUpdateResourceEarth(CCmdUI* pCmdUI)
{
    pCmdUI->Enable();
}

BOOL
CBMPTestApp::CreateDocFromResource(UINT nID, CString strDocName)
{
    // get the new document and pass the bitmap ID to use
    POSITION pos = GetFirstDocTemplatePosition();
    CDocTemplate *pDocTmpl = GetNextDocTemplate(pos);
    ASSERT(pDocTmpl);

    // Create a new document
    CBMPTestDoc* pDocument =
        (CBMPTestDoc*)pDocTmpl->CreateNewDocument();
    if (pDocument == NULL)
```

```
{
    TRACE0("CDocTemplate::CreateNewDocument returned NULL.\n");
    AfxMessageBox(AFX_IDP_FAILED_TO_CREATE_DOC);
    return FALSE;
}
ASSERT_VALID(pDocument);

// create a new frame for the document
BOOL bAutoDelete = pDocument->m_bAutoDelete;

// don't destroy if something goes wrong
pDocument->m_bAutoDelete = FALSE;

// Create a new frame for the document
CFrameWnd* pFrame =
    pDocTmpl->CreateNewFrame(pDocument, NULL);
pDocument->m_bAutoDelete = bAutoDelete;
if (pFrame == NULL)
{
    AfxMessageBox(AFX_IDP_FAILED_TO_CREATE_DOC);
    delete pDocument; // explicit delete on error
    return FALSE;
}
ASSERT_VALID(pFrame);

CWaitCursor wait;

pDocument->SetTitle(strDocName);

if (!pDocument->OnNewDocument())
{
    // user has be alerted to what failed in OnNewDocument
    TRACE0("CDocument::OnNewDocument returned FALSE.\n");
    pFrame->DestroyWindow();
    return FALSE;
}
```

I

3

```
    // final new document processing
    pDocTmpl->InitialUpdateFrame(pFrame, pDocument, TRUE);

    pDocument->SetBitmap(nID);

    return TRUE;
}


// BMPTestDoc.h : interface of the CBMPTestDoc class
/////////////////////////////////////////////////////////////////


class CBMPTestDoc : public CDocument
{
protected: // create from serialization only
    CBMPTestDoc();
    DECLARE_DYNCREATE(CBMPTestDoc)

// Attributes
public:
    CXSBitmap     m_Bitmap;

// Operations
public:

// Overrides
    // ClassWizard generated virtual function overrides
    //{{AFX_VIRTUAL(CBMPTestDoc)
    public:
    virtual void Serialize(CArchive& ar);
    virtual BOOL OnOpenDocument(LPCTSTR lpszPathName);
    virtual BOOL OnSaveDocument(LPCTSTR lpszPathName);
    //}}AFX_VIRTUAL

// Implementation
public:
    virtual ~CBMPTestDoc();
    BOOL SetBitmap(UINT nID);
```

```
#ifdef _DEBUG
    virtual void AssertValid() const;
    virtual void Dump(CDumpContext& dc) const;
#endif

protected:

// Generated message map functions
protected:
    //{{AFX_MSG(CBMPTestDoc)
        // NOTE - the ClassWizard will add and remove member
        // functions here. DO NOT EDIT what you see in these
        // blocks of generated code!
    //}}AFX_MSG
    DECLARE_MESSAGE_MAP()
};

#endif

// BMPTestDoc.cpp : implementation of the CBMPTestDoc class

#include "stdafx.h"
#include "BMPTest.h"
#include "BMPTestDoc.h"

/////////////////////////////////////////////////////////////////
// CBMPTestDoc

IMPLEMENT_DYNCREATE(CBMPTestDoc, CDocument)

BEGIN_MESSAGE_MAP(CBMPTestDoc, CDocument)
    //{{AFX_MSG_MAP(CBMPTestDoc)
        // NOTE - the ClassWizard will add and remove mapping
        // macros here. DO NOT EDIT what you see in these blocks
        // of generated code!
    //}}AFX_MSG_MAP
END_MESSAGE_MAP()
```

```
/////////////////////////////////////////////////////////
// CBMPTestDoc construction/destruction

CBMPTestDoc::CBMPTestDoc()
{
    // TODO: add one-time construction code here
}


CBMPTestDoc::~CBMPTestDoc()
{

}


/////////////////////////////////////////////////////////
// CBMPTestDoc serialization

void CBMPTestDoc::Serialize(CArchive& ar)
{
    if (ar.IsStoring())
    {
        // TODO: add storing code here
    }
    else
    {
        // TODO: add loading code here
    }
}


/////////////////////////////////////////////////////////
// CBMPTestDoc diagnostics

#ifdef _DEBUG
void CBMPTestDoc::AssertValid() const
{
    CDocument::AssertValid();
}
```

```
void CBMPTestDoc::Dump(CDumpContext& dc) const
{
    CDocument::Dump(dc);
}
#endif //_DEBUG


/////////////////////////////////////////////////////////////////
// CBMPTestDoc commands
```

```
BOOL CBMPTestDoc::OnOpenDocument(LPCTSTR lpszPathName)
{
    if (!CDocument::OnOpenDocument(lpszPathName))
        return FALSE;

    // remove existing Bitmap, if any
    if (m_Bitmap.GetSafeHandle())
        m_Bitmap.DeleteObject();

    return m_Bitmap.DoLoad(lpszPathName);
}
```

```
BOOL CBMPTestDoc::OnSaveDocument(LPCTSTR lpszPathName)
{
    if (!(m_Bitmap.DoSave(lpszPathName)))
        return FALSE;

    SetModifiedFlag(FALSE);

    return TRUE;
}
```

```
BOOL CBMPTestDoc::SetBitmap(UINT nID)
{
    // remove existing Bitmap, if any
    if (m_Bitmap.GetSafeHandle())
        m_Bitmap.DeleteObject();
```

I

3

```
        return m_Bitmap.DoLoad(nID);
}
```

```
// BMPTestView.h : interface of the CBMPTestView class
/////////////////////////////////////////////////////////////

class CBMPTestView : public CView
{
protected: // create from serialization only
    CBMPTestView();
    DECLARE_DYNCREATE(CBMPTestView)

// Attributes
public:
    CBMPTestDoc* GetDocument();
    BOOL        m_bTile;
    BOOL        m_bStretch;

// Operations
public:

// Overrides
    // ClassWizard generated virtual function overrides
    //{{AFX_VIRTUAL(CBMPTestView)
    public:
    virtual void OnDraw(CDC* pDC);  // overridden to draw this view
    virtual BOOL PreCreateWindow(CREATESTRUCT& cs);
    protected:
    virtual BOOL OnPreparePrinting(CPrintInfo* pInfo);
    virtual void OnBeginPrinting(CDC* pDC, CPrintInfo* pInfo);
    virtual void OnEndPrinting(CDC* pDC, CPrintInfo* pInfo);
    //}}AFX_VIRTUAL
```

I

3

```cpp
// Implementation
public:
    virtual ~CBMPTestView();
#ifdef _DEBUG
    virtual void AssertValid() const;
    virtual void Dump(CDumpContext& dc) const;
#endif

protected:

// Generated message map functions
protected:
    //{{AFX_MSG(CBMPTestView)
    afx_msg void OnBitmapStretch();
    afx_msg void OnUpdateBitmapStretch(CCmdUI* pCmdUI);
    afx_msg void OnBitmapTile();
    afx_msg void OnUpdateBitmapTile(CCmdUI* pCmdUI);
    afx_msg void OnUpdateBitmapRotate(CCmdUI* pCmdUI);
    afx_msg void OnBitmapRotate();
    //}}AFX_MSG
    DECLARE_MESSAGE_MAP()
};

#ifndef _DEBUG  // debug version in BMPTestView.cpp
inline CBMPTestDoc* CBMPTestView::GetDocument()
    { return (CBMPTestDoc*)m_pDocument; }
#endif

#endif

// BMPTestView.cpp : implementation of the CBMPTestView class
//

#include "stdafx.h"
#include "BMPTest.h"
#include "BMPTestDoc.h"
#include "BMPTestView.h"
```

```
///////////////////////////////////////////////////////////
// CBMPTestView

IMPLEMENT_DYNCREATE(CBMPTestView, CView)

BEGIN_MESSAGE_MAP(CBMPTestView, CView)
    //{{AFX_MSG_MAP(CBMPTestView)
    ON_COMMAND(ID_BITMAP_STRETCH, OnBitmapStretch)
    ON_UPDATE_COMMAND_UI(ID_BITMAP_STRETCH, OnUpdateBitmapStretch)
    ON_COMMAND(ID_BITMAP_TILE, OnBitmapTile)
    ON_UPDATE_COMMAND_UI(ID_BITMAP_TILE, OnUpdateBitmapTile)
    ON_UPDATE_COMMAND_UI(ID_BITMAP_ROTATE, OnUpdateBitmapRotate)
    ON_COMMAND(ID_BITMAP_ROTATE, OnBitmapRotate)
    //}}AFX_MSG_MAP
    // Standard printing commands
    ON_COMMAND(ID_FILE_PRINT, CView::OnFilePrint)
    ON_COMMAND(ID_FILE_PRINT_DIRECT, CView::OnFilePrint)
    ON_COMMAND(ID_FILE_PRINT_PREVIEW, CView::OnFilePrintPreview)
END_MESSAGE_MAP()

///////////////////////////////////////////////////////////
// CBMPTestView construction/destruction

CBMPTestView::CBMPTestView()
{
    m_bTile = FALSE;
    m_bStretch = FALSE;
}

CBMPTestView::~CBMPTestView()
{
}
```

```
BOOL CBMPTestView::PreCreateWindow(CREATESTRUCT& cs)
{
    // TODO: Modify the Window class or styles here by
    // modifying the CREATESTRUCT cs

    return CView::PreCreateWindow(cs);
}


/////////////////////////////////////////////////////////////////
// CBMPTestView drawing
```

```
void CBMPTestView::OnDraw(CDC* pDC)
{
    CBMPTestDoc* pDoc = GetDocument();
    ASSERT_VALID(pDoc);

    // Check for valid object to draw
    if (!(pDoc->m_Bitmap.GetSafeHandle()))
        return;

    CRect rect;
    GetClientRect(&rect);

    // stretch is user asked for it, otherwise
    // paint (maybe with tile)
    if (m_bStretch)
        pDoc->m_Bitmap.DoPaintStretch(pDC, rect);
    else
        pDoc->m_Bitmap.DoPaintNormal(pDC, rect, m_bTile);
}
```

I

3

```
////////////////////////////////////////////////////////////
// CBMPTestView printing

BOOL CBMPTestView::OnPreparePrinting(CPrintInfo* pInfo)
{
    // default preparation
    return DoPreparePrinting(pInfo);
}

void CBMPTestView::OnBeginPrinting(CDC* /*pDC*/, CPrintInfo*
/*pInfo*/)
{
    // TODO: add extra initialization before printing
}

void CBMPTestView::OnEndPrinting(CDC* /*pDC*/, CPrintInfo* /*pInfo*/)
{
    // TODO: add cleanup after printing
}


////////////////////////////////////////////////////////////
// CBMPTestView diagnostics

#ifdef _DEBUG
void CBMPTestView::AssertValid() const
{
    CView::AssertValid();
}

void CBMPTestView::Dump(CDumpContext& dc) const
{
    CView::Dump(dc);
}
```

```
// non-debug version is inline
CBMPTestDoc* CBMPTestView::GetDocument()
{
    ASSERT(m_pDocument->IsKindOf(RUNTIME_CLASS(CBMPTestDoc)));
    return (CBMPTestDoc*)m_pDocument;
}
#endif //_DEBUG


//////////////////////////////////////////////////////////////////
// CBMPTestView message handlers
```

```
void CBMPTestView::OnUpdateBitmapStretch(CCmdUI* pCmdUI)
{
    pCmdUI->Enable();
    pCmdUI->SetCheck(m_bStretch);
}
```

```
void CBMPTestView::OnBitmapStretch()
{
    m_bStretch = !m_bStretch;
    Invalidate();
}
```

```
void CBMPTestView::OnUpdateBitmapTile(CCmdUI* pCmdUI)
{
    pCmdUI->Enable(!m_bStretch);
    if (!m_bStretch)
        pCmdUI->SetCheck(m_bTile);
}
```

```
void CBMPTestView::OnBitmapTile()
{
    m_bTile = !m_bTile;
    Invalidate();
}
```

```
void CBMPTestView::OnUpdateBitmapRotate(CCmdUI* pCmdUI)
{
    pCmdUI->Enable();
}
```

```
void CBMPTestView::OnBitmapRotate()
{
    CBMPTestDoc* pDoc = GetDocument();
    ASSERT_VALID(pDoc);

    // Check for valid object to draw
    if (!(pDoc->m_Bitmap.GetSafeHandle()))
        return;

    pDoc->m_Bitmap.Rotate(FALSE);
    Invalidate();
}
```

Summary

In this chapter, we discussed the CXSBitmap class and it's functionality. This class will become increasingly more important as we traverse through the chapters of this book. It is a very good class in itself just for the painting operation functions, not to mention the loading, saving, and serialization of DIBs. I have found this class to be one of the most convenient and useful pieces of code that I have ever written. I use it for just about all of my projects because it saves me time in writing code. You just gotta love C++.

I

3

Section II

Subclassers

Chapter 4

Super Subclassing

Introduction

In this chapter, we're going to examine a way of making our classes more generic. For example, we could create a class extension for `CTreeCtrl` that would also work for `CTreeView`. MFC's lack of support for true multiple inheritance is somewhat problematic. To get the same functionality in a derived class of `CTreeCtrl`, you also have to derive a new class for `CTree-View`. You would then have to maintain identical source in two different files, essentially throwing away the object-oriented concept of reuse. Through subclassing, we are going to work around this issue in an unusual way. Instead of deriving from `CTreeCtrl` or `CTreeView`, we're going to create classes with our subclass handler that will be used as member variables in our MFC derived classes.

You use the subclass handler by keeping a member variable of it's derived type in your derived MFC class declaration. This is what is known as pseudo-multiple inheritance through aggregation. After MFC has created the window, you call the `SubclassWindow` function of the handler to install a new window procedure for that window. The `CXSSubWndCtrl` class then works in conjunction with the `CXSSubWndCtrlMap` class. This second class is used to keep a map of all subclassed procedures, creating a chained effect. If your procedure does not handle a windows message, the subclass handler will call the next window procedure in line, and so on.

There is a stand-alone function, XSSubclass_WndProc, that becomes the subclassed replacement procedure. XSSubclass_WndProc finds the appropriate CXSSubWndCtrl derived window procedure and makes the appropriate call. XSSubclass_WndProc also looks for the window message WM_NCDESTROY, which is the final window message a window receives, and uses this message to disengage the subclass handler for that window. For this reason, there are a few window messages you will not be able to respond to with the subclass handler. Of course, you will not be able to handle WM_CREATE. You cannot subclass a window that has not been created. You also cannot handle WM_NCDESTROY. However, before the subclass handler is disengaged, it does a SendMessage with WM_PRENCDESTROY. This is the location at which you can now put your regular WM_NCDESTROY handling code and get the same effect.

Right now, this code doesn't look like much. When we start to derive classes from the code that work with multiple MFC classes to create a sort of a pseudo-multiple inheritance, I think you'll see the bigger picture.

XSSUBWNDCTRL.H

Global Messages

There are a couple of messages we want to be able to send. We'll get to the reasons why in just a bit, but we have to provide the extern declarations for them so other source code can see them. Remember from Chapter 1 that the XSDATA macro is used to import or export data when building a DLL. When not being use for a DLL, the XSDATA macro is ignored.

```
// --------------------------------------------------------------
// Global messages
extern const UINT XSDATA WM_SETPARENTNOTIFY;
extern const UINT XSDATA WM_PRENCDESTROY;
```

Forward Declarations

```
// ------------------------------------------------------------
// Forward declaration
class CXSSubWndCtrlMap;
```

CXSSubWndCtrl **Class Declaration**

```
class XSCLASS
CXSSubWndCtrl : public CObject
{
protected:
    DECLARE_DYNAMIC(CXSSubWndCtrl);


    CWnd*            m_pSubWnd;      // The subclassed window
    WNDPROC          m_pOldWndProc;  // Pointer to replaced wndproc
    CXSSubWndCtrl*   m_pNext;        // Next subclass handler
    CWnd*            m_pWindow;      // For passed HWND's


    // Derive this to handle specific messages
    virtual LRESULT DoWindowProc(UINT nMsg, WPARAM wParam,
        LPARAM lParam);


    // Call this at the end of a message handler
    LRESULT Default();

public:
    CXSSubWndCtrl();
    virtual ~CXSSubWndCtrl();


    BOOL SubclassWindow(CWnd* pWnd);
    BOOL SubclassWindow(HWND hWnd);
    BOOL IsSubclassed();
    BOOL Remove();
    virtual CWnd* DoGetWnd();
```

II

4

```
LRESULT CallWindowProc(UINT nMsg, WPARAM wParam,
    LPARAM lParam);
};
```

CXSSubWndCtrlMap **Class Declaration**

The CXSSubWndCtrlMap class is used to keep a list of CXSSubWndCtrl classes in a map based on the HWND of the applicable window. We can then subclass a window multiple times, adding functionality to various aspects of the window. For instance, in upcoming chapters, we will be creating a background control and a caption control. You could subclass with each of these objects on the same window and each would still work. This helps you to keep your work modularized instead of getting a single bulky class. You will also have more breathing room to make these classes reusable, as they can become more generic by not being tied to any particular window's behavior. This is where pseudo-multiple inheritance comes from.

```
class XSCLASS
CXSSubWndCtrlMap : private CMapPtrToPtr
{
public:
    CXSSubWndCtrlMap();
    virtual ~CXSSubWndCtrlMap();

    // static function to return "this"
    static CXSSubWndCtrlMap& GetSubWndCtrlMap();

    // Mapping functions
    void Add(HWND hwnd, CXSSubWndCtrl* pSubWnd);
    void Remove(CXSSubWndCtrl* pSubWnd);
    void RemoveAll(HWND hwnd);
    CXSSubWndCtrl* Lookup(HWND hwnd);
};
```

macXSSubWndCtrlMap

The `GetSubWndCtrlMap` function of the `CXSSubWndCtrlMap` class is a static function. The `macXSSubWndCtrlMap` macro is used to make the `CXSSubWndC-trlMap::GetSubWndCtrlMap` function easily accessible.

```
// ------------------------------------------------------------
// Macro    :
//    macXSSubWndCtrlMap
// Purpose  :
//    This macro allows us to access the static function
//    CXSSubWndCtrlMap::GetSubclassWndMap in a nice and clean
//    manner that makes it very readable.
#define macXSSubWndCtrlMap (CXSSubWndCtrlMap::GetSubWndCtrlMap())
```

II

4

XSSUBWNDCTRL.CPP

Header Files

```
#include "stdafx.h"
#include "XSSubWndCtrl.h"
```

Global Messages

As promised, let's discuss the `WM_SETPARENTNOTIFY` and `WM_PRENCDESTROY` user-defined window messages. As you may notice, I am using the SDK function `RegisterWindowMessage` to get a unique message number back from the operating system. This number is guaranteed to be unique, yet shared if multiple programs are run that use these messages. For instance, if you have two programs that use this source, each program will have the same number assigned for each of the respective messages.

The first message, `WM_SETPARENTNOTIFY`, will be used when we want to handle our own message reflection. It is not used by these classes, but will be used by derived classes. `WM_SETPARENTNOTIFY` is placed in this location for convenience. The second message, `WM_PRENCDESTROY`, is called by the `XSSubclass_WndProc` API function when it sees a `WM_NCDESTROY` message from Windows. Because the `XSSubclass_WndProc` API function uses the `WM_NCDESTROY` message to disengage the subclass handler, this framework cannot handle this message. A `SendMessage` call is made with our registered `WM_PRENCDESTROY` message, instead.

```
// ------------------------------------------------------------
// Register global messages
const UINT WM_SETPARENTNOTIFY = ::RegisterWindowMessage
(_T("WM_SETPARENTNOTIFY"));
const UINT WM_PRENCDESTROY     = ::RegisterWindowMessage
(_T("WM_PRENCDESTROY"));
```

Dynamic Implementation

`IMPLEMENT_DYNAMIC` generates the C++ code necessary for a dynamic `CObject`-derived class with run-time access to the class name and position within the hierarchy.

```
IMPLEMENT_DYNAMIC(CXSSubWndCtrl, CWnd);
```

CXSSubWndCtrl::CXSSubWndCtrl

The constructor is used to set a number of pointers initially to `NULL`.

```
// ------------------------------------------------------------
// Function  :
//     CXSSubWndCtrl::CXSSubWndCtrl
// Purpose   :
//     Constructor, initializes memory
// ------------------------------------------------------------
CXSSubWndCtrl::CXSSubWndCtrl()
{
    m_pNext = NULL;
    m_pOldWndProc = NULL;
    m_pSubWnd = NULL;
    m_pWindow = NULL;
}
```

CXSSubWndCtrl::~CXSSubWndCtrl

The destructor, of course, does our clean up for this class. If you are running in _DEBUG mode, the code checks to make sure the subclass handler has been disengaged before it is destroyed. Otherwise, it forces an `ASSERT` condition.

The m_pWindow variable is used to create a CWnd if an HWND was passed instead. If m_pWindow is valid, we delete it.

```
// ------------------------------------------------------------------
// Function  :
//     CXSSubWndCtrl::~CXSSubWndCtrl
// Purpose   :
//     Destructor, cleans up memory
// ------------------------------------------------------------------
CXSSubWndCtrl::~CXSSubWndCtrl()
{
    ASSERT(m_pSubWnd == NULL);
    ASSERT(m_pOldWndProc==NULL);

    // Clean up any allocated memory
    if (m_pWindow)
    {
        // Because we "attached" the HWND to the CWnd,
        // we "detach" it when we're done with it
        m_pWindow->Detach();
        delete m_pWindow;
    }
}
```

CXSSubWndCtrl::SubclassWindow

The SubclassWindow function does the dirty work of verifying the validity of the passed CWnd before installing the subclasser. Once all tests pass, CXS-SubWndCtrlMap::Add is called to do the actual subclassing and then adds the subclasser to the map.

```
// ------------------------------------------------------------------
// Function  :
//     CXSSubWndCtrl::SubclassWindow
// Purpose   :
//     Subclasses a window procedure.  This function installs a
//     new window procedure that directs messages to the
//     CXSSubWndCtrl.
```

```
// Parameters:
//    CWnd* pWnd - window to subclass
// Returns   :
//    BOOL - TRUE on success, FALSE on failure
// Comments  :
//    Set pWnd = NULL to remove (uninstall) the subclassed
//      procedure
// -------------------------------------------------------------
BOOL
CXSSubWndCtrl::SubclassWindow(CWnd* pWnd)
{
    ASSERT_VALID(pWnd);

    // Make sure this instance has not already been set up
    // to be a subclasser
    ASSERT(m_pSubWnd == NULL);

    // Verify window exists and make assignment
    ASSERT(pWnd->m_hWnd && ::IsWindow(pWnd->m_hWnd));
    HWND hwnd = pWnd->m_hWnd;

    // Add window to the mapper
    theXSSubWndCtrlMap.Add(hwnd, this);

    m_pSubWnd = pWnd;

    return TRUE;
}
```

CXSSubWndCtrl::SubclassWindow

This is the same function as the previous one, except that in this case you pass a raw HWND instead of MFC's CWnd. A new CWnd is created and then the

HWND attached to it. To finish off its processing, it calls the other Subclass-
Window function to reuse the code.

```
// ------------------------------------------------------------------
// Function :
//   CXSSubWndCtrl::SubclassWindow
// Purpose  :
//   Subclasses the passes HWND
// Parameters:
//   HWND hWnd - the window to subclass
// Returns  :
//   BOOL - TRUE on success, FALSE on failue
// Comments :
//   Call SubclassWindow(NULL) to remove (uninstall) the
//   subclassed procedure.
// Notes    :
//   The prefered method is to call the other SubclassWindow with
//   a CWnd.  This function may not be available in future
//   releases.
// ------------------------------------------------------------------
BOOL
CXSSubWndCtrl::SubclassWindow(HWND hWnd)
{
    ASSERT(::IsWindow(hWnd));

    m_pWindow = new CWnd;
    m_pWindow->Attach(hWnd);
    return SubclassWindow(m_pWindow);
}
```

CXSSubWndCtrl::IsSubclassed

IsSubclassed is a quick utility function to determine whether this object has been subclassed. As I mentioned earlier, functions like this deserve to be inline. However, it's more readable in a book to have them in the source file.

```
// --------------------------------------------------------------
// Function  :
//   CXSSubWndCtrl::IsSubclassed
// Purpose   :
//   Verifies that this object has a subclassed window
// Parameters:
//   None
// Returns   :
//   BOOL - TRUE if the object has subclassed a window
//        - FALSE if the object has not subclassed a window
// --------------------------------------------------------------
BOOL
CXSSubWndCtrl::IsSubclassed()
{
    return m_pSubWnd != NULL;
}
```

CXSSubWndCtrl::Remove()

The Remove function calls CXSSubWndCtrlMap::Remove to disengage the subclass handler from the Windows window and remove it from the map.

```
// --------------------------------------------------------------
// Function  :
//   CXSSubWndCtrl::Remove
// Purpose   :
//   Removes (uninstall/disengage) the subclass handler
// Parameters:
//   None
// Returns   :
//   BOOL - TRUE on success
//        - FALSE on failure
```

```
// ---------------------------------------------------------------
BOOL
CXSSubWndCtrl::Remove()
{
    // The subclasser is uninstalling. Verify we've been
    // subclassed before proceeding
    ASSERT(m_pSubWnd != NULL);

    // Remove the window from the map
    theXSSubWndCtrlMap.Remove(this);
    m_pOldWndProc = NULL;


    m_pSubWnd = NULL;


    return TRUE;
}
```

CXSSubWndCtrl::DoGetWnd

DoGetWnd is a virtual function that returns the CWnd associated with this sub-class handler (i.e., the window that has been subclassed).

```
// ---------------------------------------------------------------
// Function  :
//   CXSSubWndCtrl::DoGetWnd
// Purpose   :
//   Returns a pointer to the passed CWnd
// Parameters:
//   None
// Returns   :
//   CWnd* - pointer to the passed CWnd
// ---------------------------------------------------------------
CWnd*
CXSSubWndCtrl::DoGetWnd()
```

```
{
    ASSERT_VALID(m_pSubWnd);
    return m_pSubWnd;
}
```

CXSSubWndCtrl::DoWindowProc

DoWindowProc is the function that makes sure the next subclass handler is
called when multi-chained subclass handlers exist.

```
// ------------------------------------------------------------
// Function  :
//      CXSSubWndCtrl::DoWindowProc
// Purpose   :
//      Chains through the old window procedures and calls each.
//      Typically, when you derive from this class, you will write
//      your own DoWindowProc procedure.  Anything you do not
//      handle, should call the base class function.
//      If you have subclassed a window more than once, this
//      function will call the previous subclassed procedure. If
//      you have not subclassed, or the last subclassed procedure
//      is reached, then the original window's procedure is called.
//      The chaining only happens until one of the procedures does
//      not call the base implementation.
// Parameters:
//      UINT nMsg - The windows message
//      WPARAM wParam - parameter applicable for windows message
//      LPARAM lParam - parameter applicable for windows message
// Returns   :
//      LRESULT - Depends on windows message
// ------------------------------------------------------------
LRESULT
CXSSubWndCtrl::DoWindowProc(UINT nMsg, WPARAM wParam, LPARAM lParam)
{
    ASSERT(m_pOldWndProc);
```

```
        // Calls the next chained subclassed window procedure,
        // or call the window's implementation.
        return m_pNext - m_pNext->DoWindowProc(nMsg, wParam, lParam) :
            ::CallWindowProc(m_pOldWndProc, m_pSubWnd->m_hWnd,
                nMsg, wParam, lParam);
}
```

CXSSubWndCtrl::CallWindowProc

The utility function `CallWindowProc` calls `DoWindowProc` for convenience purposes only.

```
// ----------------------------------------------------------------
// Function  :
//   CXSSubWndCtrl::CallWindowProc
// Purpose   :
//   For convenience only.  Calls CXSSubWndCtrl::DoWindowProc
// Parameters:
// Returns   :
// ----------------------------------------------------------------
LRESULT
CXSSubWndCtrl::CallWindowProc(UINT nMsg, WPARAM wParam,
                              LPARAM lParam)
{
    return DoWindowProc(nMsg, wParam, lParam);
}
```

CXSSubWndCtrl::Default

The `Default` function was created to give you similar benefits to MFC's `Default` function. That is, you do not have to pass this function the parameters, as you would have to if you called `DoWindowProc` directly. In MFC, you can call `AfxGetThreadState` to get at the last message passed by Windows.

You can then get access to the `MSG` structure of that message, which is then used to call `DoWindowProc` directly.

```
// -----------------------------------------------------------
// Function  :
//     CXSSubWndCtrl::Default
// Purpose   :
//     Provides default message handling.  You can call this
//     function when you have not stored the message parameters
//     from the last Windows message.  MFC stores the message in
//     its thread state.
// Parameters:
//     None
// Returns   :
//     LRESULT of the called procedure
// -----------------------------------------------------------
LRESULT
CXSSubWndCtrl::Default()
{
    // MFC stores current MSG in thread state
    MSG& msgCur = AfxGetThreadState()->m_lastSentMsg;

    // Note: must explicitly call CXSSubWndCtrl::DoWindowProc to
    // avoid infinite recursion on virtual function
    return CXSSubWndCtrl::DoWindowProc(msgCur.message,
        msgCur.wParam, msgCur.lParam);
}
```

XSSubclass_WndProc

`XSSubclass_WndProc` is a stand-alone function that becomes the subclass handler replacement. When Windows sends a message to a window, this function looks up the specific class handler for that window. Once the window is located, the handler checks to see whether the Windows message is `WM_NCDESTROY`; if not, it passes the message on to the class handler for that window.

If the Windows message is `WM_NCDESTROY`, this handler sends the registered message of `WM_PRENCDESTROY`. The subclass procedure uses the

WM_NCDESTROY message to disengage itself as the handler for that window. WM_NCDESTROY is the last message a window receives, so this is a logical place to send the WM_PRENCDESTROY message. Programmers occasionally put critical code in their own WM_NCDESTROY handlers, but the same code can now go into a WM_PRENCDESTROY handler.

```
// -----------------------------------------------------------------
// Function :
//    XSSubclass_WndProc
// Purpose  :
//    This is the actual function that gets subclassed and is
//    eventually called by Windows. This function then calls
//    the appropriate subclassed window proc. If this function
//    receives a WM_NCDESTROY window message, it uninstalls
//    itself as the window proc handler. This save the
//    programmer from having to uninstall the handler when the
//    window is destroyed.
// Parameters:
//    UINT nMsg - The windows message
//    WPARAM wParam - parameter applicable for windows message
//    LPARAM lParam - parameter applicable for windows message
// Returns  :
//    LRESULT - Depends on windows message
// Comments:
//    Subclassed window proc for message hooks.  Replaces
//    AfxWndProc or previously installed wnd proc.
// -----------------------------------------------------------------
LRESULT CALLBACK
XSSubclass_WndProc(HWND hWnd, UINT nMsg,
                   WPARAM wParam, LPARAM lParam)
{
#ifdef _USRDLL
    // if this code is in a user DLL,
    // we need to set up the MFC state
    AFX_MANAGE_STATE(AfxGetStaticModuleState());
#endif
```

```
// This looks just like AfxCallWindowProc, but we
// can't use that because CXSSubWndCtrl is not really
// derived from CWnd.
MSG& msgCur = AfxGetThreadState()->m_lastSentMsg;
MSG msgOld = msgCur;
msgCur.hwnd = hWnd;
msgCur.message = nMsg;
msgCur.wParam = wParam;
msgCur.lParam = lParam;

// Look up the wndproc handler
CXSSubWndCtrl* pSubWnd =
    macXSSubWndCtrlMap.Lookup(hWnd);
ASSERT(pSubWnd);

LRESULT lResult = 0;

if (nMsg == WM_NCDESTROY)
{
    // Just in case we need a handler
    ::SendMessage(hWnd, WM_PRENCDESTROY, 0, 0);

    // Disengage all hooks for this window before it is
    // destoyed and pass msg to original window proc
    WNDPROC wndProc = pSubWnd->m_pOldWndProc;
    macXSSubWndCtrlMap.RemoveAll(hWnd);
    lResult = ::CallWindowProc(wndProc, hWnd, nMsg,
        wParam, lParam);
}
else
{
    // Call the appropriate wndproc handler
    lResult = pSubWnd->DoWindowProc(nMsg, wParam, lParam);
```

```
    }

    msgCur = msgOld;

    return lResult;
}
```

CXSSubWndCtrlMap **Usage**

CXSSubWndCtrlMap contains a map of all CXSSubWndCtrl objects and associates each object with the HWND of the subclassed window. This HWND is then used to retrieve the CXSSubWndCtrl object when a subclassed procedure needs to be called. You should never have to call this class directly. It is used exclusively by the CXSSubWndCtrl class and XSSubclass_WndProc.

CXSSubWndCtrlMap::CXSSubWndCtrlMap

```
// ----------------------------------------------------------
// Function  :
//     CXSSubWndCtrlMap::CXSSubWndCtrlMap
// Purpose   :
//     Constructor, initializes memory
// ----------------------------------------------------------
CXSSubWndCtrlMap::CXSSubWndCtrlMap()
{
}
```

CXSSubWndCtrlMap::~CXSSubWndCtrlMap()

The CXSSubWndCtrlMap destructor checks whether the map is empty; if not, all mapped items are removed.

```
//-----------------------------------------------------------
// Function  :
//     CXSSubWndCtrlMap::~CXSSubWndCtrlMap
// Purpose   :
//     Destructor, cleans up memory.
// ----------------------------------------------------------
CXSSubWndCtrlMap::~CXSSubWndCtrlMap()
```

```
{
    if (!IsEmpty())
        CMapPtrToPtr::RemoveAll();

    ASSERT(IsEmpty());
}
```

CXSSubWndCtrlMap::GetSubWndCtrlMap()

The `GetSubWndCtrlMap` function is declared as static. The first time this function is called, the actual `CXSSubWndCtrlMap` object is created in a static variable within this function. A reference to this object is returned on this and subsequent calls. This function is typically accessed by the `macXSSubWndCtrlMap` macro.

```
// ------------------------------------------------------------
// Function  :
//     CXSSubWndCtrlMap::GetSubWndCtrlMap
// Purpose   :
//     Returns the static CXSSubWndCtrlMap variable.  It is
//     initialized the first time this function is called.
// Parameters:
//     None
// Returns   :
//     See above.
// ------------------------------------------------------------
CXSSubWndCtrlMap&
CXSSubWndCtrlMap::GetSubWndCtrlMap()
{
    // By creating the static variable here, C++ doesn't
    // instantiate it until/unless it's ever used.  This is a
    // good way of encapsulating a static object.
    static CXSSubWndCtrlMap XSSubWndCtrlMap;
    return XSSubWndCtrlMap;
}
```

CXSSubWndCtrlMap::Add

The Add function adds a new CXSSubWndCtrl object to the map through its association of the passed HWND. It automatically adjusts the chain of subclass handlers so that the previous handler can be called properly, as determined by the code.

```
// -------------------------------------------------------------
// Function  :
//     CXSSubWndCtrlMap::Add
// Purpose   :
//     Associates a new CXSSubWndCtrl procedure to a windows
//       handle (HWND)
// Parameters:
//     HWND hwnd - the window to deal with
//     CXSSubWndCtrl* pSubclassWnd - pointer to new procedure
// Returns   :
//     Nothing
// -------------------------------------------------------------
void
CXSSubWndCtrlMap::Add(HWND hWnd, CXSSubWndCtrl* pSubWnd)
{
    ASSERT(hwnd && ::IsWindow(hWnd));

    // Add to front of list
    pSubWnd->m_pNext = Lookup(hWnd);
    SetAt(hwnd, pSubWnd);

    if (pSubWnd->m_pNext == NULL)
    {
        // If this is the first hook added,
        // then subclass the window
        pSubWnd->m_pOldWndProc =
            (WNDPROC)SetWindowLong(hWnd, GWL_WNDPROC,
            (DWORD)XSSubclass_WndProc);
    }
    else
```

II

4

```
    {
        // Just copy wndproc from next hook as this class has
        // already been subclassed
        pSubWnd->m_pOldWndProc =
            pSubWnd->m_pNext->m_pOldWndProc;
    }

    ASSERT(pSubWnd->m_pOldWndProc);
}
```

CXSSubWndCtrlMap::Remove

The Remove function disengages (removes) the passed CXSSubWndCtrl object from the chain of mapped handlers andt automatically adjusts the chain so that nothing is broken. Remove gets the HWND of the passed CXSSubWndCtrl object, locates the object in the map, and then adjusts the chain as appropriate.

```
// ---------------------------------------------------------------
// Function  :
//     CXSSubWndCtrlMap::Remove
// Purpose   :
//     Removes a subclassed window procedure
// Parameters:
//     CXSSubWndCtrl* pUnSubclassWnd - Pointer to the
//        CXSSubWndCtrl to remove
// Returns   :
//     Nothing
// ---------------------------------------------------------------
void
CXSSubWndCtrlMap::Remove(CXSSubWndCtrl* pUnSubWnd)
{
    HWND hwnd = pUnSubWnd->m_pSubWnd->GetSafeHwnd();
    ASSERT(hwnd && ::IsWindow(hwnd));

    // Look up the proceedure
    CXSSubWndCtrl* pSubWnd = Lookup(hwnd);
    ASSERT(pSubWnd);
```

```
    if (pUnSubWnd == pSubWnd)
    {
        if (pSubWnd->m_pNext)
        {
            // If there are chained handlers, set the next one
            // to be the current one
            SetAt(hwnd, pSubWnd->m_pNext);
        }
        else
        {
            // last hook; restore original wndproc
            RemoveKey(hwnd);
            SetWindowLong(hwnd, GWL_WNDPROC,
                (DWORD)pSubWnd->m_pOldWndProc);
        }
    }
    else
    {
        // The hook is in the middle, so remove and patch
        // linked list
        while (pSubWnd->m_pNext != pUnSubWnd)
            pSubWnd = pSubWnd->m_pNext;

        ASSERT(pSubWnd && pSubWnd->m_pNext ==
            pUnSubWnd);

        pSubWnd->m_pNext = pUnSubWnd->m_pNext;
    }
}
```

CXSSubWndCtrlMap::RemoveAll

The RemoveAll function looks at all of the chained handlers for the passed
HWND and disengages each handler as the subclasser for that window.
RemoveAll finds each CXSSubWndCtrl object for the passed HWND, gets the

CXSSubWndCtrl object from the map, and then calls the object's Remove function.

```
// -----------------------------------------------------------
// Function  :
//     CXSSubWndCtrlMap::RemoveAll
// Purpose  :
//     Removes all of the subclassed window procedures
// Parameters:
//     HWND hwnd - The HWND of the window to remove the
//       procedures from
// Returns  :
//     Nothing
// -----------------------------------------------------------
void
CXSSubWndCtrlMap::RemoveAll(HWND hwnd)
{
    CXSSubWndCtrl* pSubWnd;

    while ((pSubWnd = Lookup(hwnd)) != NULL)
        pSubWnd->Remove();  // Unhook
}
```

CXSSubWndCtrlMap::Lookup

The Lookup function returns the CXSSubWndCtrl object that has been mapped for the passed HWND and returns a pointer to that object.

```
// -----------------------------------------------------------
// Function  :
//     CXSSubWndCtrlMap::Lookup
// Purpose  :
//     Returns the CXSSubWndCtrl pointer with the procedure for
//       the passed window
// Parameters:
//     HWND hwnd - The HWND of the window to search for
// Returns  :
```

```
//    See above.
// ----------------------------------------------------------
CXSSubWndCtrl*
CXSSubWndCtrlMap::Lookup(HWND hwnd)
{
    CXSSubWndCtrl* pSubWnd = NULL;

    // Look up the window and make sure it is in our map
    if (!CMapPtrToPtr::Lookup(hwnd, (void*&)pSubWnd))
        return NULL;

    // Make sure the procedure has been derived from
    // CXSSubWndCtrl
    ASSERT_KINDOF(CXSSubWndCtrl, pSubWnd);

    // Return it
    return pSubWnd;
}
```

Summary

In this chapter, we examined a way of subclassing window procedures and replacing them with our own handler. There wasn't much to get excited about just looking at the code. There are some interesting aspects presented, but from an outside view, this code looks pretty generic. However, interest is in the eye of the beholder. Some readers may be grinning while all kinds of concoctions for using this code come to mind. In Chapter 5, I'll give you a peek at the possibilities by using this code to help give us automatic message reflection for the framework extension we're building. Chapter 6 is where the real significance of what we've done here is brought to light as we build our own message handler for all Windows messages, including notification messages.

Chapter 5

Handling Your Own Message Reflection

Introduction

In Windows, child controls send message notifications to their parent window whenever something happens to the control. A notification message could be sent from the control because of user input, data requirements, or control changes resulting from another message response. The methodology used here allows the parent window to then handle the message. However, with C++ and the concept of encapsulation, this methodology is problematic.

Classes are written around controls to direct their behavior and to handle messages. If the control sends a message to its parent, some other class written for the parent will, most likely, get the message. We would need to have the message that was fired off to the parent sent back to the control so we can handle it — this is called "message reflection."

In the previous chapter, we discussed our subclass handler, CXSSubWndCtrl. In this chapter, we are going to derive from that class a new handler that will subclass the parent window of our subclassed child window and will be solely responsible for sending message notifications back to the child control. Our C++ class wrappers for controls will then be able to handle the messages properly with a fully encapsulated C++ class.

XSNOTIFY.H

Forward Declarations

We have one forward declaration for a class named CXSObject. This class will be presented in the next chapter and will be used for main message handling for subclassed windows. You will notice its use in the following declaration as only a friend object to the CXSNotify class.

```
// --------------------------------------------------------------
// Forward declarations
class CXSObject;
```

CXSNotify Class Declaration

As stated earlier, the CXSNotify class is publicly derived from the CXSSubWndCtrl so we can get the subclass handler benefits in our derived class. This is necessary to subclass the parent window so it will generate the needed message reflection. Once we have the message notification taken care of, we'll be able to program our controls with a better object-oriented approach.

```
class XSCLASS
CXSNotify : public CXSSubWndCtrl
{
// Construction
public:
                CXSNotify();
    virtual     ~CXSNotify();

    virtual BOOL DoInstall(CWnd* pParentWnd,
                        CXSSubWndCtrl* pChild);
    virtual BOOL DoPreInstall();
```

```
protected:
    // Our wndproc
    virtual LRESULT DoWindowProc(UINT nMsg, WPARAM wParam,
        LPARAM lParam);

protected:
    CWnd*&          m_pWnd;
    CXSSubWndCtrl* m_pChild;

protected:
    // create from serialization only
    DECLARE_DYNCREATE(CXSNotify);

public:
    friend CXSObject;
};
```

II

5

XSNOTIFY.CPP

Header Files

```
#include "stdafx.h"
#include "XSSubWndCtrl.h"
#include "XSNotify.h"
```

Dynamic Implementation

```
IMPLEMENT_DYNCREATE(CXSNotify, CXSSubWndCtrl)
```

CXSNotify::CXSNotify

In the constructor for the CXSNotify class, we want to grab the reference to the m_pSubWnd variable that exists in the CXSSubWndCtrl class.

```
// -------------------------------------------------------------
// Function :
//     CXSNotify::CXSNotify
// Purpose   :
//     Constructor, initializes memory
// -------------------------------------------------------------
CXSNotify::CXSNotify() :
    m_pWnd((CWnd*&)m_pSubWnd)
{
    m_pChild = NULL;
}
```

CXSNotify::~CXSNotify

No clean up is necessary for the class destructor.

```
// -------------------------------------------------------------
// Function :
//     CXSNotify::~CXSNotify
// Purpose   :
//     Destructor, cleans up memory
// -------------------------------------------------------------
CXSNotify::~CXSNotify()
{
}
```

CXSNotify::DoInstall

We call the virtual function DoInstall to install the CXSNotify object as the subclass handler for the desired parent window. The first parameter is a pointer to the CWnd that represents the parent window of the control we want to subclass for message reflection. The second parameter is a pointer to the subclass handler of the child control that will handle messages for that control.

You will also notice that the virtual function DoPreInstall is called just before the subclassing takes place so any pre-initialization can happen before the actual subclassing event.

```cpp
// ------------------------------------------------------------
// Function  :
//     CXSNotify::DoInstall
// Purpose   :
//     Installs the CXSNotify instance as the handler for the
//     passed CWnd pointer
// Parameters:
//     CWnd* pParentWnd - The parent CWnd to attach to
//     CWnd* pChild - Child to receive ON_NOTIFY messages
// Returns   :
//     TRUE on success, FALSE on failure
// ------------------------------------------------------------
BOOL
CXSNotify::DoInstall(CWnd* pParentWnd, CXSSubWndCtrl* pChild)
{
    ASSERT_KINDOF(CWnd, pParentWnd);
    ASSERT_KINDOF(CXSSubWndCtrl, pChild);
    ASSERT(pParentWnd->m_hWnd);

    m_pChild = pChild;

    if (!DoPreInstall())
        return FALSE;

    BOOL bResult = SubclassWindow(pParentWnd);

    return bResult;
}
```

II

5

CXSNotify::DoPreInstall

`DoPreInstall` is an empty virtual function that is to be used for derived classes. In your derived class, put any preinitialization code that needs to be run before the subclassing event into this function.

```
// ------------------------------------------------------------
// Function  :
//   CXSNotify::DoPreInstall
// Purpose   :
//   Virtual function to be used by derived classes to have
//   functionality called before the subclassing takes place.
// Parameters:
//   None
// Returns   :
//   BOOL - Return TRUE if DoPreInstall is successful,
//          otherwise return FALSE.
// ------------------------------------------------------------
BOOL
CXSNotify::DoPreInstall()
{
    return TRUE;
}
```

CXSNotify::DoWindowProc

`DoWindowProc` is a virtual function that overrides the base class implementation. The subclass handler calls this function whenever a message needs to be processed. If the message is not processed, it is then sent on to the next subclass handler (if it exists) or to the original handler for this window.

`DoWindowProc` only handles the WM_NOTIFY window message. When it sees one of these messages come through, it verifies that the previously passed parent window is still the parent. (Occasionally, programmers need to change the parent of a control with the SetParent function.) In future implementations of this framework extension library, CXSNotify will be expanded to work with other notification messages like BN_CLICKED of the WM_COMMAND message.

When notification messages are sent, they have a NMHDR structure sent in the LPARAM parameter of the message, as in the following example.

```
typedef struct tagNMHDR
{
    HWND hwndFrom;
    UINT idFrom;
    UINT code;
} NMHDR;
```

The WPARAM parameter of the message contains the identifier of the control sending the message. However, this is not guaranteed to be unique. Instead, we use the hwndFrom member variable of the NMHDR structure. The code member variable of the NMHDR structure gives us the window message that was sent, which we then use to pass it in a call to the derived subclass handler's CallWindowProc function.

If any areas of the function fail, the base class implementation of DoWindowProc is called. This will ensure that the window message is appropriately handled.

II

5

```
// ------------------------------------------------------------
// Function   :
//     CXSNotify::DoWindowProc
// Purpose    :
//     The WindowProc that is used by the subclasser. This
//     function calls the appropriate member functions that we
//     want for processing based on the received windows
//     messages.
// Parameters:
//     UINT nMsg - The windows message
//     WPARAM wParam - parameter applicable for windows message
//     LPARAM lParam - parameter applicable for windows message
// Returns    :
//     LRESULT - Depends on windows message
// ------------------------------------------------------------
LRESULT
CXSNotify::DoWindowProc(UINT nMsg, WPARAM wParam, LPARAM lParam)
{
```

```
switch(nMsg)
{
case WM_NOTIFY:
    {
        ASSERT_VALID(m_pWnd);

        // Check the validity of the child handler
        // Make sure it hasn't been destroyed
        ASSERT_VALID(m_pChild);
        if (m_pChild && m_pChild->DoGetWnd() &&
            ::IsWindow(m_pChild->DoGetWnd()->m_hWnd))
        {
            // Check to see if the parent<=>child
            // relationship is still valid
            if (m_pChild->DoGetWnd()->GetParent() != m_pWnd)
                break;

            // Get the Msg
            NMHDR* pNMHDR = (NMHDR*)lParam;
            UINT nMsg = pNMHDR->code;

            // Verify the Notify message is for this control
            UINT nID = ((UINT)(WORD)::GetDlgCtrlID(
                m_pChild->DoGetWnd()->m_hWnd));
            if (pNMHDR->idFrom != nID)
                break;

            // If the child handles this message, return TRUE
            if (m_pChild->CallWindowProc(nMsg, 0, lParam))
                return TRUE;
        }
    }
    break;
```

```
default:
    break;
}


// default - call base class
return CXSSubWndCtrl::DoWindowProc(nMsg, wParam, lParam);
}
```

Summary

In this chapter, we looked at the implementation for message reflection used by this framework. Message reflection is an essential ingredient for encapsulating controls with an object-oriented approach. It allows our C++ classes that wrap the controls to properly handle the messages that the control sends to its parent window.

In the next chapter, we will be looking at writing our own base class, CXSObject, for regular message handling. The CXSNotify class will then be used by the CXSObject class to provide seamless message handling with automatic message reflection.

II

5

Chapter 6

Roll Your Own Message Handler

Introduction

MFC implements a sophisticated message map methodology for handling messages. This extension framework does not implement something so extravagant. Instead, it uses a virtual function system for handling each Windows-, MFC-, or XSEL-defined message. The main code for handling this is in the `CXSObject` class. In conjunction with the virtual function methodology, which I mentioned earlier in this book, each virtual function that handles a message begins with `On`. All other virtual functions begin with `Do`.

The virtual message handling functions are simplistic in nature. In fact, more so than in MFC. In this extension framework, all message-handling virtual functions return a `BOOL`. You return `TRUE` if you handle the message and `FALSE` if you do not. Each of the message handling functions in the `CXSObject` class returns `FALSE` by default, with a few exceptions. You derive from this class and override any functions you want to handle. However, even if you handle the message, there may be times when you may want to return FALSE. A return of FALSE indicates to the extension framework that it should call the next window procedure to handle that message. You can have more control of this process by calling the base function Default to have the extension framework call the next window procedure. This allows you to provide code after the base implementation does its work.

To maintain the simplicity of the message handling, each virtual function takes either two or three arguments. For messages that do not need to return a value, the parameters for that function have two arguments. The WPARAM and LPARAM of the message are simply passed on directly to the virtual function. If you do not know what these variables contain, you will need to look up the corresponding message that's related to that function. For messages that expect a return value, the virtual function will have a third parameter, a reference to an LRESULT. Simply assign the LRESULT variable to the expected return value.

The CXSObject class will become the backbone for creating classes that subclass a window. We will derive from it and supply the appropriate functionality based on the subclassed window. This class comprises over 300 functions. Most of it is repetitive, since the functionality exists in stub functions.

The WIN32_IE Definition

With the addition of Internet Explorer technology incorporated into Windows, more messages have been added that need handling. There are new messages for both Internet Explorer 3.0 and 4.0. For messages that are IE 3.0 additions, you will see this wrapper around the message handling functions

```
#if (_WIN32_IE >= 0x0300)
```

For IE 4.0 additions, you will see this wrapper around the message handling functions

```
#if (_WIN32_IE >= 0x0400)
```

XSOBJECT.H

Forward Declarations

In the CXSObject class, we are going to add an instance of the CXSNotify class. This will allow us to add automatic message reflection to our desired handling by passing TRUE to our DoInstall function when we subclass the desired window.

```
// -----------------------------------------------------------
// Forward declarations
class CXSNotify;
```

CXSObject **Class Declaration**

The CXSObject class inherits from CXSSubWndCtrl. It overrides the DoWindowProc to handle all Window messages. Most of the functions are stubbed, returning FALSE to indicate they are not handled. As mentioned previously, if you derive from this class and handle a particular Window message by overriding the appropriate virtual function, you should return TRUE.

You subclass the appropriate window by calling the DoInstall function. Pass the CWnd pointer of the window you want to subclass. If you want message reflection, then also pass TRUE as the second parameter; otherwise, the default is FALSE.

If you are using the automatic message reflection, you should be very careful not to change the parent window of the subclassed window with the Windows SDK or MFC. Instead, you should use the SetParentNotify function of this class. This function will uninstall the message reflection handler for the current parent, set the new parent, and then install the message reflection for that window. When you call SetParentNotify, a Windows registered message is sent and then handled in OnSetParentNotify. This message was created in case you need more handling for when the parent window is changed.

One more item before we get into the actual code. The CXSObject class has the function CallParentDefault. This is similar to the Default function but is for messages that require message reflection. Where Default calls the next handler for a particular message, CallParentDefault will call the current handler for the parent. If you understand message reflection, you know that normal Windows behavior is to have the parent window handle the child messages. Calling Default would not work in these cases. The message, if not handled, needs to be sent to the parent to imitate the default behavior expected by Windows. You will notice that the default handling in

II

6

the code for messages that are handled by message reflection is to call Call-
ParentDefault if it is not handled by your derived class.

```
class XSCLASS
CXSObject : public CXSSubWndCtrl
{
// Construction
public:
                CXSObject();
    virtual     ~CXSObject();

    virtual BOOL  DoInstall(CWnd* pWnd, BOOL bNotify = FALSE);
    virtual BOOL  DoPreInstall();

    LRESULT CallParentDefault();

    // XSEL message helpers
    BOOL    SetParentNotify(CWnd* pWnd);

protected:
    // Our window proc
    virtual LRESULT DoWindowProc(UINT nMsg, WPARAM wParam,
        LPARAM lParam);

    // XSEL (Registered) Message handlers
    virtual BOOL OnSetParentNotify(WPARAM wParam, LPARAM lParam);
    virtual BOOL OnPreNcDestroy(WPARAM wParam, LPARAM lParam);

protected:
    CWnd*&          m_pWnd;

    //  For parent message reflection of common controls
    CXSNotify       m_Notify;

protected:
    // create from serialization only
    DECLARE_DYNCREATE(CXSObject);
```

```
protected:
    virtual BOOL OnCreate(WPARAM wParam, LPARAM lParam,
        LRESULT& lResult);
    virtual BOOL OnDestroy(WPARAM wParam, LPARAM lParam);
    virtual BOOL OnMove(WPARAM wParam, LPARAM lParam);
    virtual BOOL OnSize(WPARAM wParam, LPARAM lParam);
    virtual BOOL OnActivate(WPARAM wParam, LPARAM lParam);
    virtual BOOL OnSetFocus(WPARAM wParam, LPARAM lParam);
    virtual BOOL OnKillFocus(WPARAM wParam, LPARAM lParam);
    virtual BOOL OnEnable(WPARAM wParam, LPARAM lParam);
    virtual BOOL OnSetRedraw(WPARAM wParam, LPARAM lParam);
    virtual BOOL OnSetText(WPARAM wParam, LPARAM lParam,
        LRESULT& lResult);
    virtual BOOL OnGetText(WPARAM wParam, LPARAM lParam,
        LRESULT& lResult);
    virtual BOOL OnGetTextLength(WPARAM wParam, LPARAM lParam,
        LRESULT& lResult);
    virtual BOOL OnPaint(WPARAM wParam, LPARAM lParam);
    virtual BOOL OnClose(WPARAM wParam, LPARAM lParam);
    virtual BOOL OnQueryEndSession(WPARAM wParam, LPARAM lParam,
        LRESULT& lResult);
    virtual BOOL OnQuit(WPARAM wParam, LPARAM lParam);
    virtual BOOL OnQueryOpen(WPARAM wParam, LPARAM lParam,
        LRESULT& lResult);
    virtual BOOL OnEraseBkgnd(WPARAM wParam, LPARAM lParam,
        LRESULT& lResult);
    virtual BOOL OnSysColorChange(WPARAM wParam, LPARAM lParam);
    virtual BOOL OnEndSession(WPARAM wParam, LPARAM lParam);
    virtual BOOL OnShowWindow(WPARAM wParam, LPARAM lParam);
    virtual BOOL OnSettingChange(WPARAM wParam, LPARAM lParam);
    virtual BOOL OnDevModeChange(WPARAM wParam, LPARAM lParam);
    virtual BOOL OnActivateApp(WPARAM wParam, LPARAM lParam);
    virtual BOOL OnFontChange(WPARAM wParam, LPARAM lParam);
    virtual BOOL OnTimeChange(WPARAM wParam, LPARAM lParam);
    virtual BOOL OnCancelMode(WPARAM wParam, LPARAM lParam);
    virtual BOOL OnSetCursor(WPARAM wParam, LPARAM lParam);
    virtual BOOL OnMouseActivate(WPARAM wParam, LPARAM lParam,
```

```
      LRESULT& lResult);
virtual BOOL OnChildActivate(WPARAM wParam, LPARAM lParam);
virtual BOOL OnQueueSync(WPARAM wParam, LPARAM lParam);
virtual BOOL OnGetMinMaxInfo(WPARAM wParam, LPARAM lParam);
virtual BOOL OnPaintIcon(WPARAM wParam, LPARAM lParam);
virtual BOOL OnIconEraseBkgnd(WPARAM wParam, LPARAM lParam);
virtual BOOL OnNextDlgCtl(WPARAM wParam, LPARAM lParam);
virtual BOOL OnSpoolerStatus(WPARAM wParam, LPARAM lParam);
virtual BOOL OnDrawItem(WPARAM wParam, LPARAM lParam);
virtual BOOL OnMeasureItem(WPARAM wParam, LPARAM lParam);
virtual BOOL OnDeleteItem(WPARAM wParam, LPARAM lParam);
virtual BOOL OnVKeyToItem(WPARAM wParam, LPARAM lParam,
      LRESULT& lResult);
virtual BOOL OnCharToItem(WPARAM wParam, LPARAM lParam,
      LRESULT& lResult);
virtual BOOL OnSetFont(WPARAM wParam, LPARAM lParam);
virtual BOOL OnGetFont(WPARAM wParam, LPARAM lParam,
      LRESULT& lResult);
virtual BOOL OnSetHotKey(WPARAM wParam, LPARAM lParam,
      LRESULT& lResult);
virtual BOOL OnGetHotKey(WPARAM wParam, LPARAM lParam,
      LRESULT& lResult);
virtual BOOL OnQueryDragIcon(WPARAM wParam, LPARAM lParam,
      LRESULT& lResult);
virtual BOOL OnCompareItem(WPARAM wParam, LPARAM lParam,
      LRESULT& lResult);
virtual BOOL OnCompacting(WPARAM wParam, LPARAM lParam);
virtual BOOL OnWindowPosChanging(WPARAM wParam, LPARAM lParam);
virtual BOOL OnWindowPosChanged(WPARAM wParam, LPARAM lParam);
virtual BOOL OnPower(WPARAM wParam, LPARAM lParam,
      LRESULT& lResult);
virtual BOOL OnCopyData(WPARAM wParam, LPARAM lParam);
virtual BOOL OnNotify(WPARAM wParam, LPARAM lParam,
      LRESULT& lResult);
virtual BOOL OnInputLangChangeRequest(WPARAM wParam, LPARAM lParam);
virtual BOOL OnInputLangChange(WPARAM wParam, LPARAM lParam);
virtual BOOL OnTCard(WPARAM wParam, LPARAM lParam);
```

```
virtual BOOL OnHelp(WPARAM wParam, LPARAM lParam);
virtual BOOL OnUserChanged(WPARAM wParam, LPARAM lParam);
virtual BOOL OnNotifyFormat(WPARAM wParam, LPARAM lParam,
    LRESULT& lResult);
virtual BOOL OnContextMenu(WPARAM wParam, LPARAM lParam);
virtual BOOL OnStyleChanging(WPARAM wParam, LPARAM lParam);
virtual BOOL OnStyleChanged(WPARAM wParam, LPARAM lParam);
virtual BOOL OnDisplayChange(WPARAM wParam, LPARAM lParam);
virtual BOOL OnGetIcon(WPARAM wParam, LPARAM lParam,
    LRESULT& lResult);
virtual BOOL OnSetIcon(WPARAM wParam, LPARAM lParam,
    LRESULT& lResult);
virtual BOOL OnNcCreate(WPARAM wParam, LPARAM lParam);
virtual BOOL OnNcDestroy(WPARAM wParam, LPARAM lParam);
virtual BOOL OnNcCalcSize(WPARAM wParam, LPARAM lParam,
    LRESULT& lResult);
virtual BOOL OnNcHitTest(WPARAM wParam, LPARAM lParam,
    LRESULT& lResult);
virtual BOOL OnNcPaint(WPARAM wParam, LPARAM lParam);
virtual BOOL OnNcActivate(WPARAM wParam, LPARAM lParam,
    LRESULT& lResult);
virtual BOOL OnNcMouseHover(WPARAM wParam, LPARAM lParam);
virtual BOOL OnNcMouseLeave(WPARAM wParam, LPARAM lParam);
virtual BOOL OnGetDlgCode(WPARAM wParam, LPARAM lParam,
    LRESULT& lResult);
virtual BOOL OnNcMouseMove(WPARAM wParam, LPARAM lParam);
virtual BOOL OnNcLButtonDown(WPARAM wParam, LPARAM lParam);
virtual BOOL OnNcLButtonUp(WPARAM wParam, LPARAM lParam);
virtual BOOL OnNcLButtonDblClk(WPARAM wParam, LPARAM lParam);
virtual BOOL OnNcRButtonDown(WPARAM wParam, LPARAM lParam);
virtual BOOL OnNcRButtonUp(WPARAM wParam, LPARAM lParam);
virtual BOOL OnNcRButtonDblClk(WPARAM wParam, LPARAM lParam);
virtual BOOL OnNcMButtonDown(WPARAM wParam, LPARAM lParam);
virtual BOOL OnNcMButtonUp(WPARAM wParam, LPARAM lParam);
virtual BOOL OnNcMButtonDblClk(WPARAM wParam, LPARAM lParam);
virtual BOOL OnKeyDown(WPARAM wParam, LPARAM lParam);
virtual BOOL OnKeyUp(WPARAM wParam, LPARAM lParam);
```

II

6

```
virtual BOOL OnChar(WPARAM wParam, LPARAM lParam);
virtual BOOL OnDeadChar(WPARAM wParam, LPARAM lParam);
virtual BOOL OnSysKeyDown(WPARAM wParam, LPARAM lParam);
virtual BOOL OnSysKeyUp(WPARAM wParam, LPARAM lParam);
virtual BOOL OnSysChar(WPARAM wParam, LPARAM lParam);
virtual BOOL OnSysDeadChar(WPARAM wParam, LPARAM lParam);
virtual BOOL OnInitDialog(WPARAM wParam, LPARAM lParam,
   LRESULT& lResult);
virtual BOOL OnCommand(WPARAM wParam, LPARAM lParam);
virtual BOOL OnSysCommand(WPARAM wParam, LPARAM lParam);
virtual BOOL OnTimer(WPARAM wParam, LPARAM lParam);
virtual BOOL OnHScroll(WPARAM wParam, LPARAM lParam);
virtual BOOL OnVScroll(WPARAM wParam, LPARAM lParam);
virtual BOOL OnInitMenu(WPARAM wParam, LPARAM lParam);
virtual BOOL OnInitMenuPopup(WPARAM wParam, LPARAM lParam);
virtual BOOL OnMenuSelect(WPARAM wParam, LPARAM lParam);
virtual BOOL OnMenuChar(WPARAM wParam, LPARAM lParam,
   LRESULT& lResult);
virtual BOOL OnEnterIdle(WPARAM wParam, LPARAM lParam);
virtual BOOL OnCtlColorMsgBox(WPARAM wParam, LPARAM lParam,
   LRESULT& lResult);
virtual BOOL OnCtlColorEdit(WPARAM wParam, LPARAM lParam,
   LRESULT& lResult);
virtual BOOL OnCtlColorListBox(WPARAM wParam, LPARAM lParam,
   LRESULT& lResult);
virtual BOOL OnCtlColorBtn(WPARAM wParam, LPARAM lParam,
   LRESULT& lResult);
virtual BOOL OnCtlColorDlg(WPARAM wParam, LPARAM lParam,
   LRESULT& lResult);
virtual BOOL OnCtlColorScrollBar(WPARAM wParam, LPARAM lParam,
   LRESULT& lResult);
virtual BOOL OnCtlColorStatic(WPARAM wParam, LPARAM lParam,
   LRESULT& lResult);
virtual BOOL OnMouseMove(WPARAM wParam, LPARAM lParam);
virtual BOOL OnLButtonDown(WPARAM wParam, LPARAM lParam);
virtual BOOL OnLButtonUp(WPARAM wParam, LPARAM lParam);
virtual BOOL OnLButtonDblClk(WPARAM wParam, LPARAM lParam);
```

```
virtual BOOL OnRButtonDown(WPARAM wParam, LPARAM lParam);
virtual BOOL OnRButtonUp(WPARAM wParam, LPARAM lParam);
virtual BOOL OnRButtonDblClk(WPARAM wParam, LPARAM lParam);
virtual BOOL OnMButtonDown(WPARAM wParam, LPARAM lParam);
virtual BOOL OnMButtonUp(WPARAM wParam, LPARAM lParam);
virtual BOOL OnMButtonDblClk(WPARAM wParam, LPARAM lParam);
virtual BOOL OnMouseWheel(WPARAM wParam, LPARAM lParam);
virtual BOOL OnParentNotify(WPARAM wParam, LPARAM lParam);
virtual BOOL OnEnterMenuLoop(WPARAM wParam, LPARAM lParam);
virtual BOOL OnExitMenuLoop(WPARAM wParam, LPARAM lParam);
virtual BOOL OnNextMenu(WPARAM wParam, LPARAM lParam);
virtual BOOL OnSizing(WPARAM wParam, LPARAM lParam);
virtual BOOL OnCaptureChanged(WPARAM wParam, LPARAM lParam);
virtual BOOL OnMoving(WPARAM wParam, LPARAM lParam);
virtual BOOL OnPowerBroadcast(WPARAM wParam, LPARAM lParam,
    LRESULT& lResult);
virtual BOOL OnDeviceChange(WPARAM wParam, LPARAM lParam,
    LRESULT& lResult);
virtual BOOL OnMdiCreate(WPARAM wParam, LPARAM lParam,
    LRESULT& lResult);
virtual BOOL OnMdiDestroy(WPARAM wParam, LPARAM lParam);
virtual BOOL OnMdiActivate(WPARAM wParam, LPARAM lParam);
virtual BOOL OnMdiRestore(WPARAM wParam, LPARAM lParam);
virtual BOOL OnMdiNext(WPARAM wParam, LPARAM lParam);
virtual BOOL OnMdiMaximize(WPARAM wParam, LPARAM lParam);
virtual BOOL OnMdiTile(WPARAM wParam, LPARAM lParam,
    LRESULT& lResult);
virtual BOOL OnMdiCascade(WPARAM wParam, LPARAM lParam,
    LRESULT& lResult);
virtual BOOL OnMdiIconArrange(WPARAM wParam, LPARAM lParam);
virtual BOOL OnMdiGetActive(WPARAM wParam, LPARAM lParam,
    LRESULT& lResult);
virtual BOOL OnMdiSetMenu(WPARAM wParam, LPARAM lParam,
    LRESULT& lResult);
virtual BOOL OnEnterSizeMove(WPARAM wParam, LPARAM lParam);
virtual BOOL OnExitSizeMove(WPARAM wParam, LPARAM lParam);
virtual BOOL OnDropFiles(WPARAM wParam, LPARAM lParam);
```

II

6

```cpp
    virtual BOOL OnMdiRefreshMenu(WPARAM wParam, LPARAM lParam,
        LRESULT& lResult);
    virtual BOOL OnMouseHover(WPARAM wParam, LPARAM lParam);
    virtual BOOL OnMouseLeave(WPARAM wParam, LPARAM lParam);
    virtual BOOL OnCut(WPARAM wParam, LPARAM lParam);
    virtual BOOL OnCopy(WPARAM wParam, LPARAM lParam);
    virtual BOOL OnPaste(WPARAM wParam, LPARAM lParam);
    virtual BOOL OnClear(WPARAM wParam, LPARAM lParam);
    virtual BOOL OnUndo(WPARAM wParam, LPARAM lParam,
        LRESULT& lResult);
    virtual BOOL OnRenderFormat(WPARAM wParam, LPARAM lParam);
    virtual BOOL OnRenderAllFormats(WPARAM wParam, LPARAM lParam);
    virtual BOOL OnDestroyClipboard(WPARAM wParam, LPARAM lParam);
    virtual BOOL OnDrawClipboard(WPARAM wParam, LPARAM lParam);
    virtual BOOL OnPaintClipboard(WPARAM wParam, LPARAM lParam);
    virtual BOOL OnVScrollClipboard(WPARAM wParam, LPARAM lParam);
    virtual BOOL OnSizeClipboard(WPARAM wParam, LPARAM lParam);
    virtual BOOL OnAskCbFormatName(WPARAM wParam, LPARAM lParam);
    virtual BOOL OnChangeCbChain(WPARAM wParam, LPARAM lParam);
    virtual BOOL OnHScrollClipboard(WPARAM wParam, LPARAM lParam);
    virtual BOOL OnQueryNewPalette(WPARAM wParam, LPARAM lParam,
        LRESULT& lResult);
    virtual BOOL OnPaletteIsChanging(WPARAM wParam, LPARAM lParam);
    virtual BOOL OnPaletteChanged(WPARAM wParam, LPARAM lParam);
    virtual BOOL OnHotKey(WPARAM wParam, LPARAM lParam);
    virtual BOOL OnPrint(WPARAM wParam, LPARAM lParam);
    virtual BOOL OnPrintClient(WPARAM wParam, LPARAM lParam);
    virtual BOOL OnNotifyOutOfMemory(WPARAM wParam, LPARAM lParam);
    virtual BOOL OnNotifyClick(WPARAM wParam, LPARAM lParam);
    virtual BOOL OnNotifyDblClk(WPARAM wParam, LPARAM lParam);
    virtual BOOL OnNotifyReturn(WPARAM wParam, LPARAM lParam);
    virtual BOOL OnNotifyRClick(WPARAM wParam, LPARAM lParam,
        LRESULT& lResult);
    virtual BOOL OnNotifyRDblClk(WPARAM wParam, LPARAM lParam,
        LRESULT& lResult);
    virtual BOOL OnNotifySetFocus(WPARAM wParam, LPARAM lParam);
    virtual BOOL OnNotifyKillFocus(WPARAM wParam, LPARAM lParam);
```

```
virtual BOOL OnNotifyCustomDraw(WPARAM wParam, LPARAM lParam,
    LRESULT& lResult);
virtual BOOL OnNotifyHover(WPARAM wParam, LPARAM lParam,
    LRESULT& lResult);
virtual BOOL OnNotifyNcHitTest(WPARAM wParam, LPARAM lParam,
    LRESULT& lResult);
virtual BOOL OnNotifyKeyDown(WPARAM wParam, LPARAM lParam,
    LRESULT& lResult);
virtual BOOL OnNotifyReleasedCapture(WPARAM wParam, LPARAM lParam);
virtual BOOL OnNotifySetCursor(WPARAM wParam, LPARAM lParam,
    LRESULT& lResult);
virtual BOOL OnNotifyChar(WPARAM wParam, LPARAM lParam);
virtual BOOL OnNotifyTooltipsCreated(WPARAM wParam, LPARAM lParam);
virtual BOOL OnPropSheetApply(WPARAM wParam, LPARAM lParam,
    LRESULT& lResult);
virtual BOOL OnPropSheetGetObject(WPARAM wParam, LPARAM lParam);
virtual BOOL OnPropSheetHelp(WPARAM wParam, LPARAM lParam);
virtual BOOL OnPropSheetKillActive(WPARAM wParam, LPARAM lParam,
    LRESULT& lResult);
virtual BOOL OnPropSheetQueryCancel(WPARAM wParam, LPARAM lParam,
    LRESULT& lResult);
virtual BOOL OnPropSheetReset(WPARAM wParam, LPARAM lParam,
    LRESULT& lResult);
virtual BOOL OnPropSheetSetActive(WPARAM wParam, LPARAM lParam,
    LRESULT& lResult);
virtual BOOL OnPropSheetWizBack(WPARAM wParam, LPARAM lParam,
    LRESULT& lResult);
virtual BOOL OnPropSheetWizFinish(WPARAM wParam, LPARAM lParam,
    LRESULT& lResult);
virtual BOOL OnPropSheetWizNext(WPARAM wParam, LPARAM lParam,
    LRESULT& lResult);
virtual BOOL OnHeaderBeginDrag(WPARAM wParam, LPARAM lParam,
    LRESULT& lResult);
virtual BOOL OnHeaderEndDrag(WPARAM wParam, LPARAM lParam,
    LRESULT& lResult);
virtual BOOL OnHeaderItemChanging(WPARAM wParam, LPARAM lParam,
    LRESULT& lResult);
```

II

6

```
    virtual BOOL OnHeaderItemChanged(WPARAM wParam, LPARAM lParam);
    virtual BOOL OnHeaderItemClick(WPARAM wParam, LPARAM lParam);
    virtual BOOL OnHeaderItemDblClick(WPARAM wParam, LPARAM lParam);
    virtual BOOL OnHeaderDividerDblClick(WPARAM wParam, LPARAM lParam);
    virtual BOOL OnHeaderBeginTrack(WPARAM wParam, LPARAM lParam,
        LRESULT& lResult);
    virtual BOOL OnHeaderEndTrack(WPARAM wParam, LPARAM lParam);
    virtual BOOL OnHeaderTrack(WPARAM wParam, LPARAM lParam,
        LRESULT& lResult);
    virtual BOOL OnHeaderGetDispInfo(WPARAM wParam, LPARAM lParam);
    virtual BOOL OnToolbarGetButtonInfo(WPARAM wParam, LPARAM lParam,
        LRESULT& lResult);
    virtual BOOL OnToolbarBeginDrag(WPARAM wParam, LPARAM lParam);
    virtual BOOL OnToolbarEndDrag(WPARAM wParam, LPARAM lParam);
    virtual BOOL OnToolbarBeginAdjust(WPARAM wParam, LPARAM lParam);
    virtual BOOL OnToolbarEndAdjust(WPARAM wParam, LPARAM lParam);
    virtual BOOL OnToolbarReset(WPARAM wParam, LPARAM lParam);
    virtual BOOL OnToolbarQueryInsert(WPARAM wParam, LPARAM lParam,
        LRESULT& lResult);
    virtual BOOL OnToolbarQueryDelete(WPARAM wParam, LPARAM lParam,
        LRESULT& lResult);
    virtual BOOL OnToolbarToolbarChange(WPARAM wParam, LPARAM lParam);
    virtual BOOL OnToolbarCustHelp(WPARAM wParam, LPARAM lParam);
    virtual BOOL OnToolbarDropDown(WPARAM wParam, LPARAM lParam,
        LRESULT& lResult);
    virtual BOOL OnToolbarGetObject(WPARAM wParam, LPARAM lParam);
    virtual BOOL OnToolbarHotItemChange(WPARAM wParam, LPARAM lParam,
        LRESULT& lResult);
    virtual BOOL OnToolbarDragOut(WPARAM wParam, LPARAM lParam);
    virtual BOOL OnToolbarDeletingButton(WPARAM wParam, LPARAM lParam);
    virtual BOOL OnToolbarGetDispInfo(WPARAM wParam, LPARAM lParam);
    virtual BOOL OnToolbarGetInfoTip(WPARAM wParam, LPARAM lParam);
    virtual BOOL OnRebarHeightChange(WPARAM wParam, LPARAM lParam);
    virtual BOOL OnRebarGetObject(WPARAM wParam, LPARAM lParam);
    virtual BOOL OnRebarLayoutChanged(WPARAM wParam, LPARAM lParam);
    virtual BOOL OnRebarAutoSize(WPARAM wParam, LPARAM lParam);
    virtual BOOL OnRebarBeginDrag(WPARAM wParam, LPARAM lParam,
```

```
      LRESULT& lResult);
virtual BOOL OnRebarEndDrag(WPARAM wParam, LPARAM lParam);
virtual BOOL OnRebarDeletingBand(WPARAM wParam, LPARAM lParam);
virtual BOOL OnRebarDeleteBand(WPARAM wParam, LPARAM lParam);
virtual BOOL OnRebarChildSize(WPARAM wParam, LPARAM lParam);
virtual BOOL OnTooltipGetDispInfo(WPARAM wParam, LPARAM lParam);
virtual BOOL OnTooltipNeedText(WPARAM wParam, LPARAM lParam);
virtual BOOL OnTooltipShow(WPARAM wParam, LPARAM lParam);
virtual BOOL OnTooltipPop(WPARAM wParam, LPARAM lParam);
virtual BOOL OnStatusBarSimpleModeChange(WPARAM wParam,
      LPARAM lParam);
virtual BOOL OnUpDownDeltaPos(WPARAM wParam, LPARAM lParam,
      LRESULT& lResult);
virtual BOOL OnListviewItemChanging(WPARAM wParam, LPARAM lParam,
      LRESULT& lResult);
virtual BOOL OnListviewItemChanged(WPARAM wParam, LPARAM lParam);
virtual BOOL OnListviewInsertItem(WPARAM wParam, LPARAM lParam);
virtual BOOL OnListviewDeleteItem(WPARAM wParam, LPARAM lParam);
virtual BOOL OnListviewDeleteAllItems(WPARAM wParam, LPARAM lParam,
      LRESULT& lResult);
virtual BOOL OnListviewBeginLabelEdit(WPARAM wParam, LPARAM lParam,
      LRESULT& lResult);
virtual BOOL OnListviewEndLabelEdit(WPARAM wParam, LPARAM lParam,
      LRESULT& lResult);
virtual BOOL OnListviewColumnClick(WPARAM wParam, LPARAM lParam);
virtual BOOL OnListviewBeginDrag(WPARAM wParam, LPARAM lParam);
virtual BOOL OnListviewBeginRDrag(WPARAM wParam, LPARAM lParam);
virtual BOOL OnListviewOdCacheHit(WPARAM wParam, LPARAM lParam);
virtual BOOL OnListviewOdFindItem(WPARAM wParam, LPARAM lParam);
virtual BOOL OnListviewItemActivate(WPARAM wParam, LPARAM lParam);
virtual BOOL OnListviewOdStateChanged(WPARAM wParam, LPARAM lParam);
virtual BOOL OnListviewHotTrack(WPARAM wParam, LPARAM lParam,
      LRESULT& lResult);
virtual BOOL OnListviewGetInfoTip(WPARAM wParam, LPARAM lParam);
virtual BOOL OnListviewMarqueeBegin(WPARAM wParam, LPARAM lParam,
      LRESULT& lResult);
virtual BOOL OnListviewGetDispInfo(WPARAM wParam, LPARAM lParam);
```

II

6

```
virtual BOOL OnListviewSetDispInfo(WPARAM wParam, LPARAM lParam);
virtual BOOL OnListviewKeyDown(WPARAM wParam, LPARAM lParam);
virtual BOOL OnTreeviewSelChanging(WPARAM wParam, LPARAM lParam,
    LRESULT& lResult);
virtual BOOL OnTreeviewSelChanged(WPARAM wParam, LPARAM lParam);
virtual BOOL OnTreeviewGetDispInfo(WPARAM wParam, LPARAM lParam);
virtual BOOL OnTreeviewSetDispInfo(WPARAM wParam, LPARAM lParam);
virtual BOOL OnTreeviewItemExpanding(WPARAM wParam, LPARAM lParam,
    LRESULT& lResult);
virtual BOOL OnTreeviewItemExpanded(WPARAM wParam, LPARAM lParam);
virtual BOOL OnTreeviewBeginDrag(WPARAM wParam, LPARAM lParam);
virtual BOOL OnTreeviewBeginRDrag(WPARAM wParam, LPARAM lParam);
virtual BOOL OnTreeviewDeleteItem(WPARAM wParam, LPARAM lParam);
virtual BOOL OnTreeviewBeginLabelEdit(WPARAM wParam, LPARAM lParam,
    LRESULT& lResult);
virtual BOOL OnTreeviewEndLabelEdit(WPARAM wParam, LPARAM lParam,
    LRESULT& lResult);
virtual BOOL OnTreeviewKeyDown(WPARAM wParam, LPARAM lParam);
virtual BOOL OnTreeviewGetInfoTip(WPARAM wParam, LPARAM lParam);
virtual BOOL OnTreeviewSingleExpand(WPARAM wParam, LPARAM lParam);
virtual BOOL OnCbeGetDispInfo(WPARAM wParam, LPARAM lParam);
virtual BOOL OnCbeInsertItem(WPARAM wParam, LPARAM lParam);
virtual BOOL OnCbeDeleteItem(WPARAM wParam, LPARAM lParam);
virtual BOOL OnCbeBeginEdit(WPARAM wParam, LPARAM lParam);
virtual BOOL OnCbeEndEdit(WPARAM wParam, LPARAM lParam,
    LRESULT& lResult);
virtual BOOL OnCbeDragBegin(WPARAM wParam, LPARAM lParam);
virtual BOOL OnTabKeyDown(WPARAM wParam, LPARAM lParam);
virtual BOOL OnTabSelChange(WPARAM wParam, LPARAM lParam);
virtual BOOL OnTabSelChanging(WPARAM wParam, LPARAM lParam,
    LRESULT& lResult);
virtual BOOL OnTabGetObject(WPARAM wParam, LPARAM lParam);
virtual BOOL OnMonCalSelChange(WPARAM wParam, LPARAM lParam);
virtual BOOL OnMonCalGetDayState(WPARAM wParam, LPARAM lParam);
virtual BOOL OnMonCalSelect(WPARAM wParam, LPARAM lParam);
virtual BOOL OnDateTimeChange(WPARAM wParam, LPARAM lParam);
virtual BOOL OnDateTimeUserString(WPARAM wParam, LPARAM lParam);
```

```
virtual BOOL OnDateTimeWmKeyDown(WPARAM wParam, LPARAM lParam);
virtual BOOL OnDateTimeFormat(WPARAM wParam, LPARAM lParam);
virtual BOOL OnDateTimeFormatQuery(WPARAM wParam, LPARAM lParam);
virtual BOOL OnDateTimeDropDown(WPARAM wParam, LPARAM lParam);
virtual BOOL OnDateTimeCloseUp(WPARAM wParam, LPARAM lParam);
virtual BOOL OnPagerScroll(WPARAM wParam, LPARAM lParam);
virtual BOOL OnPagerCalcSize(WPARAM wParam, LPARAM lParam);
virtual BOOL OnQueryAfxWndProc(WPARAM wParam, LPARAM lParam,
    LRESULT& lResult);
virtual BOOL OnSizeParent(WPARAM wParam, LPARAM lParam,
    LRESULT& lResult);
virtual BOOL OnSetMessageString(WPARAM wParam, LPARAM lParam,
    LRESULT& lResult);
virtual BOOL OnIdleUpdateCmdUi(WPARAM wParam, LPARAM lParam,
    LRESULT& lResult);
virtual BOOL OnInitialUpdate(WPARAM wParam, LPARAM lParam);
virtual BOOL OnCommandHelp(WPARAM wParam, LPARAM lParam);
virtual BOOL OnHelpHitTest(WPARAM wParam, LPARAM lParam,
    LRESULT& lResult);
virtual BOOL OnExitHelpMode(WPARAM wParam, LPARAM lParam);
virtual BOOL OnRecalcParent(WPARAM wParam, LPARAM lParam,
    LRESULT& lResult);
virtual BOOL OnSizeChild(WPARAM wParam, LPARAM lParam,
    LRESULT& lResult);
virtual BOOL OnKickIdle(WPARAM wParam, LPARAM lParam);
virtual BOOL OnQueryCenterWnd(WPARAM wParam, LPARAM lParam);
virtual BOOL OnDisableModal(WPARAM wParam, LPARAM lParam,
    LRESULT& lResult);
virtual BOOL OnFloatStatus(WPARAM wParam, LPARAM lParam,
    LRESULT& lResult);
virtual BOOL OnActivateTopLevel(WPARAM wParam, LPARAM lParam);
virtual BOOL OnQuery3dControls(WPARAM wParam, LPARAM lParam,
    LRESULT& lResult);
virtual BOOL OnSocketNotify(WPARAM wParam, LPARAM lParam);
virtual BOOL OnSocketDead(WPARAM wParam, LPARAM lParam);
virtual BOOL OnPopMessageString(WPARAM wParam, LPARAM lParam,
    LRESULT& lResult);
```

```
    virtual BOOL OnQueueSentinel(WPARAM wParam, LPARAM lParam);

public:
    friend CXSNotify;
};
```

XSOBJECT.CPP

Except for a few member functions, as I mentioned earlier, this class contains a numerous amount of stub functions. For derived classes, just add the appropriate virtual function where you need functionality for handling a windows or MFC message.

Header Files

```
#include "stdafx.h"
#include "XSSubWndCtrl.h"
#include "XSNotify.h"
#include "XSObject.h"



IMPLEMENT_DYNCREATE(CXSObject, CXSSubWndCtrl)
```

CXSObject::CXSObject()

CXSObject has a member variable m_pWnd. We set this to the m_pSubWnd member variable of the base class CXSSubWndCtrl.

```
// -----------------------------------------------------------
// Function  :
//     CXSObject::CXSObject
// Purpose   :
//     Constructor, initializes memory
// -----------------------------------------------------------
CXSObject::CXSObject() :
    m_pWnd((CWnd*&)m_pSubWnd)
{
}
```

CXSObject::~CXSObject

When the destructor for this class is called, we must uninstall the message reflection handler for the parent window, if it has been installed. If we don't, we will get an exception error when the destructor for the CXSNotify is called.

```
// ------------------------------------------------------------
// Function  :
//      CXSObject::~CXSObject
// Purpose   :
//      Destructor, cleans up memory
// ------------------------------------------------------------
CXSObject::~CXSObject()
{
    // Because children are destroyed before parents, we have
    // to explicitly remove the subclass notify handler for
    // the parent
    if (m_Notify.IsSubclassed())
        m_Notify.Remove();
}
```

CXSObject::DoPreInstall

When DoInstall is called to subclass a window, the virtual function DoPre-Install is called before the actual subclassing takes place. This allows your derived class to override this function instead of overriding DoInstall.

```
// ------------------------------------------------------------
// Function  :
//   CXSObject::DoPreInstall
// Purpose   :
//   Virtual function to be used by derived classes to have
//   functionality called before the subclassing takes place.
// Parameters:
//   None
// Returns   :
//   BOOL - Return TRUE if DoPreInstall is successful,
```

II

6

```
//           otherwise return FALSE.
// ------------------------------------------------------------
BOOL
CXSObject::DoPreInstall()
{
    return TRUE;
}
```

CXSObject::DoInstall

The DoInstall function does the work of subclassing the passed CWnd and setting up the message reflection notifier, if desired. You would typically call this function in the MFC function OnCreate immediately after the window is created. An example of calling this function is as follows:

```
MyVariable.DoInstall(this, TRUE);
```

MyVariable is a derived class instance of CXSObject. For instance, it may be a class for handling the caption. A caption control subclass handler derived from CXSObject will be discussed later in this book.

```
// ------------------------------------------------------------
// Function  :
//     CXSObject::DoInstall
// Purpose   :
//     Installs the CXSObject instance as the handler for the
//     passed CWnd pointer
// Parameters:
//     CWnd* pWnd - The CWnd to attach to
//     BOOL bNotify - Install message reflection into parent
// Returns   :
//     TRUE on success, FALSE on failure
// ------------------------------------------------------------
BOOL
CXSObject::DoInstall(CWnd* pWnd, BOOL bNotify)
{
    ASSERT_KINDOF(CWnd, pWnd);
```

```
    if (!DoPreInstall())
        return FALSE;

    BOOL bResult = SubclassWindow(pWnd);

    // The User asked to have WM_NOTIFY messages sent from
    // the parent to this class
    if (bNotify)
    {
        CWnd* pParent = pWnd->GetParent();
        if (pParent)
            m_Notify.DoInstall(pParent, this);
    }

    return bResult;
}
```

CXSObject::DoWindowProc

DoWindowProc is the heart of the CXSObject class. This function is called by the base class functionality of CXSSubWndCtrl. Every Windows and MFC message is routed through this function, which in turn calls the appropriate virtual function.

DoWindowProc returns a variable of type LRESULT. A reference to this variable is passed to several of the virtual functions that need to pass back information depending on the message. Set this instance of the variable to the data to pass back in your derived function.

You may want to note that this framework extension does not handle Journal or IME Window messages.

This framework does some extra work for the Windows message WM_PALETTECHANGED. To prevent a recursion problem in Windows, if a palette is changed as a result of a window, then that window should not handle the message. If you look in the following code for this message, you will see that the code compares the m_hWnd of the subclassed window to that of the passed HWND found in the WPARAM variable. This code is in the switch statement, not the virtual function for handling this message, because it is too dangerous not to handle this message properly. The result is that the virtual function will only be called if the WM_PALETTECHANGED message was not sent by this window.

```
// ----------------------------------------------------------
// Function :
//     CXSObject::DoWindowProc
// Purpose  :
//     The WindowProc that is used by the subclasser. This
//     function calls the appropriate member functions that we
//     want for processing based on the received windows
//     messages.
// Parameters:
//     UINT nMsg - The windows message
//     WPARAM wParam - parameter applicable for windows message
//     LPARAM lParam - parameter applicable for windows message
// Returns  :
//     LRESULT - Depends on windows message
// ----------------------------------------------------------
LRESULT
CXSObject::DoWindowProc(UINT nMsg, WPARAM wParam, LPARAM lParam)
{
    LRESULT lResult = 0;

    switch(nMsg)
    {
    // ----------------------------------------------------------
    // Regular messages
    case WM_CREATE:                           // 0x0001 - returns an int
        if (!OnCreate(wParam, lParam, lResult))
            return Default();
        return lResult;

    case WM_DESTROY:                          // 0x0002
        if (!OnDestroy(wParam, lParam))
            return Default();
        return 0;

    case WM_MOVE:                             // 0x0003
        if (!OnMove(wParam, lParam))
            return Default();
        return 0;
```

```
    case WM_SIZE:                                  // 0x0005
        if (!OnSize(wParam, lParam))
            return Default();
        return 0;

    case WM_ACTIVATE:                              // 0x0006
        if (!OnActivate(wParam, lParam))
            return Default();
        return 0;

    case WM_SETFOCUS:                              // 0x0007
        if (!OnSetFocus(wParam, lParam))
            return Default();
        return 0;

    case WM_KILLFOCUS:                             // 0x0008
        if (!OnKillFocus(wParam, lParam))
            return Default();
        return 0;

    case WM_ENABLE:                                // 0x000A
        if (!OnEnable(wParam, lParam))
            return Default();
        return 0;

    case WM_SETREDRAW:                             // 0x000B
        if (!OnSetRedraw(wParam, lParam))
            return Default();
        return 0;

    case WM_SETTEXT:                               // 0x000C - returns an int
        if (!OnSetText(wParam, lParam, lResult))
            return Default();
        return lResult;

    case WM_GETTEXT:                               // 0x000D - returns an int
        if (!OnGetText(wParam, lParam, lResult))
            return Default();
        return lResult;
```

```
    case WM_GETTEXTLENGTH:                           // 0x000E - returns an int
        if (!OnGetTextLength(wParam, lParam, lResult))
            return Default();
        return lResult;

    case WM_PAINT:                                   // 0x000F
        if (!OnPaint(wParam, lParam))
            return Default();
        return 0;

    case WM_CLOSE:                                   // 0x0010
        if (!OnClose(wParam, lParam))
            return Default();
        return 0;

    case WM_QUERYENDSESSION:                         // 0x0011
        if (!OnQueryEndSession(wParam, lParam, lResult))
            return Default();
        return lResult;

    case WM_QUIT:                                    // 0x0012
        if (!OnQuit(wParam, lParam))
            Default();
        return 0;

    case WM_QUERYOPEN:                               // 0x0013
        if (!OnQueryOpen(wParam, lParam, lResult))
            return Default();
        return lResult;

    case WM_ERASEBKGND:                              // 0x0014
        if (!OnEraseBkgnd(wParam, lParam, lResult))
            return Default();
        return lResult;

    case WM_SYSCOLORCHANGE:                          // 0x0015
        if (!OnSysColorChange(wParam, lParam))
            Default();
        return 0;
```

```
case WM_ENDSESSION:                               // 0x0016
    if (!OnEndSession(wParam, lParam))
        return Default();
    return 0;

case WM_SHOWWINDOW:                               // 0x0018
    if (!OnShowWindow(wParam, lParam))
        return Default();
    return 0;

case WM_SETTINGCHANGE:                            // 0x001A
    if (!OnSettingChange(wParam, lParam))
        return Default();
    return 0;

case WM_DEVMODECHANGE:                            // 0x001B
    if (!OnDevModeChange(wParam, lParam))
        return Default();
    return 0;

case WM_ACTIVATEAPP:                              // 0x001C
    if (!OnActivateApp(wParam, lParam))
        return Default();
    return 0;

case WM_FONTCHANGE:                               // 0x001D
    if (!OnFontChange(wParam, lParam))
        Default();
    return 0;

case WM_TIMECHANGE:                               // 0x001E
    if (!OnTimeChange(wParam, lParam))
        return Default();
    return 0;

case WM_CANCELMODE:                               // 0x001F
    if (!OnCancelMode(wParam, lParam))
        return Default();
    return 0;
```

II

6

```
case WM_SETCURSOR:                                // 0x0020
    if (!OnSetCursor(wParam, lParam))
        return Default();
    return lResult;

case WM_MOUSEACTIVATE:                            // 0x0021 - returns an int
    if (!OnMouseActivate(wParam, lParam, lResult))
        return Default();
    return lResult;

case WM_CHILDACTIVATE:                            // 0x0022
    if (!OnChildActivate(wParam, lParam))
        return Default();
    return 0;

case WM_QUEUESYNC:                                // 0x0023
    if (!OnQueueSync(wParam, lParam))
        return Default();
    return 0;

case WM_GETMINMAXINFO:                            // 0x0024
    if (!OnGetMinMaxInfo(wParam, lParam))
        return Default();
    return 0;

case WM_PAINTICON:                                // 0x0026
    if (!OnPaintIcon(wParam, lParam))
        return Default();
    return 0;

case WM_ICONERASEBKGND:                           // 0x0027
    if (!OnIconEraseBkgnd(wParam, lParam))
        return Default();
    return 0;

case WM_NEXTDLGCTL:                               // 0x0028
    if (!OnNextDlgCtl(wParam, lParam))
        return Default();
    return 0;
```

```cpp
case WM_SPOOLERSTATUS:                          // 0x002A
    if (!OnSpoolerStatus(wParam, lParam))
        return Default();
    return 0;

case WM_DRAWITEM:                               // 0x002B
    if (!OnDrawItem(wParam, lParam))
        return Default();
    return TRUE;

case WM_MEASUREITEM:                            // 0x002C
    if (!OnMeasureItem(wParam, lParam))
        return Default();
    return TRUE;

case WM_DELETEITEM:                             // 0x002D
    if (!OnDeleteItem(wParam, lParam))
        return Default();
    return TRUE;

case WM_VKEYTOITEM:                             // 0x002E - returns an int
    if (!OnVKeyToItem(wParam, lParam, lResult))
        return Default();
    return lResult;

case WM_CHARTOITEM:                             // 0x002F - returns an int
    if (!OnCharToItem(wParam, lParam, lResult))
        return Default();
    return lResult;

case WM_SETFONT:                                // 0x0030
    if (!OnSetFont(wParam, lParam))
        Default();
    return 0;

case WM_GETFONT:                                // 0x0031 - returns an LRESULT
    if (!OnGetFont(wParam, lParam, lResult))
        return Default();
    return lResult;
```

II

6

```
        case WM_SETHOTKEY:                              // 0x0032 - returns an int
            if (!OnSetHotKey(wParam, lParam, lResult))
                return Default();
            return 0;


        case WM_GETHOTKEY:                              // 0x0033 - returns an int
            if (!OnGetHotKey(wParam, lParam, lResult))
                return Default();
            return lResult;


        case WM_QUERYDRAGICON:                          // 0x0037 - returns an LRESULT
            if (!OnQueryDragIcon(wParam, lParam, lResult))
                return Default();
            return lResult;


        case WM_COMPAREITEM:                            // 0x0039 - returns an int
            if (!OnCompareItem(wParam, lParam, lResult))
                return Default();
            return lResult;


        case WM_COMPACTING:                             // 0x0041
            if (!OnCompacting(wParam, lParam))
                return Default();
            return 0;


        case WM_WINDOWPOSCHANGING:                      // 0x0046
            if (!OnWindowPosChanging(wParam, lParam))
                return Default();
            return 0;


        case WM_WINDOWPOSCHANGED:                       // 0x0047
            if (!OnWindowPosChanged(wParam, lParam))
                return Default();
            return 0;

// ** OBSOLETE in 32-bit**
//  case WM_POWER:                                      // 0x0048 - returns an int
// ** Use WM_POWERBROADCAST instead **
```

```
    case WM_COPYDATA:                               // 0x004A
        if (!OnCopyData(wParam, lParam))
            return Default();
        return TRUE;


// We're not handling Journals
//      case WM_CANCELJOURNAL:                      // 0x004B


    case WM_NOTIFY:                                 // 0x004E - returns an LRESULT
        if (!OnNotify(wParam, lParam, lResult))
            return Default();
        return lResult;


    case WM_INPUTLANGCHANGEREQUEST:                 // 0x0050
        if (!OnInputLangChangeRequest(wParam, lParam))
            Default();
        return 0;


    case WM_INPUTLANGCHANGE:                        // 0x0051
        if (!OnInputLangChange(wParam, lParam))
            return Default();
        return TRUE;


    case WM_TCARD:                                  // 0x0052
        if (!OnTCard(wParam, lParam))
            Default();
        return 0;


    case WM_HELP:                                   // 0x0053
        if (!OnHelp(wParam, lParam))
            return Default();
        return TRUE;


    case WM_USERCHANGED:                            // 0x0054
        if (!OnUserChanged(wParam, lParam))
            return Default();
        return 0;
```

II

6

```
    case WM_NOTIFYFORMAT:                              // 0x0055 - returns an int
        if (!OnNotifyFormat(wParam, lParam, lResult))
            return Default();
        return lResult;

    case WM_CONTEXTMENU:                               // 0x007B
        if (!OnContextMenu(wParam, lParam))
            Default();
        return 0;

    case WM_STYLECHANGING:                             // 0x007C
        if (!OnStyleChanging(wParam, lParam))
            return Default();
        return 0;

    case WM_STYLECHANGED:                              // 0x007D
        if (!OnStyleChanged(wParam, lParam))
            return Default();
        return 0;

    case WM_DISPLAYCHANGE:                             // 0x007E
        if (!OnDisplayChange(wParam, lParam))
            Default();
        return 0;

    case WM_GETICON:                                   // 0x007F - returns an LRESULT
        if (!OnGetIcon(wParam, lParam, lResult))
            return Default();
        return lResult;

    case WM_SETICON:                                   // 0x0080 - returns an LRESULT
        if (!OnSetIcon(wParam, lParam, lResult))
            return Default();
        return lResult;

    case WM_NCCREATE:                                  // 0x0081
        if (!OnNcCreate(wParam, lParam))
            return Default();
        return TRUE;
```

```
    case WM_NCDESTROY:                                    // 0x0082
        if (!OnNcDestroy(wParam, lParam))
            return Default();
        return 0;


    case WM_NCCALCSIZE:                                   // 0x0083 - returns an int
        if (!OnNcCalcSize(wParam, lParam, lResult))
            return Default();
        return lResult;


    case WM_NCHITTEST:                                    // 0x0084 - returns an int
        if (!OnNcHitTest(wParam, lParam, lResult))
            return Default();
        return lResult;


    case WM_NCPAINT:                                      // 0x0085
        if (!OnNcPaint(wParam, lParam))
            return Default();
        return 0;


    case WM_NCACTIVATE:                                   // 0x0086
        if (!OnNcActivate(wParam, lParam, lResult))
            return Default();
        return lResult;


    case WM_GETDLGCODE:                                   // 0x0087 - returns an int
        if (!OnGetDlgCode(wParam, lParam, lResult))
            return Default();
        return lResult;


    case WM_NCMOUSEMOVE:                                  // 0x00A0
        if (!OnNcMouseMove(wParam, lParam))
            return Default();
        return 0;


    case WM_NCLBUTTONDOWN:                                // 0x00A1
        if (!OnNcLButtonDown(wParam, lParam))
            return Default();
        return 0;
```

II

6

```
    case WM_NCLBUTTONUP:                              // 0x00A2
        if (!OnNcLButtonUp(wParam, lParam))
            return Default();
        return 0;

    case WM_NCLBUTTONDBLCLK:                          // 0x00A3
        if (!OnNcLButtonDblClk(wParam, lParam))
            return Default();
        return 0;

    case WM_NCRBUTTONDOWN:                            // 0x00A4
        if (!OnNcRButtonDown(wParam, lParam))
            return Default();
        return 0;

    case WM_NCRBUTTONUP:                              // 0x00A5
        if (!OnNcRButtonUp(wParam, lParam))
            return Default();
        return 0;

    case WM_NCRBUTTONDBLCLK:                          // 0x00A6
        if (!OnNcRButtonDblClk(wParam, lParam))
            return Default();
        return 0;

    case WM_NCMBUTTONDOWN:                            // 0x00A7
        if (!OnNcMButtonDown(wParam, lParam))
            return Default();
        return 0;

    case WM_NCMBUTTONUP:                              // 0x00A8
        if (!OnNcMButtonUp(wParam, lParam))
            return Default();
        return 0;

    case WM_NCMBUTTONDBLCLK:                          // 0x00A9
        if (!OnNcMButtonDblClk(wParam, lParam))
            return Default();
        return 0;
```

```
#if WINVER >= 0x0500
    case WM_MOUSEHOVER:                              // 0x02A1 - TrackMouseEvent
        if (!OnMouseHover(wParam, lParam))
            return Default();
        return 0;


    case WM_MOUSELEAVE:                              // 0x02A3 - TrackMouseEvent
        if (!OnMouseLeave(wParam, lParam))
            return Default();
        return 0;
#endif


// Not a real message
//    case WM_KEYFIRST:                              // 0x0100


    case WM_KEYDOWN:                                 // 0x0100
        if (!OnKeyDown(wParam, lParam))
            return Default();
        return 0;


    case WM_KEYUP:                                   // 0x0101
        if (!OnKeyUp(wParam, lParam))
            return Default();
        return 0;


    case WM_CHAR:                                    // 0x0102
        if (!OnChar(wParam, lParam))
            return Default();
        return 0;


    case WM_DEADCHAR:                                // 0x0103
        if (!OnDeadChar(wParam, lParam))
            return Default();
        return 0;


    case WM_SYSKEYDOWN:                              // 0x0104
        if (!OnSysKeyDown(wParam, lParam))
            return Default();
        return 0;
```

II

6

```
        case WM_SYSKEYUP:                              // 0x0105
            if (!OnSysKeyUp(wParam, lParam))
                return Default();
            return 0;


        case WM_SYSCHAR:                               // 0x0106
            if (!OnSysChar(wParam, lParam))
                return Default();
            return 0;


        case WM_SYSDEADCHAR:                           // 0x0107
            if (!OnSysDeadChar(wParam, lParam))
                return Default();
            return 0;


// Not a real message
//    case WM_KEYLAST:                                 // 0x0108


// We're not handling IME
//    case WM_IME_STARTCOMPOSITION:                    // 0x010D
//    case WM_IME_ENDCOMPOSITION:                      // 0x010E
//    case WM_IME_COMPOSITION:                         // 0x010F
//    case WM_IME_KEYLAST:                             // 0x010F - unknown message

        case WM_INITDIALOG:                            // 0x0110
            if (!OnInitDialog(wParam, lParam, lResult))
                return Default();
            return lResult;


        case WM_COMMAND:                               // 0x0111
            if (!OnCommand(wParam, lParam))
                return Default();
            return 0;


        case WM_SYSCOMMAND:                            // 0x0112
            if (!OnSysCommand(wParam, lParam))
                return Default();
            return 0;
```

```
case WM_TIMER:                                  // 0x0113
    if (!OnTimer(wParam, lParam))
        return Default();
    return 0;

case WM_HSCROLL:                                // 0x0114
    if (!OnHScroll(wParam, lParam))
        return Default();
    return 0;

case WM_VSCROLL:                                // 0x0115
    if (!OnVScroll(wParam, lParam))
        return Default();
    return 0;

case WM_INITMENU:                               // 0x0116
    if (!OnInitMenu(wParam, lParam))
        return Default();
    return 0;

case WM_INITMENUPOPUP:                          // 0x0117
    if (!OnInitMenuPopup(wParam, lParam))
        return Default();
    return 0;

case WM_MENUSELECT:                             // 0x011F
    if (!OnMenuSelect(wParam, lParam))
        return Default();
    return 0;

case WM_MENUCHAR:                               // 0x0120 - returns an int
    if (!OnMenuChar(wParam, lParam, lResult))
        return Default();
    return lResult;

case WM_ENTERIDLE:                              // 0x0121
    if (!OnEnterIdle(wParam, lParam))
        return Default();
    return 0;
```

```
case WM_CTLCOLORMSGBOX:                         // 0x0132 - returns an LRESULT
    if (!OnCtlColorMsgBox(wParam, lParam, lResult))
        return Default();
    return lResult;

case WM_CTLCOLOREDIT:                           // 0x0133 - returns an LRESULT
    if (!OnCtlColorEdit(wParam, lParam, lResult))
        return Default();
    return lResult;

case WM_CTLCOLORLISTBOX:                         // 0x0134 - returns an LRESULT
    if (!OnCtlColorListBox(wParam, lParam, lResult))
        return Default();
    return lResult;

case WM_CTLCOLORBTN:                             // 0x0135 - returns an LRESULT
    if (!OnCtlColorBtn(wParam, lParam, lResult))
        return Default();
    return lResult;

case WM_CTLCOLORDLG:                             // 0x0136 - returns an LRESULT
    if (!OnCtlColorDlg(wParam, lParam, lResult))
        return Default();
    return lResult;

case WM_CTLCOLORSCROLLBAR:                       // 0x0137 - returns an LRESULT
    if (!OnCtlColorScrollBar(wParam, lParam, lResult))
        return Default();
    return lResult;

case WM_CTLCOLORSTATIC:                          // 0x0138 - returns an LRESULT
    if (!OnCtlColorStatic(wParam, lParam, lResult))
        return Default();
    return lResult;

case WM_MOUSEMOVE:                               // 0x0200
    if (!OnMouseMove(wParam, lParam))
        Default();
    return 0;
```

```
    case WM_LBUTTONDOWN:                           // 0x0201
        if (!OnLButtonDown(wParam, lParam))
            return Default();
        return 0;

    case WM_LBUTTONUP:                             // 0x0202
        if (!OnLButtonUp(wParam, lParam))
            return Default();
        return 0;

    case WM_LBUTTONDBLCLK:                         // 0x0203
        if (!OnLButtonDblClk(wParam, lParam))
            return Default();
        return 0;

    case WM_RBUTTONDOWN:                           // 0x0204
        if (!OnRButtonDown(wParam, lParam))
            return Default();
        return 0;

    case WM_RBUTTONUP:                             // 0x0205
        if (!OnRButtonUp(wParam, lParam))
            return Default();
        return 0;

    case WM_RBUTTONDBLCLK:                         // 0x0206
        if (!OnRButtonDblClk(wParam, lParam))
            return Default();
        return 0;

    case WM_MBUTTONDOWN:                           // 0x0207
        if (!OnMButtonDown(wParam, lParam))
            return Default();
        return 0;

    case WM_MBUTTONUP:                             // 0x0208
        if (!OnMButtonUp(wParam, lParam))
            return Default();
        return 0;
```

II

6

```
case WM_MBUTTONDBLCLK:                              // 0x0209
    if (!OnMButtonDblClk(wParam, lParam))
        return Default();
    return 0;

case WM_MOUSEWHEEL:                                 // 0x020A
    if (!OnMouseWheel(wParam, lParam))
        Default();
    return 0;

case WM_PARENTNOTIFY:                               // 0x0210
    if (!OnParentNotify(wParam, lParam))
        return Default();
    return 0;

case WM_ENTERMENULOOP:                              // 0x0211
    if (!OnEnterMenuLoop(wParam, lParam))
        return Default();
    return 0;

case WM_EXITMENULOOP:                               // 0x0212
    if (!OnExitMenuLoop(wParam, lParam))
        return Default();
    return 0;

case WM_NEXTMENU:                                   // 0x0213
    if (!OnNextMenu(wParam, lParam))
        Default();
    return 0;

case WM_SIZING:                                     // 0x0214
    if (!OnSizing(wParam, lParam))
        return Default();
    return TRUE;

case WM_CAPTURECHANGED:                             // 0x0215
    if (!OnCaptureChanged(wParam, lParam))
        return Default();
    return 0;
```

```
      case WM_MOVING:                              // 0x0216
          if (!OnMoving(wParam, lParam))
              return Default();
          return TRUE;


      case WM_POWERBROADCAST:                      // 0x0218 - returns an int
          if (!OnPowerBroadcast(wParam, lParam, lResult))
              return Default();
          return lResult;


      case WM_DEVICECHANGE:                        // 0x0219 - returns an int
          if (!OnDeviceChange(wParam, lParam, lResult))
              return Default();
          return lResult;


// We're not handling IME
//    case WM_IME_SETCONTEXT:                      // 0x0281
//    case WM_IME_NOTIFY:                          // 0x0282
//    case WM_IME_CONTROL:                         // 0x0283
//    case WM_IME_COMPOSITIONFULL:                 // 0x0284
//    case WM_IME_SELECT:                          // 0x0285
//    case WM_IME_CHAR:                            // 0x0286
//    case WM_IME_KEYDOWN:                         // 0x0290
//    case WM_IME_KEYUP:                           // 0x0291


      case WM_MDICREATE:                           // 0x0220 - returns an LRESULT
          if (!OnMdiCreate(wParam, lParam, lResult))
              return Default();
          return lResult;


      case WM_MDIDESTROY:                          // 0x0221
          if (!OnMdiDestroy(wParam, lParam))
              return Default();
          return 0;


      case WM_MDIACTIVATE:                         // 0x0222
          if (!OnMdiActivate(wParam, lParam))
              return Default();
          return 0;
```

```
case WM_MDIRESTORE:                              // 0x0223
    if (!OnMdiRestore(wParam, lParam))
        return Default();
    return 0;

case WM_MDINEXT:                                 // 0x0224
    if (!OnMdiNext(wParam, lParam))
        return Default();
    return 0;

case WM_MDIMAXIMIZE:                             // 0x0225
    if (!OnMdiMaximize(wParam, lParam))
        return Default();
    return 0;

case WM_MDITILE:                                 // 0x0226
    if (!OnMdiTile(wParam, lParam, lResult))
        return Default();
    return lResult;

case WM_MDICASCADE:                              // 0x0227
    if (!OnMdiCascade(wParam, lParam, lResult))
        return Default();
    return lResult;

case WM_MDIICONARRANGE:                          // 0x0228
    if (!OnMdiIconArrange(wParam, lParam))
        Default();
    return 0;

case WM_MDIGETACTIVE:                            // 0x0229 - returns an LRESULT
    if (!OnMdiGetActive(wParam, lParam, lResult))
        return Default();
    return lResult;

case WM_MDISETMENU:                              // 0x0230 - returns an LRESULT
    if (!OnMdiSetMenu(wParam, lParam, lResult))
        return Default();
    return lResult;
```

```
        case WM_ENTERSIZEMOVE:                          // 0x0231
            if (!OnEnterSizeMove(wParam, lParam))
                return Default();
            return 0;


        case WM_EXITSIZEMOVE:                           // 0x0232
            if (!OnExitSizeMove(wParam, lParam))
                return Default();
            return 0;


        case WM_DROPFILES:                              // 0x0233
            if (!OnDropFiles(wParam, lParam))
                return Default();
            return 0;


        case WM_MDIREFRESHMENU:                         // 0x0234 - returns an LRESULT
            if (!OnMdiRefreshMenu(wParam, lParam, lResult))
                return Default();
            return lResult;

#if WINVER >= 0x500
        case WM_MOUSEHOVER:                             // 0x02A1 - TrackMouseEvent
            if (!OnMouseHover(wParam, lParam, lResult))
                return Default();
            return lResult;


        case WM_MOUSELEAVE:                             // 0x02A3 - TrackMouseEvent
            if (!OnMouseLeave(wParam, lParam))
                return Default();
            return 0;
#endif


        case WM_CUT:                                    // 0x0300
            if (!OnCut(wParam, lParam))
                Default();
            return 0;
```

```
case WM_COPY:                                      // 0x0301
    if (!OnCopy(wParam, lParam))
        Default();
    return 0;

case WM_PASTE:                                     // 0x0302
    if (!OnPaste(wParam, lParam))
        Default();
    return 0;

case WM_CLEAR:                                     // 0x0303
    if (!OnClear(wParam, lParam))
        Default();
    return 0;

case WM_UNDO:                                      // 0x0304
    if (!OnUndo(wParam, lParam, lResult))
        return Default();
    return lResult;

case WM_RENDERFORMAT:                              // 0x0305
    if (!OnRenderFormat(wParam, lParam))
        return Default();
    return 0;

case WM_RENDERALLFORMATS:                          // 0x0306
    if (!OnRenderAllFormats(wParam, lParam))
        return Default();
    return 0;

case WM_DESTROYCLIPBOARD:                          // 0x0307
    if (!OnDestroyClipboard(wParam, lParam))
        return Default();
    return 0;

case WM_DRAWCLIPBOARD:                             // 0x0308
    if (!OnDrawClipboard(wParam, lParam))
        Default();
    return 0;
```

```
    case WM_PAINTCLIPBOARD:                      // 0x0309
        if (!OnPaintClipboard(wParam, lParam))
            return Default();
        return 0;

    case WM_VSCROLLCLIPBOARD:                    // 0x030A
        if (!OnVScrollClipboard(wParam, lParam))
            return Default();
        return 0;

    case WM_SIZECLIPBOARD:                       // 0x030B
        if (!OnSizeClipboard(wParam, lParam))
            Default();
        return 0;

    case WM_ASKCBFORMATNAME:                     // 0x030C
        if (!OnAskCbFormatName(wParam, lParam))
            return Default();
        return 0;

    case WM_CHANGECBCHAIN:                       // 0x030D
        if (!OnChangeCbChain(wParam, lParam))
            return Default();
        return 0;

    case WM_HSCROLLCLIPBOARD:                    // 0x030E
        if (!OnHScrollClipboard(wParam, lParam))
            return Default();
        return 0;

    case WM_QUERYNEWPALETTE:                     // 0x030F
        if (!OnQueryNewPalette(wParam, lParam, lResult))
            return Default();
        return lResult;

    case WM_PALETTEISCHANGING:                   // 0x0310
        if (!OnPaletteIsChanging(wParam, lParam))
            return Default();
        return 0;
```

II

6

```
case WM_PALETTECHANGED:                                // 0x0311
    {
        // To prevent recursion, do not process this
        // message if it was originally sent from this
        // class. To see if it was sent from this class,
        // check the HWND against the one used by this
        // class. If they are the same, do not process.
        HWND hWnd = (HWND)wParam;
        ASSERT(hWnd && ::IsWindow(hWnd));
        ASSERT(DoGetWnd() && DoGetWnd()->m_hWnd &&
            ::IsWindow(DoGetWnd()->m_hWnd));

        if (hWnd != DoGetWnd()->m_hWnd)
            if (!OnPaletteChanged(wParam, lParam))
                return Default();
            else
                return 0;
        else
            return Default();
    }

case WM_HOTKEY:                                        // 0x0312
    if (!OnHotKey(wParam, lParam))
        Default();
    return 0;

case WM_PRINT:                                         // 0x0317
    if (!OnPrint(wParam, lParam))
        Default();
    return 0;

case WM_PRINTCLIENT:                                   // 0x0318
    if (!OnPrintClient(wParam, lParam))
        Default();
    return 0;


// ---------------------------------------------------------
// Generic notification messages
case NM_OUTOFMEMORY:
    if (!OnNotifyOutOfMemory(wParam, lParam))
```

```
        {
            // We didn't handle it, so call
            // the parent's default handler
            return CallParentDefault();
        }
        return 0;

    case NM_CLICK:
        if (!OnNotifyClick(wParam, lParam))
        {
            // We didn't handle it, so call
            // the parent's default handler
            return CallParentDefault();
        }
        return 0;

    case NM_DBLCLK:
        if (!OnNotifyDblClk(wParam, lParam))
        {
            // We didn't handle it, so call
            // the parent's default handler
            return CallParentDefault();
        }
        return 0;

    case NM_RETURN:
        if (!OnNotifyReturn(wParam, lParam))
        {
            // We didn't handle it, so call
            // the parent's default handler
            return CallParentDefault();
        }
        return 0;

    case NM_RCLICK:
        if (!OnNotifyRClick(wParam, lParam, lResult))
        {
            // We didn't handle it, so call
            // the parent's default handler
            return CallParentDefault();
```

II

6

```
        }
        return lResult;

    case NM_RDBLCLK:
        if (!OnNotifyRDblClk(wParam, lParam, lResult))
        {
            // We didn't handle it, so call
            // the parent's default handler
            return CallParentDefault();
        }
        return lResult;

    case NM_SETFOCUS:
        if (!OnNotifySetFocus(wParam, lParam))
        {
            // We didn't handle it, so call
            // the parent's default handler
            return CallParentDefault();
        }
        return 0;

    case NM_KILLFOCUS:
        if (!OnNotifyKillFocus(wParam, lParam))
        {
            // We didn't handle it, so call
            // the parent's default handler
            return CallParentDefault();
        }
        return 0;

#if (_WIN32_IE >= 0x0300)
    case NM_CUSTOMDRAW:
        if (!OnNotifyCustomDraw(wParam, lParam, lResult))
        {
            // We didn't handle it, so call
            // the parent's default handler
            return CallParentDefault();
        }
        return lResult;
```

```
        case NM_HOVER:
            if (!OnNotifyHover(wParam, lParam, lResult))
            {
                // We didn't handle it, so call
                // the parent's default handler
                return CallParentDefault();
            }
            return lResult;
#endif

#if (_WIN32_IE >= 0x0400)
        case NM_NCHITTEST:
            if (!OnNotifyNcHitTest(wParam, lParam, lResult))
            {
                // We didn't handle it, so call
                // the parent's default handler
                return CallParentDefault();
            }
            return lResult;

        case NM_KEYDOWN:
            if (!OnNotifyKeyDown(wParam, lParam, lResult))
            {
                // We didn't handle it, so call
                // the parent's default handler
                return CallParentDefault();
            }
            return lResult;

        case NM_RELEASEDCAPTURE:
            if (!OnNotifyReleasedCapture(wParam, lParam))
            {
                // We didn't handle it, so call
                // the parent's default handler
                return CallParentDefault();
            }
            return 0;

        case NM_SETCURSOR:
            if (!OnNotifySetCursor(wParam, lParam, lResult))
```

II

6

```
        {
            // We didn't handle it, so call
            // the parent's default handler
            return CallParentDefault();
        }
        return lResult;

    case NM_CHAR:
        if (!OnNotifyChar(wParam, lParam))
        {
            // We didn't handle it, so call
            // the parent's default handler
            return CallParentDefault();
        }
        return 0;
#endif

#if WINVER >= 0x500
    case NM_TOOLTIPSCREATED:
        if(!OnNotifyTooltipsCreated(wParam, lParam))
        {
            // We didn't handle it, so call
            // the parent's default handler
            return CallParentDefault();
        }
        return 0;
#endif

    // -----------------------------------------------------------
    // Property Sheet notification messages

    case PSN_APPLY:
        if (!OnPropSheetApply(wParam, lParam, lResult))
        {
            // We didn't handle it, so call
            // the parent's default handler
            return CallParentDefault();
        }
        return lResult;
```

```
    case PSN_GETOBJECT:
    if (!OnPropSheetGetObject(wParam, lParam))
        {
            // We didn't handle it, so call
            // the parent's default handler
            return CallParentDefault();
        }
        return lResult;

    case PSN_HELP:
    if (!OnPropSheetHelp(wParam, lParam))
        {
            // We didn't handle it, so call
            // the parent's default handler
            return CallParentDefault();
        }
        return lResult;

    case PSN_KILLACTIVE:
    if (!OnPropSheetKillActive(wParam, lParam, lResult))
        {
            // We didn't handle it, so call
            // the parent's default handler
            return CallParentDefault();
        }
        return lResult;

    case PSN_QUERYCANCEL:
    if (!OnPropSheetQueryCancel(wParam, lParam, lResult))
        {
            // We didn't handle it, so call
            // the parent's default handler
            return CallParentDefault();
        }
        return lResult;

    case PSN_RESET:
    if (!OnPropSheetReset(wParam, lParam, lResult))
        {
            // We didn't handle it, so call
```

```
                    // the parent's default handler
                    return CallParentDefault();
            }
        return lResult;

    case PSN_SETACTIVE:
    if (!OnPropSheetSetActive(wParam, lParam, lResult))
        {
            // We didn't handle it, so call
            // the parent's default handler
            return CallParentDefault();
        }
        return lResult;

    case PSN_WIZBACK:
    if (!OnPropSheetWizBack(wParam, lParam, lResult))
        {
            // We didn't handle it, so call
            // the parent's default handler
            return CallParentDefault();
        }
        return lResult;

    case PSN_WIZFINISH:
    if (!OnPropSheetWizFinish(wParam, lParam, lResult))
        {
            // We didn't handle it, so call
            // the parent's default handler
            return CallParentDefault();
        }
        return lResult;

    case PSN_WIZNEXT:
    if (!OnPropSheetWizNext(wParam, lParam, lResult))
        {
            // We didn't handle it, so call
            // the parent's default handler
            return CallParentDefault();
        }
        return lResult;
```

```
// ----------------------------------------------------------
// Header notification messages

case HDN_ITEMCHANGING:
    if (!OnHeaderItemChanging(wParam, lParam, lResult))
    {
        // We didn't handle it, so call
        // the parent's default handler
        return CallParentDefault();
    }
    return lResult;

case HDN_ITEMCHANGED:
    if (!OnHeaderItemChanged(wParam, lParam))
    {
        // We didn't handle it, so call
        // the parent's default handler
        return CallParentDefault();
    }
    return 0;

case HDN_ITEMCLICK:
    if (!OnHeaderItemClick(wParam, lParam))
    {
        // We didn't handle it, so call
        // the parent's default handler
        return CallParentDefault();
    }
    return 0;

case HDN_ITEMDBLCLICK:
    if (!OnHeaderItemDblClick(wParam, lParam))
    {
        // We didn't handle it, so call
        // the parent's default handler
        return CallParentDefault();
    }
    return 0;
```

II

6

```
    case HDN_DIVIDERDBLCLICK:
        if (!OnHeaderDividerDblClick(wParam, lParam))
        {
            // We didn't handle it, so call
            // the parent's default handler
            return CallParentDefault();
        }
        return 0;

    case HDN_BEGINTRACK:
        if (!OnHeaderBeginTrack(wParam, lParam, lResult))
        {
            // We didn't handle it, so call
            // the parent's default handler
            return CallParentDefault();
        }
        return lResult;

    case HDN_ENDTRACK:
        if (!OnHeaderEndTrack(wParam, lParam))
        {
            // We didn't handle it, so call
            // the parent's default handler
            return CallParentDefault();
        }
        return 0;

    case HDN_TRACK:
        if (!OnHeaderTrack(wParam, lParam, lResult))
        {
            // We didn't handle it, so call
            // the parent's default handler
            return CallParentDefault();
        }
        return lResult;

#if (_WIN32_IE >= 0x0300)
    case HDN_GETDISPINFO:
        if (!OnHeaderGetDispInfo(wParam, lParam))
        {
```

```
                // We didn't handle it, so call
                // the parent's default handler
                return CallParentDefault();
            }
            return lResult;


        case HDN_BEGINDRAG:
            if (!OnHeaderBeginDrag(wParam, lParam, lResult))
            {
                // We didn't handle it, so call
                // the parent's default handler
                return CallParentDefault();
            }
            return lResult;


        case HDN_ENDDRAG:
            if (!OnHeaderEndDrag(wParam, lParam, lResult))
            {
                // We didn't handle it, so call
                // the parent's default handler
                return CallParentDefault();
            }
            return lResult;
#endif

        // ----------------------------------------------------------
        // Toolbar notification messages

        case TBN_GETBUTTONINFO:
            if (!OnToolbarGetButtonInfo(wParam, lParam, lResult))
            {
                // We didn't handle it, so call
                // the parent's default handler
                return CallParentDefault();
            }
            return lResult;


        case TBN_BEGINDRAG:
            if (!OnToolbarBeginDrag(wParam, lParam))
            {
```

```
                // We didn't handle it, so call
                // the parent's default handler
                return CallParentDefault();
            }
            return 0;

    case TBN_ENDDRAG:
        if (!OnToolbarEndDrag(wParam, lParam))
        {
            // We didn't handle it, so call
            // the parent's default handler
            return CallParentDefault();
        }
        return 0;

    case TBN_BEGINADJUST:
        if (!OnToolbarBeginAdjust(wParam, lParam))
        {
            // We didn't handle it, so call
            // the parent's default handler
            return CallParentDefault();
        }
        return 0;

    case TBN_ENDADJUST:
        if (!OnToolbarEndAdjust(wParam, lParam))
        {
            // We didn't handle it, so call
            // the parent's default handler
            return CallParentDefault();
        }
        return 0;

    case TBN_RESET:
        if (!OnToolbarReset(wParam, lParam))
        {
            // We didn't handle it, so call
            // the parent's default handler
            return CallParentDefault();
        }
        return 0;
```

```
    case TBN_QUERYINSERT:
        if (!OnToolbarQueryInsert(wParam, lParam, lResult))
        {
            // We didn't handle it, so call
            // the parent's default handler
            return CallParentDefault();
        }
        return lResult;

    case TBN_QUERYDELETE:
        if (!OnToolbarQueryDelete(wParam, lParam, lResult))
        {
            // We didn't handle it, so call
            // the parent's default handler
            return CallParentDefault();
        }
        return lResult;

    case TBN_TOOLBARCHANGE:
        if (!OnToolbarToolbarChange(wParam, lParam))
        {
            // We didn't handle it, so call
            // the parent's default handler
            return CallParentDefault();
        }
        return 0;

    case TBN_CUSTHELP:
        if (!OnToolbarCustHelp(wParam, lParam))
        {
            // We didn't handle it, so call
            // the parent's default handler
            return CallParentDefault();
        }
        return 0;

#if (_WIN32_IE >= 0x0300)
    case TBN_DROPDOWN:
        if (!OnToolbarDropDown(wParam, lParam, lResult))
```

II

6

```
        {
            // We didn't handle it, so call
            // the parent's default handler
            return CallParentDefault();
        }
        return lResult;
#endif

#if (_WIN32_IE >= 0x0400)
    case TBN_GETOBJECT:
        if (!OnToolbarGetObject(wParam, lParam))
        {
            // We didn't handle it, so call
            // the parent's default handler
            return CallParentDefault();
        }
        return 0;

    case TBN_HOTITEMCHANGE:
        if (!OnToolbarHotItemChange(wParam, lParam, lResult))
        {
            // We didn't handle it, so call
            // the parent's default handler
            return CallParentDefault();
        }
        return lResult;

    case TBN_DRAGOUT:
        if (!OnToolbarDragOut(wParam, lParam))
        {
            // We didn't handle it, so call
            // the parent's default handler
            return CallParentDefault();
        }
        return 0;

    case TBN_DELETINGBUTTON:
        if (!OnToolbarDeletingButton(wParam, lParam))
        {
            // We didn't handle it, so call
```

```
                    // the parent's default handler
                    return CallParentDefault();
            }
            return 0;

        case TBN_GETDISPINFO:
            if (!OnToolbarGetDispInfo(wParam, lParam))
            {
                // We didn't handle it, so call
                // the parent's default handler
                return CallParentDefault();
            }
            return 0;

        case TBN_GETINFOTIP:
            if (!OnToolbarGetInfoTip(wParam, lParam))
            {
                // We didn't handle it, so call
                // the parent's default handler
                return CallParentDefault();
            }
            return 0;
#endif

        // ----------------------------------------------------------
        // Rebar notification messages
        case RBN_HEIGHTCHANGE:
            if (!OnRebarHeightChange(wParam, lParam))
            {
                // We didn't handle it, so call
                // the parent's default handler
                return CallParentDefault();
            }
            return 0;

#if (_WIN32_IE >= 0x0400)
        case RBN_GETOBJECT:
            if (!OnRebarGetObject(wParam, lParam))
            {
                // We didn't handle it, so call
```

```
                        // the parent's default handler
                        return CallParentDefault();
                }
                return 0;


        case RBN_LAYOUTCHANGED:
                if (!OnRebarLayoutChanged(wParam, lParam))
                {
                        // We didn't handle it, so call
                        // the parent's default handler
                        return CallParentDefault();
                }
                return 0;


        case RBN_AUTOSIZE:
                if (!OnRebarAutoSize(wParam, lParam))
                {
                        // We didn't handle it, so call
                        // the parent's default handler
                        return CallParentDefault();
                }
                return 0;


        case RBN_BEGINDRAG:
                if (!OnRebarBeginDrag(wParam, lParam, lResult))
                {
                        // We didn't handle it, so call
                        // the parent's default handler
                        return CallParentDefault();
                }
                return lResult;


        case RBN_ENDDRAG:
                if (!OnRebarEndDrag(wParam, lParam))
                {
                        // We didn't handle it, so call
                        // the parent's default handler
                        return CallParentDefault();
                }
                return 0;
```

```
        case RBN_DELETINGBAND:
            if (!OnRebarDeletingBand(wParam, lParam))
            {
                // We didn't handle it, so call
                // the parent's default handler
                return CallParentDefault();
            }
            return 0;

        case RBN_DELETEDBAND:
            if (!OnRebarDeleteBand(wParam, lParam))
            {
                // We didn't handle it, so call
                // the parent's default handler
                return CallParentDefault();
            }
            return 0;

        case RBN_CHILDSIZE:
            if (!OnRebarChildSize(wParam, lParam))
            {
                // We didn't handle it, so call
                // the parent's default handler
                return CallParentDefault();
            }
            return 0;
#endif

    // --------------------------------------------------------
    // Tooltip notification messages
//    case TTN_GETDISPINFO:  // same as TTN_NEEDTEXT
    case TTN_NEEDTEXT:
            if (!OnTooltipNeedText(wParam, lParam))
            {
                // We didn't handle it, so call
                // the parent's default handler
                return CallParentDefault();
            }
            return 0;
```

```
    case TTN_SHOW:
        if (!OnTooltipShow(wParam, lParam))
        {
            // We didn't handle it, so call
            // the parent's default handler
            return CallParentDefault();
        }
        return 0;

    case TTN_POP:
        if (!OnTooltipPop(wParam, lParam))
        {
            // We didn't handle it, so call
            // the parent's default handler
            return CallParentDefault();
        }
        return 0;


    // -----------------------------------------------------------
    // Status bar notification messages
#if (_WIN32_IE >= 0x0400)
    case SBN_SIMPLEMODECHANGE:
        if (!OnStatusBarSimpleModeChange(wParam, lParam))
        {
            // We didn't handle it, so call
            // the parent's default handler
            return CallParentDefault();
        }
        return 0;

#endif


    // -----------------------------------------------------------
    // Up/Down Ctrl notification messages
    case UDN_DELTAPOS:
        if (!OnUpDownDeltaPos(wParam, lParam, lResult))
        {
            // We didn't handle it, so call
            // the parent's default handler
```

```
            return CallParentDefault();
        }
        return lResult;


    // --------------------------------------------------------
    // Listview notification messages
    case LVN_ITEMCHANGING:
        if (!OnListviewItemChanging(wParam, lParam, lResult))
        {
            // We didn't handle it, so call
            // the parent's default handler
            return CallParentDefault();
        }
        return lResult;


    case LVN_ITEMCHANGED:
        if (!OnListviewItemChanged(wParam, lParam))
        {
            // We didn't handle it, so call
            // the parent's default handler
            return CallParentDefault();
        }
        return 0;


    case LVN_INSERTITEM:
        if (!OnListviewInsertItem(wParam, lParam))
        {
            // We didn't handle it, so call
            // the parent's default handler
            return CallParentDefault();
        }
        return 0;


    case LVN_DELETEITEM:
        if (!OnListviewDeleteItem(wParam, lParam))
        {
            // We didn't handle it, so call
            // the parent's default handler
            return CallParentDefault();
        }
        return 0;
```

II

6

```
case LVN_DELETEALLITEMS:
    if (!OnListviewDeleteAllItems(wParam, lParam, lResult))
    {
        // We didn't handle it, so call
        // the parent's default handler
        return CallParentDefault();
    }
    return lResult;

case LVN_BEGINLABELEDIT:
    if (!OnListviewBeginLabelEdit(wParam, lParam, lResult))
    {
        // We didn't handle it, so call
        // the parent's default handler
        return CallParentDefault();
    }
    return lResult;

case LVN_ENDLABELEDIT:
    if (!OnListviewEndLabelEdit(wParam, lParam, lResult))
    {
        // We didn't handle it, so call
        // the parent's default handler
        return CallParentDefault();
    }
    return lResult;

case LVN_COLUMNCLICK:
    if (!OnListviewColumnClick(wParam, lParam))
    {
        // We didn't handle it, so call
        // the parent's default handler
        return CallParentDefault();
    }
    return 0;

case LVN_BEGINDRAG:
    if (!OnListviewBeginDrag(wParam, lParam))
    {
```

```
                // We didn't handle it, so call
                // the parent's default handler
                return CallParentDefault();
            }
            return 0;

        case LVN_BEGINRDRAG:
            if (!OnListviewBeginRDrag(wParam, lParam))
            {
                // We didn't handle it, so call
                // the parent's default handler
                return CallParentDefault();
            }
            return 0;

#if (_WIN32_IE >= 0x0300)
        case LVN_ODCACHEHINT:
            if (!OnListviewOdCacheHit(wParam, lParam))
            {
                // We didn't handle it, so call
                // the parent's default handler
                return CallParentDefault();
            }
            return 0;

        case LVN_ODFINDITEM:
            if (!OnListviewOdFindItem(wParam, lParam))
            {
                // We didn't handle it, so call
                // the parent's default handler
                return CallParentDefault();
            }
            return 0;

        case LVN_ITEMACTIVATE:
            if (!OnListviewItemActivate(wParam, lParam))
            {
                // We didn't handle it, so call
                // the parent's default handler
                return CallParentDefault();
```

```
            }
        return 0;

    case LVN_ODSTATECHANGED:
        if (!OnListviewOdStateChanged(wParam, lParam))
        {
            // We didn't handle it, so call
            // the parent's default handler
            return CallParentDefault();
        }
        return 0;
#endif

#if (_WIN32_IE >= 0x0400)
    case LVN_HOTTRACK:
        if (!OnListviewHotTrack(wParam, lParam, lResult))
        {
            // We didn't handle it, so call
            // the parent's default handler
            return CallParentDefault();
        }
        return lResult;

    case LVN_GETINFOTIP:
        if (!OnListviewGetInfoTip(wParam, lParam))
        {
            // We didn't handle it, so call
            // the parent's default handler
            return CallParentDefault();
        }
        return 0;

    case LVN_MARQUEEBEGIN:
        if (!OnListviewMarqueeBegin(wParam, lParam, lResult))
        {
            // We didn't handle it, so call
            // the parent's default handler
            return CallParentDefault();
        }
        return lResult;
```

```
#endif

    case LVN_GETDISPINFO:
        if (!OnListviewGetDispInfo(wParam, lParam))
        {
            // We didn't handle it, so call
            // the parent's default handler
            return CallParentDefault();
        }
        return 0;

    case LVN_SETDISPINFO:
        if (!OnListviewSetDispInfo(wParam, lParam))
        {
            // We didn't handle it, so call
            // the parent's default handler
            return CallParentDefault();
        }
        return 0;

    case LVN_KEYDOWN:
        if (!OnListviewKeyDown(wParam, lParam))
        {
            // We didn't handle it, so call
            // the parent's default handler
            return CallParentDefault();
        }
        return 0;


    // -----------------------------------------------------------
    // Treeview notification messages

    case TVN_SELCHANGING:
        if (!OnTreeviewSelChanging(wParam, lParam, lResult))
        {
            // We didn't handle it, so call
            // the parent's default handler
            return CallParentDefault();
        }
        return 0;
```

II

6

```
case TVN_SELCHANGED:
    if (!OnTreeviewSelChanged(wParam, lParam))
    {
        // We didn't handle it, so call
        // the parent's default handler
        return CallParentDefault();
    }
    return 0;

case TVN_GETDISPINFO:
    if (!OnTreeviewGetDispInfo(wParam, lParam))
    {
        // We didn't handle it, so call
        // the parent's default handler
        return CallParentDefault();
    }
    return 0;

case TVN_SETDISPINFO:
    if (!OnTreeviewSetDispInfo(wParam, lParam))
    {
        // We didn't handle it, so call
        // the parent's default handler
        return CallParentDefault();
    }
    return 0;

case TVN_ITEMEXPANDING:
    if (!OnTreeviewItemExpanding(wParam, lParam, lResult))
    {
        // We didn't handle it, so call
        // the parent's default handler
        return CallParentDefault();
    }
    return lResult;

case TVN_ITEMEXPANDED:
    if (!OnTreeviewItemExpanded(wParam, lParam))
    {
```

```
            // We didn't handle it, so call
            // the parent's default handler
            return CallParentDefault();
        }
        return 0;

    case TVN_BEGINDRAG:
        if (!OnTreeviewBeginDrag(wParam, lParam))
        {
            // We didn't handle it, so call
            // the parent's default handler
            return CallParentDefault();
        }
        return 0;

    case TVN_BEGINRDRAG:
        if (!OnTreeviewBeginRDrag(wParam, lParam))
        {
            // We didn't handle it, so call
            // the parent's default handler
            return CallParentDefault();
        }
        return 0;

    case TVN_DELETEITEM:
        if (!OnTreeviewDeleteItem(wParam, lParam))
        {
            // We didn't handle it, so call
            // the parent's default handler
            return CallParentDefault();
        }
        return 0;

    case TVN_BEGINLABELEDIT:
        if (!OnTreeviewBeginLabelEdit(wParam, lParam, lResult))
        {
            // We didn't handle it, so call
            // the parent's default handler
            return CallParentDefault();
        }
```

```
            return lResult;

        case TVN_ENDLABELEDIT:
            if (!OnTreeviewEndLabelEdit(wParam, lParam, lResult))
            {
                // We didn't handle it, so call
                // the parent's default handler
                return CallParentDefault();
            }
            return lResult;


        case TVN_KEYDOWN:
            if (!OnTreeviewKeyDown(wParam, lParam))
            {
                // We didn't handle it, so call
                // the parent's default handler
                return CallParentDefault();
            }
            return 0;

#if (_WIN32_IE >= 0x0400)
        case TVN_GETINFOTIP:
            if (!OnTreeviewGetInfoTip(wParam, lParam))
            {
                // We didn't handle it, so call
                // the parent's default handler
                return CallParentDefault();
            }
            return 0;


        case TVN_SINGLEEXPAND:
            if (!OnTreeviewSingleExpand(wParam, lParam))
            {
                // We didn't handle it, so call
                // the parent's default handler
                return CallParentDefault();
            }
            return 0;

#endif
```

```
    // ----------------------------------------------------------
    // ComboBoxEx notification messages
#if (_WIN32_IE >= 0x0400)
    case CBEN_GETDISPINFO:                              // unknown message
        if (!OnCbeGetDispInfo(wParam, lParam))
        {
            // We didn't handle it, so call
            // the parent's default handler
            return CallParentDefault();
        }
        return 0;


    case CBEN_INSERTITEM:                               // unknown message
        if (!OnCbeInsertItem(wParam, lParam))
        {
            // We didn't handle it, so call
            // the parent's default handler
            return CallParentDefault();
        }
        return 0;


    case CBEN_DELETEITEM:                               // unknown message
        if (!OnCbeDeleteItem(wParam, lParam))
        {
            // We didn't handle it, so call
            // the parent's default handler
            return CallParentDefault();
        }
        return 0;


    case CBEN_BEGINEDIT:                                // unknown message
        if (!OnCbeBeginEdit(wParam, lParam))
        {
            // We didn't handle it, so call
            // the parent's default handler
            return CallParentDefault();
        }
        return 0;
```

II

6

```
        case CBEN_ENDEDIT:                                    // unknown message
            if (!OnCbeEndEdit(wParam, lParam, lResult))
            {
                // We didn't handle it, so call
                // the parent's default handler
                return CallParentDefault();
            }
            return lResult;

        case CBEN_DRAGBEGIN:
            if (!OnCbeDragBegin(wParam, lParam))
            {
                // We didn't handle it, so call
                // the parent's default handler
                return CallParentDefault();
            }
            return 0;

#endif

        // ----------------------------------------------------------
        // Tab Ctrl notification messages
        case TCN_KEYDOWN:
            if (!OnTabKeyDown(wParam, lParam))
            {
                // We didn't handle it, so call
                // the parent's default handler
                return CallParentDefault();
            }
            return 0;

        case TCN_SELCHANGE:
            if (!OnTabSelChange(wParam, lParam))
            {
                // We didn't handle it, so call
                // the parent's default handler
                return CallParentDefault();
            }
            return 0;
```

```
        case TCN_SELCHANGING:
            if (!OnTabSelChanging(wParam, lParam, lResult))
            {
                // We didn't handle it, so call
                // the parent's default handler
                return CallParentDefault();
            }
            return lResult;

#if (_WIN32_IE >= 0x0400)
        case TCN_GETOBJECT:
            if (!OnTabGetObject(wParam, lParam))
            {
                // We didn't handle it, so call
                // the parent's default handler
                return CallParentDefault();
            }
            return 0;
#endif

        // ----------------------------------------------------------
        // Month/Calendar Ctrl notification messages
        case MCN_SELCHANGE:
            if (!OnMonCalSelChange(wParam, lParam))
            {
                // We didn't handle it, so call
                // the parent's default handler
                return CallParentDefault();
            }
            return 0;

        case MCN_GETDAYSTATE:
            if (!OnMonCalGetDayState(wParam, lParam))
            {
                // We didn't handle it, so call
                // the parent's default handler
                return CallParentDefault();
            }
            return 0;
```

```
case MCN_SELECT:
    if (!OnMonCalSelect(wParam, lParam))
    {
        // We didn't handle it, so call
        // the parent's default handler
        return CallParentDefault();
    }
    return 0;




// ------------------------------------------------------------
// Date/Time Picker Ctrl notification messages
case DTN_DATETIMECHANGE:
    if (!OnDateTimeChange(wParam, lParam))
    {
        // We didn't handle it, so call
        // the parent's default handler
        return CallParentDefault();
    }
    return 0;

case DTN_USERSTRING:
    if (!OnDateTimeUserString(wParam, lParam))
    {
        // We didn't handle it, so call
        // the parent's default handler
        return CallParentDefault();
    }
    return 0;

case DTN_WMKEYDOWN:
    if (!OnDateTimeWmKeyDown(wParam, lParam))
    {
        // We didn't handle it, so call
        // the parent's default handler
        return CallParentDefault();
    }
    return 0;
```

```
        case DTN_FORMAT:
            if (!OnDateTimeFormat(wParam, lParam))
            {
                // We didn't handle it, so call
                // the parent's default handler
                return CallParentDefault();
            }
            return 0;

        case DTN_FORMATQUERY:
            if (!OnDateTimeFormatQuery(wParam, lParam))
            {
                // We didn't handle it, so call
                // the parent's default handler
                return CallParentDefault();
            }
            return 0;

        case DTN_DROPDOWN:
            if (!OnDateTimeDropDown(wParam, lParam))
            {
                // We didn't handle it, so call
                // the parent's default handler
                return CallParentDefault();
            }
            return 0;

        case DTN_CLOSEUP:
            if (!OnDateTimeCloseUp(wParam, lParam))
            {
                // We didn't handle it, so call
                // the parent's default handler
                return CallParentDefault();
            }
            return 0;

    // -----------------------------------------------------------
    // Pager Ctrl notification messages
#if (_WIN32_IE >= 0x0400)
```

II

6

```
    case PGN_SCROLL:
        if (!OnPagerScroll(wParam, lParam))
        {
            // We didn't handle it, so call
            // the parent's default handler
            return CallParentDefault();
        }
        return 0;

    case PGN_CALCSIZE:
        if (!OnPagerCalcSize(wParam, lParam))
        {
            // We didn't handle it, so call
            // the parent's default handler
            return CallParentDefault();
        }
        return 0;
#endif


    // ---------------------------------------------------------
    // MFC messages

    // lResult = 1 if processed by AfxWndProc
    case WM_QUERYAFXWNDPROC:                    // 0x0360
        if (!OnQueryAfxWndProc(wParam, lParam, lResult))
            return Default();
        return lResult;


    // lParam = &AFX_SIZEPARENTPARAMS
    case WM_SIZEPARENT:                         // 0x0361
        if (!OnSizeParent(wParam, lParam, lResult))
            return Default();
        return lResult;


    // wParam = nIDS (or 0), lParam = lpszOther (or NULL)
    case WM_SETMESSAGESTRING:                   // 0x0362
        if (!OnSetMessageString(wParam, lParam, lResult))
            return Default();
        return lResult;
```

```
    // wParam == bDisableIfNoHandler
    case WM_IDLEUPDATECMDUI:                    // 0x0363
        if (!OnIdleUpdateCmdUi(wParam, lParam, lResult))
            return Default();
        return lResult;


    // (params unused) - sent to children
    case WM_INITIALUPDATE:                      // 0x0364
        if (!OnInitialUpdate(wParam, lParam))
            return Default();
        return 0;


    // lResult = TRUE/FALSE, lParam = dwContext
    case WM_COMMANDHELP:                         // 0x0365
        if (!OnCommandHelp(wParam, lParam))
            return Default();
        return TRUE;


    // lResult = dwContext, lParam = MAKELONG(x,y)
    case WM_HELPHITTEST:                         // 0x0366
        if (!OnHelpHitTest(wParam, lParam, lResult))
            return Default();
        return lResult;


    // (params unused)
    case WM_EXITHELPMODE:                        // 0x0367
        if (!OnExitHelpMode(wParam, lParam))
            return Default();
        return 0;


    // force RecalcLayout on frame window
    // (only for inplace frame windows)
    case WM_RECALCPARENT:                        // 0x0368
        if (!OnRecalcParent(wParam, lParam, lResult))
            return Default();
        return lResult;


    // special notify from COleResizeBar
    // wParam = ID of child window
```

II

6

```
    // lParam = lpRectNew (new position/size)
    case WM_SIZECHILD:                           // 0x0369
        if (!OnSizeChild(wParam, lParam, lResult))
            return Default();
        return lResult;


    // (params unused) causes idles to kick in
    case WM_KICKIDLE:                            // 0x036A
        if (!OnKickIdle(wParam, lParam))
            return Default();
        return 0;


    // lParam = HWND to use as centering parent
    case WM_QUERYCENTERWND:                      // 0x036B
        if (!OnQueryCenterWnd(wParam, lParam))
            return Default();
        return 0;


    // lResult = 0, disable during modal state
    // lResult = 1, don't disable
    case WM_DISABLEMODAL:                        // 0x036C
        if (!OnDisableModal(wParam, lParam, lResult))
            return Default();
        return lResult;


    // wParam combination of FS_* flags
    // See MFC documentation
    case WM_FLOATSTATUS:                         // 0x036D
        if (!OnFloatStatus(wParam, lParam, lResult))
            return Default();
        return lResult;


    // WM_ACTIVATETOPLEVEL is like WM_ACTIVATEAPP
    // but works with hierarchies of mixed processes
    // (as is the case with OLE in-place activation)
    // wParam = nState (like WM_ACTIVATE)
    //  lParam = pointer to HWND[2]
    //  lParam[0] = hWnd getting WM_ACTIVATE
    //  lParam[1] = hWndOther
    case WM_ACTIVATETOPLEVEL:                     // 0x036E
```

```
        if (!OnActivateTopLevel(wParam, lParam))
            return Default();
        return 0;


    // lResult != 0 if 3D controls wanted
    case WM_QUERY3DCONTROLS:                    // 0x036F
        if (!OnQuery3dControls(wParam, lParam, lResult))
            return Default();
        return lResult;


    // WM_SOCKET_NOTIFY and WM_SOCKET_DEAD are used
    // internally by MFC's Windows sockets implementation.
    // For more information, see sockcore.cpp
    case WM_SOCKET_NOTIFY:                       // 0x0373
        if (!OnSocketNotify(wParam, lParam))
            return Default();
        return 0;


    case WM_SOCKET_DEAD:                         // 0x0374
        if (!OnSocketDead(wParam, lParam))
            return Default();
        return 0;


    // same as WM_SETMESSAGESTRING except not popped
    // if IsTracking()
    case WM_POPMESSAGESTRING:                    // 0x0375
        if (!OnPopMessageString(wParam, lParam, lResult))
            return Default();
        return lResult;


    // Marker used while rearranging the message queue
    case WM_QUEUE_SENTINEL:                      // 0x0379
        if (!OnQueueSentinel(wParam, lParam))
            return Default();
        return 0;
    }


// ------------------------------------------------------------
// XSEL messages
```

```
    if (WM_SETPARENTNOTIFY == nMsg)            // XSEL message
    {
        // wParam = HWND of new parent
        return OnSetParentNotify(wParam, lParam);
    }
    else if (WM_PRENCDESTROY == nMsg)          // XSEL message
    {
        // We can't handle WM_NCDESTROY as we use this message
        // to remove the subclass handler.  Instead, XSEL sends
        // the message WM_PRENCDESTROY, which is where you put
        // your code you would normally put in your
        // WM_NCDESTROY handler.

        // no valid parameters (0,0)
        return OnPreNcDestroy(wParam, lParam);
    }

    // default - call base class
    return CXSSubWndCtrl::DoWindowProc(nMsg, wParam, lParam);
}
```

CXSObject::SetParentNotify

The SetParentNotify function has been added because there are some implications if you have automatic message reflection installed and you change the parent of a control. Message reflection means that messages sent from a child control to the parent are reflected back to the code handling the control. If the parent was changed, then the automatic message reflection of this framework extension would be disrupted. So, instead of calling CWnd::SetParent, use this function for your subclassed window.

```
// --------------------------------------------------------------
// Function  :
//     CXSObject::SetParentNotify
// Purpose   :
//     Call this function to set up Parent Notification
//     Reflection for the managed child window.
//     In your own code, you should never call SetParent to
//     change the parent of your child window, unless you know
```

```
//      you have not set up Notification Reflection for the
//      parent.  If you have set up Notification Reflection, use
//      this class to change the parent.  It also uninstalls the
//      Notification event handler from the previous parent and
//      sets it up for the new parent.
// Parameters:
//      CWnd* pWnd - The CWnd to become the new parent
//                 - If pWnd is NULL, it will set up the
//                   Notification Reflection for the current
//                   parent.
// Returns   :
//      TRUE on success, FALSE on failure
//
-----------------------------------------------------------------
BOOL
CXSObject::SetParentNotify(CWnd* pWnd)
{
    HWND hWnd = pWnd - pWnd->m_hWnd : NULL;
    return DoGetWnd()->SendMessage(WM_SETPARENTNOTIFY,
        (WPARAM)hWnd, 0);
}
```

CXSObject::OnSetParentNotify

When SetParentNotify is called, it sends an XSEL message of WM_SETPARENTNOTIFY. This virtual function catches that message in case you need further processing based on the action of the parent window changing. If you derive from this class and add your own OnSetParentNotify virtual function, you should make sure to call the base implementation presented here.

```
// -----------------------------------------------------------------
// Function  :
//      CXSObject::OnSetParentNotify
// Purpose   :
//      Called when the window receives the XSEL message
//      WM_PARENTNOTIFY.  This function can be overridden by
```

```
//     derived classes.
//     See info on SetParentNotify for a full explanation.
// Parameters:
//     WPARAM wParam - HWND of new parent (may be NULL)
// Returns   :
//     TRUE on success, FALSE on failure
// --------------------------------------------------------------------
BOOL
CXSObject::OnSetParentNotify(WPARAM wParam, LPARAM lParam)
{
    // wParam = HWND of new parent

    // A request has been made to change the parent
    // We need this because if the current parent has
    // been set up to reflect notification message,
    // it will have to be removed and the new parent
    // will have to be set up

    HWND hWnd = (HWND)wParam;

    // Verify the new parent
    if (!hWnd)
    {
        // If a NULL was passed, then the code
        // retrieves the parent handle
        hWnd = ::GetParent(DoGetWnd()->m_hWnd);

        // If it's still NULL, then we are at the
        // top-most level of windows
        if (NULL == hWnd)
            return FALSE;
    }

    // Sanity check
    ASSERT(::IsWindow(hWnd));
```

```
// Make sure we're not trying to set a window to
// be its own parent
if (DoGetWnd()->m_hWnd != hWnd)
    return FALSE;

// Check to make sure the passed window is
// not already the parent
if (hWnd && DoGetWnd()->GetParent() &&
    DoGetWnd()->GetParent()->m_hWnd != hWnd)
{
    // Make windows set the new parent
    if (!::SetParent(DoGetWnd()->m_hWnd, hWnd))
        return FALSE;
}

// See if the previous parent has been set up
// for notification reflection
if (m_Notify.IsSubclassed())
{
    // Disengage it
    m_Notify.Remove();
}

// Now set up the new Parent for
// notification reflection
CWnd* pParent = DoGetWnd()->GetParent();
if (pParent && pParent->m_hWnd == hWnd)
    return m_Notify.DoInstall(pParent, this);

return FALSE;
}
```

CXSObject::CallParentDefault

CallParentDefault is much like the Default function from the base CXS-SubWndCtrl class. Default will call the next handler for a window message. CallParentDefault will send the message to the intended parent window for controls. By default, this function is called for window control messages that are not handled.

```
//
//---------------------------------------------------------------------------

// Function  :
//    CXSObject::CallParentDefault
// Purpose   :
//    Calls the parent window handler to handle the
//    Notification message.
// Parameters:
//    None
// Returns   :
//    Depends on message
// --------------------------------------------------------------------------
LRESULT
CXSObject::CallParentDefault()
{
    // Is the parent subclassed to handle the Notification
    // Reflection, and, if so, is it still a valid window?
    if (m_Notify.IsSubclassed() &&
        ::IsWindow(m_Notify.DoGetWnd()->m_hWnd))
    {
        return m_Notify.Default();
    }

    return FALSE;
}
```

CXSObject::OnPreNcDestroy

There are a couple of window messages that this framework extension cannot handle. The first message is WM_CREATE. We cannot subclass a window that does not have a valid HWND. The second message is WM_NCDESTROY. The framework extension uses this message to disengage itself automatically from any window it has subclassed. As a result, you cannot handle this message. However, just before disengagement takes place, the subclass handler will send an XSEL message of WM_PRENCDESTROY. Any code intended for an OnNcDestroy handler should be placed into the OnPreNcDestroy virtual function. However, at no time when handling code in OnPreNcDestroy should a call to the Windows API DestroyWindow be called. Since the window is in the process of being destroyed, another call to destroy the window could cause an access violation (GPF) error.

```
// -----------------------------------------------------------------
// Function  :
//     CXSObject::OnPreNcDestroy
// Purpose   :
//     Called when WM_NCDESTROY is called.  WM_NCDESTROY is the
//     last windows message received before a window is fully
//     destroyed.  The subclass handler uses this message to
//     remove (uninstall) itself as the message proc handler.
//     Because the WM_NCDESTROY message is never received by this
//     framework, the virtual function OnPreNcDestroy is called
//     before the subclass handler removes itself.
// Parameters:
//     Ignored.
// Returns   :
//     TRUE if the message was handled, FALSE if it was not.
// -----------------------------------------------------------------
BOOL
CXSObject::OnPreNcDestroy(WPARAM wParam, LPARAM lParam)
{
    return FALSE;
}
```

CXSObject::On<MessageId>

Each virtual function that handles a window or MFC message is stubbed in this class. There is no default processing and they return FALSE so that the message is handled by the next handler.

```
// -----------------------------------------------------------------
// Function :
//     CXSObject::On<MessageId>
// Purpose  :
//     The functions below are the virtual function that you will
//     override in your derived classes.  Each function returns
//     a BOOL.  This is quite simple.  If you handle the message,
//     return TRUE. If you want default processing, return FALSE.
//     Even if you handle it, but want the default processing,
//     you can return FALSE.
//     The function is passed the WPARAM and LPARAM paramaters.
//     Check with the message ID to see how they are used.
//     If the message is expected to return a value, a third
//     parameter is used, a reference to LRESULT. Set this
//     parameter to the value to return. If a function sets this
//     parameter, but returns FALSE, it will not be used.   In
this
//     case, call Default() for regular messages, of call
//     CallParentDefault() for reflected messages and return
TRUE.
// Parameters:
//     WPARAM wParam - Depends on message
//     LPARAM lParam - Depends on message
//     LRESULT& lResult - Depends on message
// Returns  :
//     BOOL - TRUE, the message was handled.
//          - FALSE, do default processing.
// -----------------------------------------------------------------
```

CXSObject::OnCreate

This message is not handled by the framework extension. You cannot sub-class a window that has not already been created and has a valid HWND.

```
BOOL
CXSObject::OnCreate(WPARAM wParam, LPARAM lParam,
                    LRESULT& lResult)
{
    // -----------------------------------------------------------
    // PLEASE NOTE!
    // -----------------------------------------------------------
    // This function will never be called.
    // -----------------------------------------------------------
    ASSERT(FALSE);
    return FALSE;
}
```

CXSObject::OnDestroy

```
BOOL
CXSObject::OnDestroy(WPARAM wParam, LPARAM lParam)
{
    return FALSE;
}
```

CXSObject::OnMove

```
BOOL
CXSObject::OnMove(WPARAM wParam, LPARAM lParam)
{
    return FALSE;
}
```

II

6

CXSObject::OnSize

```
BOOL
CXSObject::OnSize(WPARAM wParam, LPARAM lParam)
{
    return FALSE;
}
```

CXSObject::OnActivate

```
BOOL
CXSObject::OnActivate(WPARAM wParam, LPARAM lParam)
{
    return FALSE;
}
```

CXSObject::OnSetFocus

```
BOOL
CXSObject::OnSetFocus(WPARAM wParam, LPARAM lParam)
{
    return FALSE;
}
```

CXSObject::OnKillFocus

```
BOOL
CXSObject::OnKillFocus(WPARAM wParam, LPARAM lParam)
{
    return FALSE;
}
```

CXSObject::OnEnable

```
BOOL
CXSObject::OnEnable(WPARAM wParam, LPARAM lParam)
{
    return FALSE;
}
```

CXSObject::OnSetRedraw

```
BOOL
CXSObject::OnSetRedraw(WPARAM wParam, LPARAM lParam)
{
    return FALSE;
}
```

CXSObject::OnSetText

```
BOOL
CXSObject::OnSetText(WPARAM wParam, LPARAM lParam,
                     LRESULT& lResult)
{
    return FALSE;
}
```

CXSObject::OnGetText

```
BOOL
CXSObject::OnGetText(WPARAM wParam, LPARAM lParam,
                     LRESULT& lResult)
{
    return FALSE;
}
```

II

6

CXSObject::OnGetTextLength

```
BOOL
CXSObject::OnGetTextLength(WPARAM wParam, LPARAM lParam,
                            LRESULT& lResult)
{
    return FALSE;
}
```

CXSObject::OnPaint

```
BOOL
CXSObject::OnPaint(WPARAM wParam, LPARAM lParam)
{
    return FALSE;
}
```

CXSObject::OnClose

```
BOOL
CXSObject::OnClose(WPARAM wParam, LPARAM lParam)
{
    return FALSE;
}
```

CXSObject::OnQueryEndSession

```
BOOL
CXSObject::OnQueryEndSession(WPARAM wParam, LPARAM lParam,
                             LRESULT& lResult)
{
    return FALSE;
}
```

CXSObject::OnQuit

```
BOOL
CXSObject::OnQuit(WPARAM wParam, LPARAM lParam)
{
    return FALSE;
}
```

CXSObject::OnQueryOpen

```
BOOL
CXSObject::OnQueryOpen(WPARAM wParam, LPARAM lParam,
                       LRESULT& lResult)
{
    return FALSE;
}
```

CXSObject::OnEraseBkgnd

```
BOOL
CXSObject::OnEraseBkgnd(WPARAM wParam, LPARAM lParam,
                        LRESULT& lResult)
{
    return FALSE;
}
```

CXSObject::OnSysColorChange

```
BOOL
CXSObject::OnSysColorChange(WPARAM wParam, LPARAM lParam)
{
    return FALSE;
}
```

II

6

CXSObject::OnEndSession

```
BOOL
CXSObject::OnEndSession(WPARAM wParam, LPARAM lParam)
{
    return FALSE;
}
```

CXSObject::OnShowWindow

```
BOOL
CXSObject::OnShowWindow(WPARAM wParam, LPARAM lParam)
{
    return FALSE;
}
```

CXSObject::OnSettingChange

```
BOOL
CXSObject::OnSettingChange(WPARAM wParam, LPARAM lParam)
{
    return FALSE;
}
```

CXSObject::OnDevModeChange

```
BOOL
CXSObject::OnDevModeChange(WPARAM wParam, LPARAM lParam)
{
    return FALSE;
}
```

CXSObject::OnActivateApp

```
BOOL
CXSObject::OnActivateApp(WPARAM wParam, LPARAM lParam)
{
    return FALSE;
}
```

CXSObject::OnFontChange

```
BOOL
CXSObject::OnFontChange(WPARAM wParam, LPARAM lParam)
{
    return FALSE;
}
```

CXSObject::OnTimeChange

```
BOOL
CXSObject::OnTimeChange(WPARAM wParam, LPARAM lParam)
{
    return FALSE;
}
```

CXSObject::OnCancelMode

```
BOOL
CXSObject::OnCancelMode(WPARAM wParam, LPARAM lParam)
{
    return FALSE;
}
```

II

6

CXSObject::OnSetCursor

```
BOOL
CXSObject::OnSetCursor(WPARAM wParam, LPARAM lParam,
                        LRESULT& lResult)
{
    return FALSE;
}
```

CXSObject::OnMouseActivate

```
BOOL
CXSObject::OnMouseActivate(WPARAM wParam, LPARAM lParam,
                            LRESULT& lResult)
{
    return FALSE;
}
```

CXSObject::OnChildActivate

```
BOOL
CXSObject::OnChildActivate(WPARAM wParam, LPARAM lParam)
{
    return FALSE;
}
```

CXSObject::OnQueueSync

```
BOOL
CXSObject::OnQueueSync(WPARAM wParam, LPARAM lParam)
{
    return FALSE;
}
```

CXSObject::OnGetMinMaxInfo

```
BOOL
CXSObject::OnGetMinMaxInfo(WPARAM wParam, LPARAM lParam)
{
    return FALSE;
}
```

CXSObject::OnPaintIcon

```
BOOL
CXSObject::OnPaintIcon(WPARAM wParam, LPARAM lParam)
{
    return FALSE;
}
```

CXSObject::OnIconEraseBkgnd

```
BOOL
CXSObject::OnIconEraseBkgnd(WPARAM wParam, LPARAM lParam)
{
    return FALSE;
}
```

CXSObject::OnNextDlgCtl

```
BOOL
CXSObject::OnNextDlgCtl(WPARAM wParam, LPARAM lParam)
{
    return FALSE;
}
```

CXSObject::OnSpoolerStatus

```
BOOL
CXSObject::OnSpoolerStatus(WPARAM wParam, LPARAM lParam)
{
    return FALSE;
}
```

CXSObject::OnDrawItem

```
BOOL
CXSObject::OnDrawItem(WPARAM wParam, LPARAM lParam)
{
    return FALSE;
}
```

CXSObject::OnMeasureItem

```
BOOL
CXSObject::OnMeasureItem(WPARAM wParam, LPARAM lParam)
{
    return FALSE;
}
```

CXSObject::OnDeleteItem

```
BOOL
CXSObject::OnDeleteItem(WPARAM wParam, LPARAM lParam)
{
    return FALSE;
}
```

CXSObject::OnVKeyToItem

```
BOOL
CXSObject::OnVKeyToItem(WPARAM wParam, LPARAM lParam,
                        LRESULT& lResult)
{
    return FALSE;
}
```

CXSObject::OnCharToItem

```
BOOL
CXSObject::OnCharToItem(WPARAM wParam, LPARAM lParam,
                        LRESULT& lResult)
{
    return FALSE;
}
```

CXSObject::OnSetFont

```
BOOL
CXSObject::OnSetFont(WPARAM wParam, LPARAM lParam)
{
    return FALSE;
}
```

CXSObject::OnGetFont

```
BOOL
CXSObject::OnGetFont(WPARAM wParam, LPARAM lParam,
                     LRESULT& lResult)
{
    return FALSE;
}
```

II

6

CXSObject::OnSetHotKey

```
BOOL
CXSObject::OnSetHotKey(WPARAM wParam, LPARAM lParam,
                       LRESULT& lResult)
{
    return FALSE;
}
```

CXSObject::OnGetHotKey

```
BOOL
CXSObject::OnGetHotKey(WPARAM wParam, LPARAM lParam,
                       LRESULT& lResult)
{
    return FALSE;
}
```

CXSObject::OnQueryDragIcon

```
BOOL
CXSObject::OnQueryDragIcon(WPARAM wParam, LPARAM lParam,
                           LRESULT& lResult)
{
    return FALSE;
}
```

CXSObject::OnCompareItem

```
BOOL
CXSObject::OnCompareItem(WPARAM wParam, LPARAM lParam,
                         LRESULT& lResult)
{
    return FALSE;
}
```

CXSObject::OnCompacting

```
BOOL
CXSObject::OnCompacting(WPARAM wParam, LPARAM lParam)
{
    return FALSE;
}
```

CXSObject::OnWindowPosChanging

```
BOOL
CXSObject::OnWindowPosChanging(WPARAM wParam, LPARAM lParam)
{
    return FALSE;
}
```

II

CXSObject::OnWindowPosChanged

```
BOOL
CXSObject::OnWindowPosChanged(WPARAM wParam, LPARAM lParam)
{
    return FALSE;
}
```

6

CXSObject::OnPower

```
BOOL
CXSObject::OnPower(WPARAM wParam, LPARAM lParam)
{
    return FALSE;
}
```

CXSObject::OnCopyData

```
BOOL
CXSObject::OnCopyData(WPARAM wParam, LPARAM lParam)
{
    return FALSE;
}
```

CXSObject::OnNotify

```
BOOL
CXSObject::OnNotify(WPARAM wParam, LPARAM lParam,
                    LRESULT& lResult)
{
    return FALSE;
}
```

CXSObject::OnInputLangChangeRequest

```
BOOL
CXSObject::OnInputLangChangeRequest(WPARAM wParam, LPARAM
lParam)
{
    return FALSE;
}
```

CXSObject::OnInputLangChange

```
BOOL
CXSObject::OnInputLangChange(WPARAM wParam, LPARAM lParam)
{
    return FALSE;
}
```

CXSObject::OnTCard

```
BOOL
CXSObject::OnTCard(WPARAM wParam, LPARAM lParam)
{
    return FALSE;
}
```

CXSObject::OnHelp

```
BOOL
CXSObject::OnHelp(WPARAM wParam, LPARAM lParam)
{
    return FALSE;
}
```

II

CXSObject::OnUserChanged

```
BOOL
CXSObject::OnUserChanged(WPARAM wParam, LPARAM lParam)
{
    return FALSE;
}
```

6

CXSObject::OnNotifyFormat

```
BOOL
CXSObject::OnNotifyFormat(WPARAM wParam, LPARAM lParam,
                          LRESULT& lResult)
{
    return FALSE;
}
```

CXSObject::OnContextMenu

```
BOOL
CXSObject::OnContextMenu(WPARAM wParam, LPARAM lParam)
{
    return FALSE;
}
```

CXSObject::OnStyleChanging

```
BOOL
CXSObject::OnStyleChanging(WPARAM wParam, LPARAM lParam)
{
    return FALSE;
}
```

CXSObject::OnStyleChanged

```
BOOL
CXSObject::OnStyleChanged(WPARAM wParam, LPARAM lParam)
{
    return FALSE;
}
```

CXSObject::OnDisplayChange

```
BOOL
CXSObject::OnDisplayChange(WPARAM wParam, LPARAM lParam)
{
    return FALSE;
}
```

CXSObject::OnGetIcon

```
BOOL
CXSObject::OnGetIcon(WPARAM wParam, LPARAM lParam,
                     LRESULT& lResult)
{
    return FALSE;
}
```

CXSObject::OnSetIcon

```
BOOL
CXSObject::OnSetIcon(WPARAM wParam, LPARAM lParam,
                     LRESULT& lResult)
{
    return FALSE;
}
```

CXSObject::OnNcCreate

```
BOOL
CXSObject::OnNcCreate(WPARAM wParam, LPARAM lParam)
{
    return FALSE;
}
```

CXSObject::OnNcDestroy

```
BOOL
CXSObject::OnNcDestroy(WPARAM wParam, LPARAM lParam)
{
    // ------------------------------------------------------------
    // PLEASE NOTE!
    // ------------------------------------------------------------
    // This function will never be called.  The subclass handler
    // uses the WM_NCDESTROY function to uninstall it's
```

```
      // window procedure from the window.  However, before doing
      // this, it sends an XSEL message, WM_PRENCDESTROY, which
      // is caught in the virtual function OnPreNcDestroy.  Use
      // this function instead to do your WM_NCDESTROY work.
      // Immediately following this function, the subclass
      // handler
      // will be uninstalled and the HWND will be destroyed.
      // -----------------------------------------------------------
      ASSERT(FALSE);
      return FALSE;
}
```

CXSObject::OnNcCalcSize

```
BOOL
CXSObject::OnNcCalcSize(WPARAM wParam, LPARAM lParam,
                        LRESULT& lResult)

{
    return FALSE;
}
```

CXSObject::OnNcHitTest

```
BOOL
CXSObject::OnNcHitTest(WPARAM wParam, LPARAM lParam,
                       LRESULT& lResult)

{
    return FALSE;
}
```

CXSObject::OnNcPaint

```
BOOL
CXSObject::OnNcPaint(WPARAM wParam, LPARAM lParam)
{
    return FALSE;
}
```

CXSObject::OnNcActivate

```
BOOL
CXSObject::OnNcActivate(WPARAM wParam, LPARAM lParam,
                        LRESULT& lResult)
{
    return FALSE;
}
```

II

CXSObject::OnGetDlgCode

```
BOOL
CXSObject::OnGetDlgCode(WPARAM wParam, LPARAM lParam,
                        LRESULT& lResult)
{
    return FALSE;
}
```

6

CXSObject::OnNcMouseMove

```
BOOL
CXSObject::OnNcMouseMove(WPARAM wParam, LPARAM lParam)
{
    return FALSE;
}
```

CXSObject::OnNcLButtonDown

```
BOOL
CXSObject::OnNcLButtonDown(WPARAM wParam, LPARAM lParam)
{
    return FALSE;
}
```

CXSObject::OnNcLButtonUp

```
BOOL
CXSObject::OnNcLButtonUp(WPARAM wParam, LPARAM lParam)
{
    return FALSE;
}
```

CXSObject::OnNcLButtonDblClk

```
BOOL
CXSObject::OnNcLButtonDblClk(WPARAM wParam, LPARAM lParam)
{
    return FALSE;
}
```

CXSObject::OnNcRButtonDown

```
BOOL
CXSObject::OnNcRButtonDown(WPARAM wParam, LPARAM lParam)
{
    return FALSE;
}
```

CXSObject::OnNcRButtonUp

```
BOOL
CXSObject::OnNcRButtonUp(WPARAM wParam, LPARAM lParam)
{
    return FALSE;
}
```

CXSObject::OnNcRButtonDblClk

```
BOOL
CXSObject::OnNcRButtonDblClk(WPARAM wParam, LPARAM lParam)
{
    return FALSE;
}
```

II

CXSObject::OnNcButtonDown

```
BOOL
CXSObject::OnNcButtonDown(WPARAM wParam, LPARAM lParam)
{
    return FALSE;
}
```

6

CXSObject::OnNcMButtonUp

```
BOOL
CXSObject::OnNcMButtonUp(WPARAM wParam, LPARAM lParam)
{
    return FALSE;
}
```

CXSObject::OnNcMButtonDblClk

```
BOOL
CXSObject::OnNcMButtonDblClk(WPARAM wParam, LPARAM lParam)
{
    return FALSE;
}
```

CXSObject::OnNcMouseHover

```
BOOL
CXSObject::OnNcMouseHover(WPARAM wParam, LPARAM lParam)
{
    return FALSE;
}
```

CXSObject::OnNcMouseLeave

```
BOOL
CXSObject::OnNcMouseLeave(WPARAM wParam, LPARAM lParam)
{
    return FALSE;
}
```

CXSObject::OnKeyDown

```
BOOL
CXSObject::OnKeyDown(WPARAM wParam, LPARAM lParam)
{
    return FALSE;
}
```

CXSObject::OnKeyUp

```
BOOL
CXSObject::OnKeyUp(WPARAM wParam, LPARAM lParam)
{
    return FALSE;
}
```

CXSObject::OnChar

```
BOOL
CXSObject::OnChar(WPARAM wParam, LPARAM lParam)
{
    return FALSE;
}
```

CXSObject::OnDeadChar

```
BOOL
CXSObject::OnDeadChar(WPARAM wParam, LPARAM lParam)
{
    return FALSE;
}
```

CXSObject::OnSysKeyDown

```
BOOL
CXSObject::OnSysKeyDown(WPARAM wParam, LPARAM lParam)
{
    return FALSE;
}
```

II

6

CXSObject::OnSysKeyUp

```
BOOL
CXSObject::OnSysKeyUp(WPARAM wParam, LPARAM lParam)
{
    return FALSE;
}
```

CXSObject::OnSysChar

```
BOOL
CXSObject::OnSysChar(WPARAM wParam, LPARAM lParam)
{
    return FALSE;
}
```

CXSObject::OnSysDeadChar

```
BOOL
CXSObject::OnSysDeadChar(WPARAM wParam, LPARAM lParam)
{
    return FALSE;
}
```

CXSObject::OnInitDialog

```
BOOL
CXSObject::OnInitDialog(WPARAM wParam, LPARAM lParam,
                        LRESULT& lResult)
{
    return FALSE;
}
```

CXSObject::OnCommand

```
BOOL
CXSObject::OnCommand(WPARAM wParam, LPARAM lParam)
{
    return FALSE;
}
```

CXSObject::OnSysCommand

```
BOOL
CXSObject::OnSysCommand(WPARAM wParam, LPARAM lParam)
{
    return FALSE;
}
```

II

CXSObject::OnTimer

```
BOOL
CXSObject::OnTimer(WPARAM wParam, LPARAM lParam)
{
    return FALSE;
}
```

6

CXSObject::OnHScroll

```
BOOL
CXSObject::OnHScroll(WPARAM wParam, LPARAM lParam)
{
    return FALSE;
}
```

CXSObject::OnVScroll

```
BOOL
CXSObject::OnVScroll(WPARAM wParam, LPARAM lParam)
{
    return FALSE;
}
```

CXSObject::OnInitMenu

```
BOOL
CXSObject::OnInitMenu(WPARAM wParam, LPARAM lParam)
{
    return FALSE;
}
```

CXSObject::OnInitMenuPopup

```
BOOL
CXSObject::OnInitMenuPopup(WPARAM wParam, LPARAM lParam)
{
    return FALSE;
}
```

CXSObject::OnMenuSelect

```
BOOL
CXSObject::OnMenuSelect(WPARAM wParam, LPARAM lParam)
{
    return FALSE;
}
```

CXSObject::OnMenuChar

```
BOOL
CXSObject::OnMenuChar(WPARAM wParam, LPARAM lParam,
                      LRESULT& lResult)
{
    return FALSE;
}
```

CXSObject::OnEnterIdle

```
BOOL
CXSObject::OnEnterIdle(WPARAM wParam, LPARAM lParam)
{
    return FALSE;
}
```

CXSObject::OnCtlColorMsgBox

```
BOOL
CXSObject::OnCtlColorMsgBox(WPARAM wParam, LPARAM lParam,
                           LRESULT& lResult)
{
    return FALSE;
}
```

CXSObject::OnCtlColorEdit

```
BOOL
CXSObject::OnCtlColorEdit(WPARAM wParam, LPARAM lParam,
                          LRESULT& lResult)
{
    return FALSE;
}
```

CXSObject::OnCtlColorListBox

```
BOOL
CXSObject::OnCtlColorListBox(WPARAM wParam, LPARAM lParam,
                            LRESULT& lResult)
{
    return FALSE;
}
```

CXSObject::OnCtlColorBtn

```
BOOL
CXSObject::OnCtlColorBtn(WPARAM wParam, LPARAM lParam,
                        LRESULT& lResult)
{
    return FALSE;
}
```

CXSObject::OnCtlColorDlg

```
BOOL
CXSObject::OnCtlColorDlg(WPARAM wParam, LPARAM lParam,
                        LRESULT& lResult)
{
    return FALSE;
}
```

CXSObject::OnCtlColorScrollBar

```
BOOL
CXSObject::OnCtlColorScrollBar(WPARAM wParam, LPARAM lParam,
                              LRESULT& lResult)
{
    return FALSE;
}
```

CXSObject::OnCtlColorStatic

```
BOOL
CXSObject::OnCtlColorStatic(WPARAM wParam, LPARAM lParam,
                                 LRESULT& lResult)
{
    return FALSE;
}
```

CXSObject::OnMouseMove

```
BOOL
CXSObject::OnMouseMove(WPARAM wParam, LPARAM lParam)
{
    return FALSE;
}
```

CXSObject::OnLButtonDown

```
BOOL
CXSObject::OnLButtonDown(WPARAM wParam, LPARAM lParam)
{
    return FALSE;
}
```

CXSObject::OnLButtonUp

```
BOOL
CXSObject::OnLButtonUp(WPARAM wParam, LPARAM lParam)
{
    return FALSE;
}
```

II

6

CXSObject::OnLButtonDblClk

```
BOOL
CXSObject::OnLButtonDblClk(WPARAM wParam, LPARAM lParam)
{
    return FALSE;
}
```

CXSObject::OnRButtonDown

```
BOOL
CXSObject::OnRButtonDown(WPARAM wParam, LPARAM lParam)
{
    return FALSE;
}
```

CXSObject::OnRButtonUp

```
BOOL
CXSObject::OnRButtonUp(WPARAM wParam, LPARAM lParam)
{
    return FALSE;
}
```

CXSObject::OnRButtonDblClk

```
BOOL
CXSObject::OnRButtonDblClk(WPARAM wParam, LPARAM lParam)
{
    return FALSE;
}
```

CXSObject::OnMButtonDown

```
BOOL
CXSObject::OnMButtonDown(WPARAM wParam, LPARAM lParam)
{
    return FALSE;
}
```

CXSObject::OnMButtonUp

```
BOOL
CXSObject::OnMButtonUp(WPARAM wParam, LPARAM lParam)
{
    return FALSE;
}
```

II

CXSObject::OnMButtonDblClk

```
BOOL
CXSObject::OnMButtonDblClk(WPARAM wParam, LPARAM lParam)
{
    return FALSE;
}
```

6

CXSObject::OnMouseWheel

```
BOOL
CXSObject::OnMouseWheel(WPARAM wParam, LPARAM lParam)
{
    return FALSE;
}
```

CXSObject::OnParentNotify

```
BOOL
CXSObject::OnParentNotify(WPARAM wParam, LPARAM lParam)
{
    return FALSE;
}
```

CXSObject::OnEnterMenuLoop

```
BOOL
CXSObject::OnEnterMenuLoop(WPARAM wParam, LPARAM lParam)
{
    return FALSE;
}
```

CXSObject::OnExitMenuLoop

```
BOOL
CXSObject::OnExitMenuLoop(WPARAM wParam, LPARAM lParam)
{
    return FALSE;
}
```

CXSObject::OnNextMenu

```
BOOL
CXSObject::OnNextMenu(WPARAM wParam, LPARAM lParam)
{
    return FALSE;
}
```

CXSObject::OnSizing

```
BOOL
CXSObject::OnSizing(WPARAM wParam, LPARAM lParam)
{
    return FALSE;
}
```

CXSObject::OnCaptureChanged

```
BOOL
CXSObject::OnCaptureChanged(WPARAM wParam, LPARAM lParam)
{
    return FALSE;
}
```

CXSObject::OnMoving

```
BOOL
CXSObject::OnMoving(WPARAM wParam, LPARAM lParam)
{
    return FALSE;
}
```

CXSObject::OnPowerBroadcast

```
BOOL
CXSObject::OnPowerBroadcast(WPARAM wParam, LPARAM lParam,
                            LRESULT& lResult)
{
    return FALSE;
}
```

II

6

CXSObject::OnDeviceChange

```
BOOL
CXSObject::OnDeviceChange(WPARAM wParam, LPARAM lParam,
                          LRESULT& lResult)
{
    return FALSE;
}
```

CXSObject::OnMdiCreate

```
BOOL
CXSObject::OnMdiCreate(WPARAM wParam, LPARAM lParam,
                       LRESULT& lResult)
{
    return FALSE;
}
```

CXSObject::OnMdiDestroy

```
BOOL
CXSObject::OnMdiDestroy(WPARAM wParam, LPARAM lParam)
{
    return FALSE;
}
```

CXSObject::OnMdiActivate

```
BOOL
CXSObject::OnMdiActivate(WPARAM wParam, LPARAM lParam)
{
    return FALSE;
}
```

CXSObject::OnMdiRestore

```
BOOL
CXSObject::OnMdiRestore(WPARAM wParam, LPARAM lParam)
{
    return FALSE;
}
```

CXSObject::OnMdiNext

```
BOOL
CXSObject::OnMdiNext(WPARAM wParam, LPARAM lParam)
{
    return FALSE;
}
```

CXSObject::OnMdiMaximize

```
BOOL
CXSObject::OnMdiMaximize(WPARAM wParam, LPARAM lParam)
{
    return FALSE;
}
```

CXSObject::OnMdiTile

```
BOOL
CXSObject::OnMdiTile(WPARAM wParam, LPARAM lParam,
                     LRESULT& lResult)
{
    return FALSE;
}
```

CXSObject::OnMdiCascade

```
BOOL
CXSObject::OnMdiCascade(WPARAM wParam, LPARAM lParam,
                        LRESULT& lResult)

{

    return FALSE;

}
```

CXSObject::OnMdiIconArrange

```
BOOL
CXSObject::OnMdiIconArrange(WPARAM wParam, LPARAM lParam)
{

    return FALSE;

}
```

CXSObject::OnMdiGetActive

```
BOOL
CXSObject::OnMdiGetActive(WPARAM wParam, LPARAM lParam,
                          LRESULT& lResult)

{

    return FALSE;

}
```

CXSObject::OnMdiSetMenu

```
BOOL
CXSObject::OnMdiSetMenu(WPARAM wParam, LPARAM lParam,
                        LRESULT& lResult)

{

    return FALSE;

}
```

CXSObject::OnEnterSizeMove

```
BOOL
CXSObject::OnEnterSizeMove(WPARAM wParam, LPARAM lParam)
{
    return FALSE;
}
```

CXSObject::OnExitSizeMove

```
BOOL
CXSObject::OnExitSizeMove(WPARAM wParam, LPARAM lParam)
{
    return FALSE;
}
```

II

CXSObject::OnDropFiles

```
BOOL
CXSObject::OnDropFiles(WPARAM wParam, LPARAM lParam)
{
    return FALSE;
}
```

6

CXSObject::OnMdiRefreshMenu

```
BOOL
CXSObject::OnMdiRefreshMenu(WPARAM wParam, LPARAM lParam,
                            LRESULT& lResult)
{
    return FALSE;
}
```

CXSObject::OnMouseHover

```
BOOL
CXSObject::OnMouseHover(WPARAM wParam, LPARAM lParam)
{
    return FALSE;
}
```

CXSObject::OnMouseLeave

```
BOOL
CXSObject::OnMouseLeave(WPARAM wParam, LPARAM lParam)
{
    return FALSE;
}
```

CXSObject::OnCut

```
BOOL
CXSObject::OnCut(WPARAM wParam, LPARAM lParam)
{
    return FALSE;
}
```

CXSObject::OnCopy

```
BOOL
CXSObject::OnCopy(WPARAM wParam, LPARAM lParam)
{
    return FALSE;
}
```

CXSObject::OnPaste

```
BOOL
CXSObject::OnPaste(WPARAM wParam, LPARAM lParam)
{
    return FALSE;
}
```

CXSObject::OnClear

```
BOOL
CXSObject::OnClear(WPARAM wParam, LPARAM lParam)
{
    return FALSE;
}
```

CXSObject::OnUndo

```
BOOL
CXSObject::OnUndo(WPARAM wParam, LPARAM lParam)
{
    return FALSE;
}
```

CXSObject::OnRenderFormat

```
BOOL
CXSObject::OnRenderFormat(WPARAM wParam, LPARAM lParam)
{
    return FALSE;
}
```

II

6

CXSObject::OnRenderAllFormats

```
BOOL
CXSObject::OnRenderAllFormats(WPARAM wParam, LPARAM lParam)
{
    return FALSE;
}
```

CXSObject::OnDestroyClipboard

```
BOOL
CXSObject::OnDestroyClipboard(WPARAM wParam, LPARAM lParam)
{
    return FALSE;
}
```

CXSObject::OnDrawClipboard

```
BOOL
CXSObject::OnDrawClipboard(WPARAM wParam, LPARAM lParam)
{
    return FALSE;
}
```

CXSObject::OnPaintClipboard

```
BOOL
CXSObject::OnPaintClipboard(WPARAM wParam, LPARAM lParam)
{
    return FALSE;
}
```

CXSObject::OnVScrollClipboard

```
BOOL
CXSObject::OnVScrollClipboard(WPARAM wParam, LPARAM lParam)
{
    return FALSE;
}
```

CXSObject::OnSizeClipboard

```
BOOL
CXSObject::OnSizeClipboard(WPARAM wParam, LPARAM lParam)
{
    return FALSE;
}
```

II

CXSObject::OnAskCbFormatName

```
BOOL
CXSObject::OnAskCbFormatName(WPARAM wParam, LPARAM lParam)
{
    return FALSE;
}
```

6

CXSObject::OnChangeCbChain

```
BOOL
CXSObject::OnChangeCbChain(WPARAM wParam, LPARAM lParam)
{
    return FALSE;
}
```

CXSObject::OnHScrollClipboard

```
BOOL
CXSObject::OnHScrollClipboard(WPARAM wParam, LPARAM lParam)
{
    return FALSE;
}
```

CXSObject::OnQueryNewPalette

```
BOOL
CXSObject::OnQueryNewPalette(WPARAM wParam, LPARAM lParam,
                             LRESULT& lResult)
{
    return FALSE;
}
```

CXSObject::OnPaletteIsChanging

```
BOOL
CXSObject::OnPaletteIsChanging(WPARAM wParam, LPARAM lParam)
{
    return FALSE;
}
```

CXSObject::OnPaletteChanged

```
BOOL
CXSObject::OnPaletteChanged(WPARAM wParam, LPARAM lParam)
{
    return FALSE;
}
```

CXSObject::OnHotKey

```
BOOL
CXSObject::OnHotKey(WPARAM wParam, LPARAM lParam)
{
    return FALSE;
}
```

CXSObject::OnPrint

```
BOOL
CXSObject::OnPrint(WPARAM wParam, LPARAM lParam)
{
    return FALSE;
}
```

CXSObject::OnPrintClient

```
BOOL
CXSObject::OnPrintClient(WPARAM wParam, LPARAM lParam)
{
    return FALSE;
}
```

CXSObject::OnNotifyOutOfMemory

```
BOOL
CXSObject::OnNotifyOutOfMemory(WPARAM wParam, LPARAM lParam)
{
    return FALSE;
}
```

CXSObject::OnNotifyClick

```
BOOL
CXSObject::OnNotifyClick(WPARAM wParam, LPARAM lParam)
{
    return FALSE;
}
```

CXSObject::OnNotifyDblClk

```
BOOL
CXSObject::OnNotifyDblClk(WPARAM wParam, LPARAM lParam)
{
    return FALSE;
}
```

CXSObject::OnNotifyReturn

```
BOOL
CXSObject::OnNotifyReturn(WPARAM wParam, LPARAM lParam)
{
    return FALSE;
}
```

CXSObject::OnNotifyRClick

```
BOOL
CXSObject::OnNotifyRClick(WPARAM wParam, LPARAM lParam,
                          LRESULT& lResult)
{
    return FALSE;
}
```

CXSObject::OnNotifyRDblClk

```
BOOL
CXSObject::OnNotifyRDblClk(WPARAM wParam, LPARAM lParam,
                           LRESULT& lResult)
{
    return FALSE;
}
```

CXSObject::OnNotifySetFocus

```
BOOL
CXSObject::OnNotifySetFocus(WPARAM wParam, LPARAM lParam)
{
    return FALSE;
}
```

CXSObject::OnNotifyKillFocus

```
BOOL
CXSObject::OnNotifyKillFocus(WPARAM wParam, LPARAM lParam)
{
    return FALSE;
}
```

CXSObject::OnNotifyCustomDraw

```
BOOL
CXSObject::OnNotifyCustomDraw(WPARAM wParam, LPARAM lParam)
{
    return FALSE;
}
```

II

6

CXSObject::OnNotifyHover

```
BOOL
CXSObject::OnNotifyHover(WPARAM wParam, LPARAM lParam,
                         LRESULT& lResult)

{
    return FALSE;
}
```

CXSObject::OnNotifyNcHitTest

```
BOOL
CXSObject::OnNotifyNcHitTest(WPARAM wParam, LPARAM lParam,
                             LRESULT& lResult)

{
    return FALSE;
}
```

CXSObject::OnNotifyKeyDown

```
BOOL
CXSObject::OnNotifyKeyDown(WPARAM wParam, LPARAM lParam,
                           LRESULT& lResult)

{
    return FALSE;
}
```

CXSObject::OnNotifyReleasedCapture

```
BOOL
CXSObject::OnNotifyReleasedCapture(WPARAM wParam, LPARAM
lParam)
{
    return FALSE;
}
```

CXSObject::OnNotifySetCursor

```
BOOL
CXSObject::OnNotifySetCursor(WPARAM wParam, LPARAM lParam,
                            LRESULT& lResult)
{
    return FALSE;
}
```

CXSObject::OnNotifyChar

```
BOOL
CXSObject::OnNotifyChar(WPARAM wParam, LPARAM lParam)
{
    return FALSE;
}
```

CXSObject::OnNotifyTooltipsCreated

```
BOOL
CXSObject::OnNotifyTooltipsCreated(WPARAM wParam, LPARAM
lParam,
{
    return FALSE;
}
```

CXSObject::OnPropSheetApply

```
BOOL
CXSObject::OnPropSheetApply(WPARAM wParam, LPARAM lParam,
                           LRESULT& lResult)
{
    return FALSE;
}
```

CXSObject::OnPropSheetGetObject

```
BOOL
CXSObject::OnPropSheetGetObject(WPARAM wParam, LPARAM lParam)
{
    return FALSE;
}
```

CXSObject::OnPropSheetHelp

```
BOOL
CXSObject::OnPropSheetHelp(WPARAM wParam, LPARAM lParam)
{
    return FALSE;
}
```

CXSObject::OnPropSheetKillActive

```
BOOL
CXSObject::OnPropSheetKillActive(WPARAM wParam, LPARAM lParam,
                                 LRESULT& lResult)
{
    return FALSE;
}
```

CXSObject::OnPropSheetQueryCancel

```
BOOL
CXSObject::OnPropSheetQueryCancel(WPARAM wParam, LPARAM lParam,
                                  LRESULT& lResult)
{
    return FALSE;
}
```

CXSObject::OnPropSheetReset

```
BOOL
CXSObject::OnPropSheetReset(WPARAM wParam, LPARAM lParam,
                                LRESULT& lResult)
{
    return FALSE;
}
```

CXSObject::OnPropSheetSetActive

```
BOOL
CXSObject::OnPropSheetSetActive(WPARAM wParam, LPARAM lParam,
                                LRESULT& lResult)
{
    return FALSE;
}
```

CXSObject::OnPropSheetWizBack

```
BOOL
CXSObject::OnPropSheetWizBack(WPARAM wParam, LPARAM lParam,
                                LRESULT& lResult)
{
    return FALSE;
}
```

CXSObject::OnPropSheetWizFinish

```
BOOL
CXSObject::OnPropSheetWizFinish(WPARAM wParam, LPARAM lParam,
                                LRESULT& lResult)
{
    return FALSE;
}
```

CXSObject::OnPropSheetWizNext

```
BOOL
CXSObject::OnPropSheetWizNext(WPARAM wParam, LPARAM lParam,
                                  LRESULT& lResult)
{
    return FALSE;
}
```

CXSObject::OnHeaderBeginDrag

```
BOOL
CXSObject::OnHeaderBeginDrag(WPARAM wParam, LPARAM lParam)
{
    return FALSE;
}
```

CXSObject::OnHeaderEndDrag

```
BOOL
CXSObject::OnHeaderEndDrag(WPARAM wParam, LPARAM lParam)
{
    return FALSE;
}
```

CXSObject::OnHeaderItemChanging

```
BOOL
CXSObject::OnHeaderItemChanging(WPARAM wParam, LPARAM lParam,
                                  LRESULT& lResult)
{
    return FALSE;
}
```

CXSObject::OnHeaderItemChanged

```
BOOL
CXSObject::OnHeaderItemChanged(WPARAM wParam, LPARAM lParam)
{
    return FALSE;
}
```

CXSObject::OnHeaderItemClicked

```
BOOL
CXSObject::OnHeaderItemClicked(WPARAM wParam, LPARAM lParam)
{
    return FALSE;
}
```

CXSObject::OnHeaderItemDblClick

```
BOOL
CXSObject::OnHeaderItemDblClick(WPARAM wParam, LPARAM lParam)
{
    return FALSE;
}
```

CXSObject::OnHeaderDividerDblClick

```
BOOL
CXSObject::OnHeaderDividerDblClick(WPARAM wParam, LPARAM
lParam)
{
    return FALSE;
}
```

II

6

CXSObject::OnHeaderBeginTrack

```
BOOL
CXSObject::OnHeaderBeginTrack(WPARAM wParam, LPARAM lParam,
                             LRESULT& lResult)
{
    return FALSE;
}
```

CXSObject::OnHeaderEndTrack

```
BOOL
CXSObject::OnHeaderEndTrack(WPARAM wParam, LPARAM lParam)
{
    return FALSE;
}
```

CXSObject::OnHeaderTrack

```
BOOL
CXSObject::OnHeaderTrack(WPARAM wParam, LPARAM lParam,
                        LRESULT& lResult)
{
    return FALSE;
}
```

CXSObject::OnHeaderGetDispInfo

```
BOOL
CXSObject::OnHeaderGetDispInfo(WPARAM wParam, LPARAM lParam)
{
    return FALSE;
}
```

CXSObject::OnToolbarGetButtonInfo

```
BOOL
CXSObject::OnToolbarGetButtonInfo(WPARAM wParam, LPARAM lParam,
                                  LRESULT& lResult)
{
    return FALSE;
}
```

CXSObject::OnToolbarBeginDrag

```
BOOL
CXSObject::OnToolbarBeginDrag(WPARAM wParam, LPARAM lParam)
{
    return FALSE;
}
```

II

CXSObject::OnToolbarEndDrag

```
BOOL
CXSObject::OnToolbarEndDrag(WPARAM wParam, LPARAM lParam)
{
    return FALSE;
}
```

6

CXSObject::OnToolbarBeginAdjust

```
BOOL
CXSObject::OnToolbarBeginAdjust(WPARAM wParam, LPARAM lParam)
{
    return FALSE;
}
```

CXSObject::OnToolbarEndAdjust

```
BOOL
CXSObject::OnToolbarEndAdjust(WPARAM wParam, LPARAM lParam)
{
    return FALSE;
}
```

CXSObject::OnToolbarReset

```
BOOL
CXSObject::OnToolbarReset(WPARAM wParam, LPARAM lParam)
{
    return FALSE;
}
```

CXSObject::OnToolbarQueryInsert

```
BOOL
CXSObject::OnToolbarQueryInsert(WPARAM wParam, LPARAM lParam,
                                LRESULT& lResult)
{
    return FALSE;
}
```

CXSObject::OnToolbarQueryDelete

```
BOOL
CXSObject::OnToolbarQueryDelete(WPARAM wParam, LPARAM lParam,
                                LRESULT& lResult)
{
    return FALSE;
}
```

CXSObject::OnToolbarToolbarChange

```
BOOL
CXSObject::OnToolbarToolbarChange(WPARAM wParam, LPARAM lParam)
{
    return FALSE;
}
```

CXSObject::OnToolbarCustHelp

```
BOOL
CXSObject::OnToolbarCustHelp(WPARAM wParam, LPARAM lParam)
{
    return FALSE;
}
```

CXSObject::OnToolbarDropDown

```
BOOL
CXSObject::OnToolbarDropDown(WPARAM wParam, LPARAM lParam,
                            LRESULT& lResult)
{
    return FALSE;
}
```

CXSObject::OnToolbarGetObject

```
BOOL
CXSObject::OnToolbarGetObject(WPARAM wParam, LPARAM lParam)
{
    return FALSE;
}
```

II

6

CXSObject::OnToolbarHotItemChange

```
BOOL
CXSObject::OnToolbarHotItemChange(WPARAM wParam, LPARAM lParam,
                                  LRESULT& lResult)
{
    return FALSE;
}
```

CXSObject::OnToolbarDragOut

```
BOOL
CXSObject::OnToolbarDragOut(WPARAM wParam, LPARAM lParam)
{
    return FALSE;
}
```

CXSObject::OnToolbarDeletingButton

```
BOOL
CXSObject::OnToolbarDeletingButton(WPARAM wParam, LPARAM
lParam)
{
    return FALSE;
}
```

CXSObject::OnToolbarGetDispInfo

```
BOOL
CXSObject::OnToolbarGetDispInfo(WPARAM wParam, LPARAM lParam)
{
    return FALSE;
}
```

CXSObject::OnToolbarGetInfoTip

```
BOOL
CXSObject::OnToolbarGetInfoTip(WPARAM wParam, LPARAM lParam)
{
    return FALSE;
}
```

CXSObject::OnRebarHeightChange

```
BOOL
CXSObject::OnRebarHeightChange(WPARAM wParam, LPARAM lParam)
{
    return FALSE;
}
```

CXSObject::OnRebarGetObject

```
BOOL
CXSObject::OnRebarGetObject(WPARAM wParam, LPARAM lParam)
{
    return FALSE;
}
```

CXSObject::OnRebarLayoutChanged

```
BOOL
CXSObject::OnRebarLayoutChanged(WPARAM wParam, LPARAM lParam)
{
    return FALSE;
}
```

II

6

CXSObject::OnRebarAutoSize

```
BOOL
CXSObject::OnRebarAutoSize(WPARAM wParam, LPARAM lParam)
{
    return FALSE;
}
```

CXSObject::OnRebarBeginDrag

```
BOOL
CXSObject::OnRebarBeginDrag(WPARAM wParam, LPARAM lParam,
                            LRESULT& lResult)
{
    return FALSE;
}
```

CXSObject::OnRebarEndDrag

```
BOOL
CXSObject::OnRebarEndDrag(WPARAM wParam, LPARAM lParam)
{
    return FALSE;
}
```

CXSObject::OnRebarDeletingBand

```
BOOL
CXSObject::OnRebarDeletingBand(WPARAM wParam, LPARAM lParam)
{
    return FALSE;
}
```

CXSObject::OnRebarDeleteBand

```
BOOL
CXSObject::OnRebarDeleteBand(WPARAM wParam, LPARAM lParam)
{
    return FALSE;
}
```

CXSObject::OnRebarChildSize

```
BOOL
CXSObject::OnRebarChildSize(WPARAM wParam, LPARAM lParam)
{
    return FALSE;
}
```

CXSObject::OnTooltipGetDispInfo

```
BOOL
CXSObject::OnTooltipGetDispInfo(WPARAM wParam, LPARAM lParam)
{
    return FALSE;
}
```

CXSObject::OnTooltipNeedText

```
BOOL
CXSObject::OnTooltipNeedText(WPARAM wParam, LPARAM lParam)
{
    return FALSE;
}
```

II

6

CXSObject::OnTooltipShow

```
BOOL
CXSObject::OnTooltipShow(WPARAM wParam, LPARAM lParam)
{
    return FALSE;
}
```

CXSObject::OnTooltipPop

```
BOOL
CXSObject::OnTooltipPop(WPARAM wParam, LPARAM lParam)
{
    return FALSE;
}
```

CXSObject::OnStatusBarSimpleModeChange

```
BOOL
CXSObject::OnStatusBarSimpleModeChange(WPARAM wParam, LPARAM lParam)
{
    return FALSE;
}
```

CXSObject::OnUpDownDeltaPos

```
BOOL
CXSObject::OnUpDownDeltaPos(WPARAM wParam, LPARAM lParam,
                           LRESULT& lResult)
{
    return FALSE;
}
```

CXSObject::OnListviewItemChanging

```
BOOL
CXSObject::OnListviewItemChanging(WPARAM wParam, LPARAM lParam,
                                  LRESULT& lResult)
{
    return FALSE;
}
```

CXSObject::OnListviewItemChanged

```
BOOL
CXSObject::OnListviewItemChanged(WPARAM wParam, LPARAM lParam)
{
    return FALSE;
}
```

CXSObject::OnListviewInsertItem

```
BOOL
CXSObject::OnListviewInsertItem(WPARAM wParam, LPARAM lParam)
{
    return FALSE;
}
```

CXSObject::OnListviewDeleteItem

```
BOOL
CXSObject::OnListviewDeleteItem(WPARAM wParam, LPARAM lParam)
{
    return FALSE;
}
```

II

6

CXSObject::OnListviewDeleteAllItems

```
BOOL
CXSObject::OnListviewDeleteAllItems(WPARAM wParam,
                                    LPARAM lParam,
                                    LRESULT& lResult)

{
    return FALSE;
}
```

CXSObject::OnListviewBeginLabelEdit

```
BOOL
CXSObject::OnListviewBeginLabelEdit(WPARAM wParam, LPARAM
lParam,
                                    LRESULT& lResult)

{
    return FALSE;
}
```

CXSObject::OnListviewEndLabelEdit

```
BOOL
CXSObject::OnListviewEndLabelEdit(WPARAM wParam, LPARAM lParam,
                                  LRESULT& lResult)

{
    return FALSE;
}
```

CXSObject::OnListviewColumnClick

```
BOOL
CXSObject::OnListviewColumnClick(WPARAM wParam, LPARAM lParam)
{
    return FALSE;
}
```

CXSObject::OnListviewBeginDrag

```
BOOL
CXSObject::OnListviewBeginDrag(WPARAM wParam, LPARAM lParam)
{
    return FALSE;
}
```

CXSObject::OnListviewBeginRDrag

```
BOOL
CXSObject::OnListviewBeginRDrag(WPARAM wParam, LPARAM lParam)
{
    return FALSE;
}
```

II

CXSObject::OnListviewOdCacheHit

```
BOOL
CXSObject::OnListviewOdCacheHit(WPARAM wParam, LPARAM lParam)
{
    return FALSE;
}
```

6

CXSObject::OnListviewOdFindItem

```
BOOL
CXSObject::OnListviewOdFindItem(WPARAM wParam, LPARAM lParam)
{
    return FALSE;
}
```

CXSObject::OnListviewItemActivate

```
BOOL
CXSObject::OnListviewItemActivate(WPARAM wParam, LPARAM lParam)
{
    return FALSE;
}
```

CXSObject::OnListviewOdStateChanged

```
BOOL
CXSObject::OnListviewOdStateChanged(WPARAM wParam, LPARAM
lParam)
{
    return FALSE;
}
```

CXSObject::OnListviewHotTrack

```
BOOL
CXSObject::OnListviewHotTrack(WPARAM wParam, LPARAM lParam,
                             LRESULT& lResult)

{
    return FALSE;
}
```

CXSObject::OnListviewGetInfoTip

```
BOOL
CXSObject::OnListviewGetInfoTip(WPARAM wParam, LPARAM lParam)
{
    return FALSE;
}
```

CXSObject::OnListviewMarqueeBegin

```
BOOL
CXSObject::OnListviewMarqueeBegin(WPARAM wParam, LPARAM lParam,
                                  LRESULT& lResult)
{
    return FALSE;
}
```

CXSObject::OnListviewGetDispInfo

```
BOOL
CXSObject::OnListviewGetDispInfo(WPARAM wParam, LPARAM lParam)
{
    return FALSE;
}
```

CXSObject::OnListviewSetDispInfo

```
BOOL
CXSObject::OnListviewSetDispInfo(WPARAM wParam, LPARAM lParam)
{
    return FALSE;
}
```

CXSObject::OnListviewKeyDown

```
BOOL
CXSObject::OnListviewKeyDown(WPARAM wParam, LPARAM lParam)
{
    return FALSE;
}
```

II

6

CXSObject::OnTreeviewSelChanging

```
BOOL
CXSObject::OnTreeviewSelChanging(WPARAM wParam, LPARAM lParam,
                                 LRESULT& lResult)

{
    return FALSE;
}
```

CXSObject::OnTreeviewSelChanged

```
BOOL
CXSObject::OnTreeviewSelChanged(WPARAM wParam, LPARAM lParam)
{
    return FALSE;
}
```

CXSObject::OnTreeviewGetDispInfo

```
BOOL
CXSObject::OnTreeviewGetDispInfo(WPARAM wParam, LPARAM lParam)
{
    return FALSE;
}
```

CXSObject::OnTreeviewSetDispInfo

```
BOOL
CXSObject::OnTreeviewSetDispInfo(WPARAM wParam, LPARAM lParam)
{
    return FALSE;
}
```

CXSObject::OnTreeviewItemExpanding

```
BOOL
CXSObject::OnTreeviewItemExpanding(WPARAM wParam, LPARAM lParam,
                                   LRESULT& lResult)
{
    return FALSE;
}
```

CXSObject::OnTreeviewItemExpanded

```
BOOL
CXSObject::OnTreeviewItemExpanded(WPARAM wParam, LPARAM lParam)
{
    return FALSE;
}
```

CXSObject::OnTreeviewBeginDrag

```
BOOL
CXSObject::OnTreeviewBeginDrag(WPARAM wParam, LPARAM lParam)
{
    return FALSE;
}
```

CXSObject::OnTreeviewBeginRDrag

```
BOOL
CXSObject::OnTreeviewBeginRDrag(WPARAM wParam, LPARAM lParam)
{
    return FALSE;
}
```

II

6

CXSObject::OnTreeviewDeleteItem

```
BOOL
CXSObject::OnTreeviewDeleteItem(WPARAM wParam, LPARAM lParam)
{
    return FALSE;
}
```

CXSObject::OnTreeviewBeginLabelEdit

```
BOOL
CXSObject::OnTreeviewBeginLabelEdit(WPARAM wParam, LPARAM
lParam,
                                    LRESULT& lResult)
{
    return FALSE;
}
```

CXSObject::OnTreeviewEndLabelEdit

```
BOOL
CXSObject::OnTreeviewEndLabelEdit(WPARAM wParam, LPARAM lParam,
                                  LRESULT& lResult)
{
    return FALSE;
}
```

CXSObject::OnTreeviewKeyDown

```
BOOL
CXSObject::OnTreeviewKeyDown(WPARAM wParam, LPARAM lParam)
{
    return FALSE;
}
```

CXSObject::OnTreeviewGetInfoTip

```
BOOL
CXSObject::OnTreeviewGetInfoTip(WPARAM wParam, LPARAM lParam)
{
    return FALSE;
}
```

CXSObject::OnTreeviewSingleExpand

```
BOOL
CXSObject::OnTreeviewSingleExpand(WPARAM wParam, LPARAM lParam)
{
    return FALSE;
}
```

CXSObject::OnCbeGetDispInfo

```
BOOL
CXSObject::OnCbeGetDispInfo(WPARAM wParam, LPARAM lParam)
{
    return FALSE;
}
```

CXSObject::OnCbeInsertItem

```
BOOL
CXSObject::OnCbeInsertItem(WPARAM wParam, LPARAM lParam)
{
    return FALSE;
}
```

II

6

CXSObject::OnCbeDeleteItem

```
BOOL
CXSObject::OnCbeDeleteItem(WPARAM wParam, LPARAM lParam)
{
    return FALSE;
}
```

CXSObject::OnCbeBeginEdit

```
BOOL
CXSObject::OnCbeBeginEdit(WPARAM wParam, LPARAM lParam)
{
    return FALSE;
}
```

CXSObject::OnCbeEndEdit

```
BOOL
CXSObject::OnCbeEndEdit(WPARAM wParam, LPARAM lParam,
                        LRESULT& lResult)
{
    return FALSE;
}
```

CXSObject::OnCbeDragBegin

```
BOOL
CXSObject::OnCbeDragBegin(WPARAM wParam, LPARAM lParam)
{
    return FALSE;
}
```

CXSObject::OnTabKeyDown

```
BOOL
CXSObject::OnTabKeyDown(WPARAM wParam, LPARAM lParam)
{
    return FALSE;
}
```

CXSObject::OnTabSelChange

```
BOOL
CXSObject::OnTabSelChange(WPARAM wParam, LPARAM lParam)
{
    return FALSE;
}
```

CXSObject::OnTabSelChanging

```
BOOL
CXSObject::OnTabSelChanging(WPARAM wParam, LPARAM lParam,
                           LRESULT& lResult)
{
    return FALSE;
}
```

CXSObject::OnTabGetObject

```
BOOL
CXSObject::OnTabGetObject(WPARAM wParam, LPARAM lParam)
{
    return FALSE;
}
```

II

6

CXSObject::OnMonCalSelChange

```
BOOL
CXSObject::OnMonCalSelChange(WPARAM wParam, LPARAM lParam)
{
    return FALSE;
}
```

CXSObject::OnMonCalGetDayState

```
BOOL
CXSObject::OnMonCalGetDayState(WPARAM wParam, LPARAM lParam)
{
    return FALSE;
}
```

CXSObject::OnMonCalSelect

```
BOOL
CXSObject::OnMonCalSelect(WPARAM wParam, LPARAM lParam)
{
    return FALSE;
}
```

CXSObject::OnDateTimeChange

```
BOOL
CXSObject::OnDateTimeChange(WPARAM wParam, LPARAM lParam)
{
    return FALSE;
}
```

CXSObject::OnDateTimeUserString

```
BOOL
CXSObject::OnDateTimeUserString(WPARAM wParam, LPARAM lParam)
{
    return FALSE;
}
```

CXSObject::OnDateTimeWmKeyDown

```
BOOL
CXSObject::OnDateTimeWmKeyDown(WPARAM wParam, LPARAM lParam)
{
    return FALSE;
}
```

CXSObject::OnDateTimeFormat

```
BOOL
CXSObject::OnDateTimeFormat(WPARAM wParam, LPARAM lParam)
{
    return FALSE;
}
```

CXSObject::OnDateTimeFormatQuery

```
BOOL
CXSObject::OnDateTimeFormatQuery(WPARAM wParam, LPARAM lParam)
{
    return FALSE;
}
```

CXSObject::OnDateTimeDropDown

```
BOOL
CXSObject::OnDateTimeDropDown(WPARAM wParam, LPARAM lParam)
{
    return FALSE;
}
```

CXSObject::OnDateTimeCloseUp

```
BOOL
CXSObject::OnDateTimeCloseUp(WPARAM wParam, LPARAM lParam)
{
    return FALSE;
}
```

CXSObject::OnPagerScroll

```
BOOL
CXSObject::OnPagerScroll(WPARAM wParam, LPARAM lParam)
{
    return FALSE;
}
```

CXSObject::OnPagerCalcSize

```
BOOL
CXSObject::OnPagerCalcSize(WPARAM wParam, LPARAM lParam)
{
    return FALSE;
}
```

CXSObject::OnQueryAfxWndProc

```
BOOL
CXSObject::OnQueryAfxWndProc(WPARAM wParam, LPARAM lParam,
                            LRESULT& lResult)
{
    return FALSE;
}
```

CXSObject::OnSizeParent

```
BOOL
CXSObject::OnSizeParent(WPARAM wParam, LPARAM lParam,
                        LRESULT& lResult)
{
    return FALSE;
}
```

CXSObject::OnSetMessageString ·

```
BOOL
CXSObject::OnSetMessageString(WPARAM wParam, LPARAM lParam,
                              LRESULT& lResult)
{
    return FALSE;
}
```

CXSObject::OnIdleUpdateCmdUi

```
BOOL
CXSObject::OnIdleUpdateCmdUi(WPARAM wParam, LPARAM lParam,
                            LRESULT& lResult)
{
    return FALSE;
}
```

CXSObject::OnInitialUpdate

```
BOOL
CXSObject::OnInitialUpdate(WPARAM wParam, LPARAM lParam)
{
    return FALSE;
}
```

CXSObject::OnCommandHelp

```
BOOL
CXSObject::OnCommandHelp(WPARAM wParam, LPARAM lParam,
                         LRESULT& lResult)

{
    return FALSE;
}
```

CXSObject::OnHelpHitTest

```
BOOL
CXSObject::OnHelpHitTest(WPARAM wParam, LPARAM lParam,
                         LRESULT& lResult)
{
    return FALSE;
}
```

CXSObject::OnExitHelpMode

```
BOOL
CXSObject::OnExitHelpMode(WPARAM wParam, LPARAM lParam)
{
    return FALSE;
}
```

CXSObject::OnRecalcParent

```
BOOL
CXSObject::OnRecalcParent(WPARAM wParam, LPARAM lParam,
                          LRESULT& lResult)
{
    return FALSE;
}
```

CXSObject::OnSizeChild

```
BOOL
CXSObject::OnSizeChild(WPARAM wParam, LPARAM lParam,
                       LRESULT& lResult)
{
    return FALSE;
}
```

CXSObject::OnKickIdle

```
BOOL
CXSObject::OnKickIdle(WPARAM wParam, LPARAM lParam)
{
    return FALSE;
}
```

CXSObject::OnQueryCenterWnd

```
BOOL
CXSObject::OnQueryCenterWnd(WPARAM wParam, LPARAM lParam)
{
    return FALSE;
}
```

CXSObject::OnDisableModal

```
BOOL
CXSObject::OnDisableModal(WPARAM wParam, LPARAM lParam,
                          LRESULT& lResult)
{
    return FALSE;
}
```

CXSObject::OnFloatStatus

```
BOOL
CXSObject::OnFloatStatus(WPARAM wParam, LPARAM lParam,
                         LRESULT& lResult)
{
    return FALSE;
}
```

CXSObject::OnActivateTopLevel

```
BOOL
CXSObject::OnActivateTopLevel(WPARAM wParam, LPARAM lParam)
{
    return FALSE;
}
```

CXSObject::OnQuery3dControls

```
BOOL
CXSObject::OnQuery3dControls(WPARAM wParam, LPARAM lParam,
                             LRESULT& lResult)
{
    return FALSE;
}
```

CXSObject::OnSocketNotify

```
BOOL
CXSObject::OnSocketNotify(WPARAM wParam, LPARAM lParam)
{
    return FALSE;
}
```

CXSObject::OnSocketDead

```
BOOL
CXSObject::OnSocketDead(WPARAM wParam, LPARAM lParam)
{
    return FALSE;
}
```

II

CXSObject::OnPopMessageString

```
BOOL
CXSObject::OnPopMessageString(WPARAM wParam, LPARAM lParam,
                              LRESULT& lResult)
{
    return FALSE;
}
```

6

CXSObject::OnQueueSentinel

```
BOOL
CXSObject::OnQueueSentinel(WPARAM wParam, LPARAM lParam)
{
    return FALSE;
}
```

Summary

We have now completed the message handling methodology provided by this extension framework for MFC. By deriving from the CXSObject class, we can now handle any message by providing the appropriate virtual functions in our derived class. If you do not derive from this class, your other option would be to derive from the CXSSubWndCtrl class itself and provide your own derived DoWindowProc function. Believe me, it gets a bit tedious to do this. However, once the functionality is there, as in the CXSObject class, it makes it much easier to work with it logically and physically.

Section III

Extensions

Chapter 7

Creating a Background Control

Introduction

This is the first chapter in which we'll start to explore the use of the extension framework message handling described in the previous chapters. In short, we're going to create a background control. A background control manages the background of the subclassed window. It allows us to paint a bitmap on the window before any other drawing takes place. This allows us to have different colors, gradient colors, images (bitmaps), or some other custom background. The window should show different backgrounds when it is either active or inactive. For instance, let's say we want to add the background control to a dialog. When the dialog is active, we are going to show a bitmap behind other controls that may be on that dialog. When the dialog is inactive, we may want to show the same bitmap, but in a gray scale instead of color.

We first have to consider which Window messages we need the extension framework to handle for us. In terms of the virtual functions, we'll definitely want to handle `OnActivate`, `OnSetFocus`, and `OnKillFocus`. We'll be working with palettes (although it will be hidden from us, since we'll be using the `CXSBitmap` class to handle bitmaps and automatic palette handling), so we'll need to handle `OnSysColorChange` and `OnPaletteChanged`. For the painting, we'll need to handle `OnEraseBkgnd` and `OnPaint`.

We'll also need functions for creating the bitmaps and for handling swapping of active and inactive bitmaps when appropriate, depending on the state of the window. We'll also have to think about when it is appropriate to show the bitmaps. For instance, if we're subclassing a main window, like a dialog application, we don't need to draw the background if the application is iconic.

XSBGCTRL.H

Enumerated Background Types

We want to define a number of behaviors for our background control. These behaviors, or types, will be placed into the `enum BackgroundType` for easy checking. Primarily, we want to be able to provide default functionality. Whenever the background control class `CXSBgCtrl` sees `BackgroundNormal`, it will not do any further processing. Instead, it will let Windows do its default processing so that we get the desired result. For example, if a solid color is desired, use `BackgroundColor`; if a color gradient is desired, use `BackgroundGradient`. If a bitmapped image is to be displayed, we'll use `BackgroundBitmap`. To cover our bases, we'll allow a custom bitmap to be used by having a `BackgroundCustom` enum type.

```
// --------------------------------------------------------------
// Enumerated background types
enum BackgroundType
{
    BackgroundNormal = 0,
    BackgroundColor,
    BackgroundGradient,
    BackgroundBitmap,
    BackgroundCustom
};
```

CXSBgCtrl **Class Declaration**

We must also allow for background redrawing when the window is resized. Since we create our background bitmaps on the fly and store them so they can be painted on the screen quickly, we need a notification to recreate these bitmaps. We'll provide that functionality in the virtual function DoInvalidate.

There will be other times when we want to call the m_hWnd->InvalidateWindow and m_hWnd->UpdateWindow. For these two actions, we'll provide pass through functions of the same name.

Finally, we want to set up a few utility functions that will be tagged as virtual to allow derived classes to take advantage of them. We'll use the DoGetBitmapRect function to get the size of the bitmap. We'll use DoGetPaintRect to get the size of the area to be painted, in case this is different from the bitmap size. We'll use the DoGetDC function to retrieve the device context (DC) of the window to be painted. These utility functions may not seem so important right now, but we'll need them in the next chapter to create a caption control for painting just the title bar. Since the class CXSCaption will inherit from CXSBgCtrl, it makes sense to place them in this class.

```
class XSCLASS
CXSBgCtrl : public CXSObject
{
// Construction
public:
    CXSBgCtrl();
    virtual ~CXSBgCtrl();

    virtual void DoInvalidate();

    // Pass-thru messages
            void InvalidateWindow(BOOL bErase = TRUE);
            void UpdateWindow();

    // Background handling functions
    int        GetBackgroundType();

    int        SetNormal();
```

III

7

```
    int         SetColor(COLORREF crActive, COLORREF crInactive);
    void        GetColor(COLORREF& crActive, COLORREF& crInactive);
    COLORREF    GetActiveColor();
    COLORREF    GetInactiveColor();

    int         SetGradient(COLORREF crActive,
                    COLORREF crInactive, int nGradFills);
    int         GetGradientCount();

    int         SetBitmaps(HINSTANCE hinst, UINT nActiveID,
                    UINT nInactiveID, BOOL bTile = TRUE);
    int         SetBitmaps(LPCTSTR lpszActiveFileName,
                    LPCTSTR lpszInactiveFileName,
                    BOOL bTile = TRUE);

    CXSBitmap&  GetActiveBitmap();
    CXSBitmap&  GetInactiveBitmap();

    void        SetButtonBorder(BOOL bBorder = TRUE);
    BOOL        GetButtonBorder();

protected:
    // Background handling functions
    virtual void DoResetBitmaps();
    virtual void DoResetAll();

    virtual BOOL DoCreateBackgroundBmp(CDC* pDC, BOOL bState,
                    CXSBitmap& bmp, CRect& rcDim);

    BOOL        CreateGradientBmp(CDC* pDC, BOOL bState,
                    CXSBitmap& bmp, CRect& rcDim);
    BOOL        CreateBitmapBmp(CDC* pDC, BOOL bState,
                    CXSBitmap& bmp, CRect& rcDim);
    virtual BOOL DoCreateCustomBmp(CDC* pDC, BOOL bState,
                    CXSBitmap& bmp, CRect& rcDim);

    virtual BOOL DoDrawBackground(CDC* pDC, CXSBitmap& bmp,
```

```
                           CRect& rcDim) { return TRUE; }
        virtual void   DoDrawButtonBorder(CDC* pDC, CXSBitmap& bmp,
                         CRect rcDim);
        virtual BOOL   DoPaint(CDC* pDC, CXSBitmap& bmp, CRect rcDim);
        virtual CRect  DoGetBitmapRect(CWnd& wnd);
        virtual CRect  DoGetPaintRect(CWnd& wnd);
        virtual CDC*   DoGetDC(CWnd& wnd);
        virtual BOOL   DoGetState(CWnd& wnd);
        virtual BOOL   DoCheckIconic(CWnd& wnd);

protected:
    // Background handling variables
    CSize        m_szBackground;       // Size of background
    int          m_nBackgroundType;    // Background Type
    CXSBitmap    m_bmpBackground[2];    // Background Bitmaps
    BOOL         m_bState;             // Focus/Active State
    COLORREF     m_crColor[2];         // Color Fill
    int          m_nGradFills;         // Gradients for Color
    CXSBitmap    m_bmp[2];             // Original Bitmaps
    BOOL         m_bTile;              // TRUE=Tile, FALSE=Stretch
    BOOL         m_bButtonBorder;      // Draw a 3-D button Border

protected:
    // create from serialization only
    DECLARE_DYNCREATE(CXSBgCtrl);

protected:
    // The message handlers
    virtual BOOL OnActivate(WPARAM wParam, LPARAM lParam);
    virtual BOOL OnEraseBkgnd(WPARAM wParam, LPARAM lParam,
        LRESULT& lResult);
    virtual BOOL OnKillFocus(WPARAM wParam, LPARAM lParam);
    virtual BOOL OnSysColorChange(WPARAM wParam, LPARAM lParam);
    virtual BOOL OnPaletteChanged(WPARAM wParam, LPARAM lParam);
    virtual BOOL OnSetFocus(WPARAM wParam, LPARAM lParam);
    virtual BOOL OnPaint(WPARAM wParam, LPARAM lParam);
};
```

III

7

XSBGCTRL.CPP

Header Files

```
#include "stdafx.h"
#include "XSMisc.h"
#include "XSRect.h"
#include "XSPalette.h"
#include "XSDibApi.h"
#include "XSBitmap.h"
#include "XSSubWndCtrl.h"
#include "XSNotify.h"
#include "XSObject.h"
#include "XSBgCtrl.h"


IMPLEMENT_DYNCREATE(CXSBgCtrl, CXSObject)
```

CXSBgCtrl::CXSBgCtrl

The constructor initializes a number of variables for us, the most significant of which is m_bState. This variable maintains the state of the window, whether it is active or inactive. It is set to 1 initially because it is assumed that the window just subclassed is active. This variable will be used as an index to a CXSBitmap array. This array will contain our inactive (m_bmpBackground[0]) and active (m_bmpBackground[1]) bitmaps.

The rest of the constructor calls the virtual function DoResetAll, which cleans up and reinitializes memory. See the following function for further details.

```
// ----------------------------------------------------------
// Function  :
//     CXSBgCtrl::CXSBgCtrl
// Purpose   :
//     Constructor, initializes memory
// ----------------------------------------------------------
CXSBgCtrl::CXSBgCtrl()
{
    // Set defaults
```

```
    m_bState = 1;
    m_bButtonBorder = FALSE;
    m_nBackgroundType = BackgroundNormal;

    // Initialize
    DoResetAll();
}
```

CXSBgCtrl::~CXSBgCtrl

```
// ------------------------------------------------------------
// Function :
//     CXSBgCtrl::~CXSBgCtrl
// Purpose  :
//     Destructor, cleans up memory
// ------------------------------------------------------------
CXSBgCtrl::~CXSBgCtrl()
{
}
```

CXSBgCtrl::DoInvalidate

The DoInvalidate function resets the m_szBackground variable. This variable is of type CSize and contains the dimensions of the desired bitmap. The code periodically checks this variable. If it has been reset, then the bitmaps are rebuilt. Calling DoInvalidate ensures that the bitmaps are recreated and redrawn.

```
// ------------------------------------------------------------
// Function :
//     CXSBgCtrl::DoInvalidate
// Purpose  :
//     Invalidates the CXSBgCtrl so that the bitmaps are
//     recreated the next time they are redrawn
// Parameters:
//     None
// Returns  :
//     Nothing
```

III

7

```
// --------------------------------------------------------------
void
CXSBgCtrl::DoInvalidate()
{
    m_szBackground = CSize(0,0);
}
```

CXSBgCtrl::InvalidateWindow

The InvalidateWindow function is a pass-through function to the subclassed CWnd's Invalidate function.

```
// --------------------------------------------------------------
// Function  :
//   CXSBgCtrl::InvalidateWindow
// Purpose   :
//   Calls CWnd::Invalidate. Invalidates the entire client area
//   of CWnd. The client area is marked for painting when the
//   next WM_PAINT message occurs. The region can also be
//   validated before a WM_PAINT message occurs by the
//   ValidateRect or ValidateRgn member function.
// Parameters:
//   BOOL bErase - TRUE to erase background (default)
//               - FALSE to leave background unchanged
// Returns   :
//   Nothing
// --------------------------------------------------------------
void
CXSBgCtrl::InvalidateWindow(BOOL bErase)
{
    DoGetWnd()->Invalidate(bErase);
}
```

CXSBgCtrl::UpdateWindow

UpdateWindow is a pass-through function to the subclassed CWnd's UpdateWindow function.

```
// -------------------------------------------------------------
// Function :
//   CXSBgCtrl::UpdateWindow
// Purpose   :
//   Calls CWnd::UpdateWindow. Updates the client area by sending
//   a WM_PAINT message if the update region is not empty. The
//   UpdateWindow member function sends a WM_PAINT message
//   directly, bypassing the application queue. If the update
//   region is empty, WM_PAINT is not sent.
// Parameters:
//   None
// Returns   :
//   Nothing
// -------------------------------------------------------------
void
CXSBgCtrl::UpdateWindow()
{
    DoGetWnd()->UpdateWindow();
}
```

CXSBgCtrl::GetBackgroundType

GetBackgroundType returns the enum BackgroundType that is stored in m_nBackgroundType. The code uses this to know what type of background is to be painted.

```
// -------------------------------------------------------------
// Function :
//   CXSBgCtrl::GetBackgroundType
// Purpose   :
//   Returns the background type in use.
// Parameters:
//   Nothing
// Returns   :
//   int - The background type
```

```
// ------------------------------------------------------------
int
CXSBgCtrl::GetBackgroundType()
{
    return m_nBackgroundType;
}


// ------------------------------------------------------------
// Windows Message Handlers
// ------------------------------------------------------------
```

CXSBgCtrl::OnActivate

The virtual function OnActivate responds to the Windows message
WM_ACTIVATE. CXSBgCtrl maintains two distinct bitmaps. One for when the
window is active, and one for when it is inactive. The active bitmap needs to
be painted when the window receives this message, which sets into motion
the repainting of the active bitmap.

```
// ------------------------------------------------------------
// Function   :
//   CXSBgCtrl::OnActivate
// Purpose    : Handles the Windows message WM_ACTIVATE.
// Parameters: See CXSObject::OnActive
// ------------------------------------------------------------
BOOL
CXSBgCtrl::OnActivate(WPARAM wParam, LPARAM lParam)
{
    // If we're normal, then let Windows/MFC
    // do all of the work
    if (BackgroundNormal == m_nBackgroundType)
        return FALSE;

    // Make sure we repaint the background
    DoGetWnd()->InvalidateRect(DoGetPaintRect(*DoGetWnd()));

    return TRUE;
}
```

CXSBgCtrl::OnEraseBkgnd

The virtual function OnEraseBkgnd responds to the Windows message WM_ERASEBKGND. We don't want Windows to erase our background before a repaint. This would cause a flash and would not look very professional. Therefore, we return FALSE in the LRESULT to let Windows know that it should not erase the background.

```cpp
// ------------------------------------------------------------
// Function :
//   CXSBgCtrl::OnEraseBkgnd
// Purpose   : Handles the Windows message WM_ERASEBKGND.
// Parameters: See CXSObject::OnEraseBkgnd
// ------------------------------------------------------------
BOOL
CXSBgCtrl::OnEraseBkgnd(WPARAM wParam, LPARAM lParam, LRESULT& lRe-
sult)
{
    // If we're normal, then let Windows/MFC
    // do all of the work
    if (BackgroundNormal == m_nBackgroundType)
        return FALSE;

    // Don't allow background paints
    lResult = FALSE;
    return TRUE;
}
```

CXSBgCtrl::OnKillFocus

The virtual function OnKillFocus responds to the Windows message WM_KILLFOCUS. This is much the same as the OnActivate virtual function, except this time, we are going to be painting the inactive bitmap instead of the active one.

```cpp
// ------------------------------------------------------------
// Function :
//   CXSBgCtrl::OnKillFocus
// Purpose   : Handles the Windows message WM_KILLFOCUS.
// Parameters: See CXSObject::OnKillFocus
```

III

7

```
// ------------------------------------------------------------
BOOL
CXSBgCtrl::OnKillFocus(WPARAM wParam, LPARAM lParam)
{
    // If we're normal, then let Windows/MFC
    // do all of the work
    if (BackgroundNormal == m_nBackgroundType)
        return FALSE;


    // Make sure we can repaint the background
    DoGetWnd()->InvalidateRect(DoGetPaintRect(*DoGetWnd()));

    return TRUE;
}
```

CXSBgCtrl::OnSysColorChange

The virtual function OnSysColorChange responds to the Windows message
WM_SYSCOLORCHANGE. Whenever you are dealing with bitmaps that have palettes, it is a good idea to respond to this message so that your image is displayed correctly.

```
// ------------------------------------------------------------
// Function   :
//   CXSBgCtrl::OnSysColorChange
// Purpose    : Handles the Windows message WM_SYSCOLORCHANGE.
// Parameters: See CXSObject::OnSysColorChange
// ------------------------------------------------------------
BOOL
CXSBgCtrl::OnSysColorChange(WPARAM wParam, LPARAM lParam)
{
    // If we're normal, then let Windows/MFC
    // do all of the work
    if (BackgroundNormal == m_nBackgroundType)
        return FALSE;


    // Make sure we repaint the background
    // and recreate the bitmaps
```

```
      InvalidateWindow();
      DoInvalidate();
      return TRUE;
  }
```

CXSBgCtrl::OnPaletteChanged

The virtual function OnPaletteChanged responds to the Windows message
WM_PALETTECHANGED. As with OnSysColorChange, if we have an image with a
palette, we should redraw it so it is displayed correctly.

```
// -----------------------------------------------------------
// Function :
//   CXSBgCtrl::OnPaletteChanged
// Purpose   : Handles the Windows message WM_PALETTECHANGED.
// Parameters: See CXSObject::OnPaletteChanged
// -----------------------------------------------------------
BOOL
CXSBgCtrl::OnPaletteChanged(WPARAM wParam, LPARAM lParam)
{
    // If we're normal, then let Windows/MFC
    // do all of the work
    if (BackgroundNormal == m_nBackgroundType)
        return FALSE;

    InvalidateWindow();
    DoInvalidate();
    return TRUE;
}
```

III

7

CXSBgCtrl::OnSetFocus

The virtual function OnSetFocus responds to the Windows message WM_SETFOCUS. As with the OnActivate and OnKillFocus virtual functions, this tells our control that an active/inactive state change has occurred.

```
// --------------------------------------------------------------
// Function  :
//  CXSBgCtrl::OnSetFocus
// Purpose   : Handles the Windows message WM_SETFOCUS.
// Parameters: See CXSObject::OnSetFocus
// --------------------------------------------------------------
BOOL
CXSBgCtrl::OnSetFocus(WPARAM wParam, LPARAM lParam)
{
    // If we're normal, then let Windows/MFC
    // do all of the work
    if (BackgroundNormal == m_nBackgroundType)
        return FALSE;

    // Make sure we repaint the background
    DoGetWnd()->InvalidateRect(DoGetPaintRect(*DoGetWnd()));

    return TRUE;
}
```

CXSBgCtrl::OnPaint

The virtual function OnPaint responds to the Windows message WM_PAINT. This is when we are notified by Windows that our window needs repainting. In this function, we first check the selected background type. If it is BackgroundNormal, we call the base functionality and return. If BackgroundType is anything else, we proceed to do our magic.

The next step is to check to see if this window is in an iconic state by calling DoCheckIconic. We don't want to do all the processing it takes to paint the background if there is no need for it. The DoCheckIconic function is virtual because there are at times windows that will be drawn when they are iconic (e.g., MDI child windows). However, that's covered in another chapter. For now, we assume that if the subclassed window is iconic, we don't need to paint it. You should note that we call the default implementation by calling the `Default` function.

The next item on the agenda is to get the state of the window by calling the virtual function `DoGetState`. This will determine if we will be painting the active or inactive bitmap. Then we get the bitmap dimensions by calling the virtual function `DoGetBitmapRect` and we get the painting area by calling the virtual function `DoGetPaintRect`. In most cases, these two dimensions will be the same. However, we cannot always count on that. There may be times when the two will vary, especially for derived classes, and we'll need to be able to handle this scenario. Finally, we get the needed device context (DC) by calling the virtual function `DoGetDC`. The `DoGetDC` function is virtual because it is conceivable that different DC's may be used for the painting. We certainly cannot know this ahead of time, so the virtual function exists to handle this situation.

Now that we have a lot of our desired information, it is time to prepare the bitmaps. We first check to see if the size returned by `DoGetPaintRect` matches the size of our current background size variable, `m_szBackground`. If they do not match, we have to rebuild the bitmaps and any current bitmaps are deleted. The needed bitmaps are stored in an array of `CXSBitmap` objects. The first element (0) is the inactive bitmap and the next element (1) is the active bitmap. We set a new `CXSBitmap` reference to the desired bitmap that we want to change based on the state, inactive (0) or active (1). We then create a bitmap of the desired dimensions. This is the bitmap we will paint our background onto so we can use it later. The only time the bitmaps are recreated is when the size changes. Keeping our desired bitmaps in storage like this allows us to increase the speed at which the background is redrawn for subsequent paintings.

The bitmap receives the background paint in a call to the virtual function `DoDrawBackground`. Once the bitmap has the desired background, we call the virtual function `DoPaint` to do the actual work for us. It should be noted that `DoPaint` should not be confused with `OnPaint`. Now that the work is all done, we have to make sure we delete the DC given to us in the previous call to `DoGetDC`.

```
// ------------------------------------------------------------
// Function :
//    CXSBgCtrl::OnPaint
// Purpose  :
//    Paints the desired background type.  If the CWnd is in an
//    iconic state, it calls the default processing handler.
```

```
// Parameters:
//    None
// Returns   :
//    Nothing
// ------------------------------------------------------------
BOOL
CXSBgCtrl::OnPaint(WPARAM wParam, LPARAM lParam)
{
    // If we're normal, then let Windows/MFC
    // do all of the work
    if (BackgroundNormal == m_nBackgroundType)
        return CXSObject::OnPaint(wParam, lParam);

    // If the window is an icon, no need to paint a background
    if (!DoCheckIconic(*DoGetWnd()))
    {
        // Just call the default handler
        Default();
        return TRUE;
    }

    // Get the window state
    m_bState = DoGetState(*DoGetWnd());

    // Get the window dimensions
    CRect rcBitmap = DoGetBitmapRect(*DoGetWnd());
    CRect rcPaint = DoGetPaintRect(*DoGetWnd());

    // Get background DC
    CDC* pDC = DoGetDC(*DoGetWnd());
    ASSERT(pDC);
    CDC dc;
    dc.CreateCompatibleDC(pDC);

    // Are we going to be creating new bitmaps?
    if (rcPaint.Size() != m_szBackground)
    {
```

```
        // Invalidate bitmaps
        m_bmpBackground[0].DoDeleteObject();
        m_bmpBackground[1].DoDeleteObject();

        // Set new dimensions
        m_szBackground = rcPaint.Size();
    }


    // Get active/inactive bitmap and determine if
    // regeneration is required
    CXSBitmap& bmp = m_bmpBackground[m_bState];
    BOOL bPaintIt = TRUE;

    // If the bitmap does not exist, then create one
    if (!bmp.GetSafeHandle())
    {
        bmp.CreateCompatibleBitmap(pDC, rcBitmap.Width(),
            rcBitmap.Height());

        BOOL bResult = DoCreateBackgroundBmp(&dc, m_bState,
            bmp, rcBitmap);
        ASSERT(bResult);  // problems? Sanity check...

        // Get ImageSize info
        if (bResult)
            bmp.Size();
        else
            bPaintIt = FALSE;
    }

    // If it's OK to paint and we have a valid bitmap,
    // paint the background, icon, and buttons
    if (bPaintIt && bmp.GetSafeHandle())
    {
        DoDrawBackground(&dc, bmp, rcBitmap);

        // Check to see if we are drawing a button border
```

III

7

```
        if (m_bButtonBorder)
            DoDrawButtonBorder(&dc, bmp, rcBitmap);


        // Now, paint the background onto the window
        DoPaint(pDC, bmp, rcPaint);
    }


    if (pDC)
        delete pDC;


    return TRUE;
}
```

CXSBgCtrl::DoResetBitmaps

The virtual function DoResetBitmaps reinitializes the active and inactive bitmaps for the CXSBgCtrl object.

```
// -----------------------------------------------------------
// Function  :
//    CXSBgCtrl::DoResetBitmaps
// Purpose   :
//    Sets the bitmaps back to the default.  Uses system color
//    COLOR_WINDOW, which may or may not appropriate for your
//    derived control.
// Parameters:
//    None
// Returns   :
//    Nothing
// -----------------------------------------------------------
void
CXSBgCtrl::DoResetBitmaps()
{
    m_nBackgroundType = BackgroundNormal;
    m_crColor[0] = ::GetSysColor(COLOR_WINDOW);
    m_crColor[1] = ::GetSysColor(COLOR_WINDOW);
    m_nGradFills = 1;
```

```
    // initialize bitmaps
    for( int x = 0; x < 2; x++)
        m_bmp[x].DeleteObject();
}
```

CXSBgCtrl::DoResetAll

The virtual function DoResetAll is a utility function mostly for derived classes. CXSBgCtrl does call this function. Whenever you derive a class where items might need reinitialization, override this function in your derived class. However, do not forget to call the base implementation.

```
// -------------------------------------------------------------
// Function :
//    CXSBgCtrl::DoResetAll
// Purpose  :
//    Calls all appropriate reset functions.
// Parameters:
//    None
// Returns  :
//    Nothing
// -------------------------------------------------------------
void
CXSBgCtrl::DoResetAll()
{
    DoResetBitmaps();
}
```

CXSBgCtrl::SetNormal

The SetNormal function sets the CXSBgCtrl object to have a normal background. The function returns the previous background enum type.

```
// -------------------------------------------------------------
// Function :
//    CXSBgCtrl::SetNormal
// Purpose  :
//    Sets background to "Normal".  Normal is defined by this
//    class programmatically.  If you really want Normal, as
```

```
//      defined by Windows, then uninstall the handler.
// Parameters:
//    None
// Returns   :
//    Nothing
// -------------------------------------------------------------
int
CXSBgCtrl::SetNormal()
{
    int nOldBGType = m_nBackgroundType;

    // Set background type
    m_nBackgroundType = BackgroundNormal;

    // Invalidate the dimensions, the HWND, and then paint
    DoResetAll();
    DoInvalidate();
    InvalidateWindow();
    UpdateWindow();

    return nOldBGType;
}
```

CXSBgCtrl::SetColor

The SetColor function sets the CXSBgCtrl object to have a color background. The function takes the active and inactive colors to use as arguments. The function returns the previous background enum type.

```
// -------------------------------------------------------------
// Function  :
//    CXSBgCtrl::SetColor
// Purpose   :
//    Sets background to Color.
// Parameters:
//    COLORREF crActive - The color to use when active
//    COLORREF crInactive - The color to use when inactive
// Returns   :
```

```
//    int - The previous caption type
// --------------------------------------------------------------
int
CXSBgCtrl::SetColor(COLORREF crActive,
                    COLORREF crInactive)
{
    int nOldBGType = SetGradient(crActive, crInactive, 1);

    // Set background type
    m_nBackgroundType = BackgroundColor;

    return nOldBGType;
}
```

CXSBgCtrl::GetColor

The GetColor function returns the active and inactive colors in the passed COLORREF references.

```
// --------------------------------------------------------------
// Function  :
//    CXSBgCtrl::GetColor
// Purpose   :
//    Gets active and inactive background colors.
// Parameters:
//    COLORREF& crActive - The color used when active
//    COLORREF& crInactive - The color used when inactive
// Returns   :
//    int - The previous caption type
// --------------------------------------------------------------
void
CXSBgCtrl::GetColor(COLORREF& crActive, COLORREF& crInactive)
{
    crActive = m_crColor[1];
    crInactive = m_crColor[0];
}
```

III

7

CXSBgCtrl::GetActiveColor

The GetActiveColor **returns the active** COLORREF**.**

```
// ----------------------------------------------------------------
// Function :
//     CXSBgCtrl::GetActiveColor
// Purpose  :
//     Gets active background color
// Parameters:
//     None
// Returns  :
//     COLORREF - The active color
// ----------------------------------------------------------------
COLORREF
CXSBgCtrl::GetActiveColor()
{
    return m_crColor[1];
}
```

CXSBgCtrl::GetInactiveColor

The GetInactiveColor **returns the inactive** COLORREF**.**

```
// ----------------------------------------------------------------
// Function :
//     CXSBgCtrl::GetInactiveColor
// Purpose  :
//     Gets inactive background color
// Parameters:
//     None
// Returns  :
//     COLORREF - The inactive color
// ----------------------------------------------------------------
COLORREF
CXSBgCtrl::GetInactiveColor()
{
    return m_crColor[0];
}
```

CXSBgCtrl::SetGradient

The SetGradient function sets the CXSBgCtrl object to have a gradient background. The function takes the active and inactive colors to use as arguments, as well as the number of steps to create the gradient. The function returns the previous background enum type.

```
// --------------------------------------------------------------
// Function  :
//    CXSBgCtrl::SetGradient
// Purpose   :
//    Sets background to Gradient.  The passed color is used to
//    create a gradient from color to black, right to left.
// Parameters:
//    COLORREF crActive - The color to use when active
//    COLORREF crInactive - The color to use when inactive
// Returns   :
//    int - The previous caption type
// --------------------------------------------------------------
int
CXSBgCtrl::SetGradient(COLORREF crActive,
                       COLORREF crInactive,
                       int nGradFills)
{
    ASSERT(crActive >= 0 && crActive <= RGB(255,255,255));

    int nOldBGType = GetBackgroundType();

    // Reset bitmaps
    DoResetBitmaps();

    // Set background type
    m_nBackgroundType = BackgroundGradient;

    // Set color options
    m_crColor[0] = crInactive;
    m_crColor[1] = crActive;
    m_nGradFills = nGradFills;
```

III

7

```
// Invalidate the dimensions, the HWND, and then paint
DoInvalidate();
InvalidateWindow();
UpdateWindow();

return nOldBGType;
}
```

CXSBgCtrl::GetGradientCount

The GetGradientCount function returns the number of steps used to create the gradient background.

```
// ----------------------------------------------------------------
// Function  :
//     CXSBgCtrl::GetGradientCount
// Purpose   :
//   Returns the number of gradients in use when background type
//   is of type BackgroundGradient.
// Parameters:
//   Nothing
// Returns   :
//   int - The number of gradients
// ----------------------------------------------------------------
int
CXSBgCtrl::GetGradientCount()
{
    return m_nGradFills;
}
```

CXSBgCtrl::SetBitmaps

The SetBitmaps function sets the CXSBgCtrl object to have a bitmapped background. The function takes the following items as arguments: the HIN-STANCE of the bitmap resources location, the UINT ID of the active bitmap, the UINT ID of the inactive bitmap, and a BOOL that determines if the bitmaps are to be tiled when painted. The function returns the previous background enum type.

```cpp
// ------------------------------------------------------------
// Function  :
//     CXSBgCtrl::SetBitmaps
// Purpose   :
//     Sets background to Bitmaps.
// Parameters:
//     HINSTANCE hinst - HINSTANCE of the resources
//     UINT nActiveID - The bitmap to use when active
//     UINT nInactiveID - The bitmap to use when inactive
//     BOOL bTile - TRUE if the bitmaps should be tile
//                - FALSE if the bitmaps should be stretched
// Returns   :
//     int - The previous caption type, -1 on error
// ------------------------------------------------------------
int
CXSBgCtrl::SetBitmaps(HINSTANCE hinst, UINT nActiveID,
                      UINT nInactiveID, BOOL bTile)
{
    int nOldBGType = GetBackgroundType();

    // Reset bitmaps
    DoResetBitmaps();

    // Set background type
    m_nBackgroundType = BackgroundBitmap;

    // Load bitmaps
    if (!m_bmp[0].DoLoad(hinst, nInactiveID))
        return -1;

    if (!m_bmp[1].DoLoad(hinst, nActiveID))
    {
        m_bmp[0].DoDeleteObject();
        return -1;
    }
```

III

7

```
    // Set tile options
    m_bTile = bTile;

    // Invalidate the dimensions, the HWND, and then paint
    DoInvalidate();
    InvalidateWindow();
    UpdateWindow();

    return nOldBGType;
}
```

CXSBgCtrl::SetBitmaps

The SetBitmaps function sets the CXSBgCtrl object to have a bitmapped background. The function takes the following items as arguments: the LPCTSTR path of the active bitmap, the LPCTSTR path of the inactive bitmap, and a BOOL that determines if the bitmaps are to be tiled when painted. The function returns the previous background enum type.

```
// -------------------------------------------------------------
// Function :
//     CXSBgCtrl::SetBitmaps
// Purpose  :
//     Sets background to Bitmaps.
// Parameters:
//     LPCTSTR lpszActiveFileName - The bitmap file to use when
//      active.
//     LPCTSTR lpszInactiveFileName - The bitmap file to use
//     when inactive
//     BOOL bTile - TRUE if the bitmaps should be tile
//                - FALSE if the bitmaps should be stretched
// Returns  :
//     int - The previous caption type, -1 on error
//     This function does not verify that the files exist.
// -------------------------------------------------------------
int
CXSBgCtrl::SetBitmaps(LPCTSTR lpszActiveFileName,
```

```
                       LPCTSTR lpszInactiveFileName,
                       BOOL bTile)
{
    int nOldBGType = GetBackgroundType();

    // Reset bitmaps
    DoResetBitmaps();

    // Set background type
    m_nBackgroundType = BackgroundBitmap;

    // Load bitmaps
    if (!m_bmp[0].DoLoad(lpszInactiveFileName))
        return -1;

    if (!m_bmp[1].DoLoad(lpszActiveFileName))
    {
        m_bmp[0].DoDeleteObject();
        return -1;
    }

    // Set tile options
    m_bTile = bTile;

    // Invalidate the dimensions, the HWND, and then paint
    DoInvalidate();
    InvalidateWindow();
    UpdateWindow();

    return nOldBGType;
}
```

III

7

CXSBgCtrl::GetActiveBitmap

The GetActiveBitmap returns a reference to the active bitmap's CXSBitmap object.

```
// ------------------------------------------------------------
// Function :
//   CXSBgCtrl::GetActiveBitmap
// Purpose  :
//   Returns a reference to the active bitmap
// Parameters:
//   None
// Returns  :
//   CXSBitmap& - The active bitmap
// ------------------------------------------------------------
CXSBitmap&
CXSBgCtrl::GetActiveBitmap()
{
    return m_bmp[1];
}
```

CXSBgCtrl::GetInactiveBitmap

The GetInactiveBitmap returns a reference to the inactive bitmap's CXSBitmap object.

```
// ------------------------------------------------------------
// Function :
//   CXSBgCtrl::GetInactiveBitmap
// Purpose  :
//   Returns a reference to the inactive bitmap
// Parameters:
//   None
// Returns  :
//   CXSBitmap& - The inactive bitmap
// ------------------------------------------------------------
CXSBitmap&
```

```
CXSBgCtrl::GetInactiveBitmap()
{
    return m_bmp[0];
}
```

CXSBgCtrl::SetButtonBorder

The SetButtonBorder function turns on button border painting when the background is painted.

```
// ---------------------------------------------------------------
// Function  :
//   CXSBgCtrl::SetButtonBorder
// Purpose   :
//   Turns button border use on or off
// Parameters:
//   BOOL bBorder - TRUE to turn on button border (default)
//                - FALSE to turn off button border
// Returns   :
//   Nothing
// ---------------------------------------------------------------
void
CXSBgCtrl::SetButtonBorder(BOOL bBorder)
{
    m_bButtonBorder = bBorder;
}
```

CXSBgCtrl::GetButtonBorder

The GetButtonBorder function returns the button border state flag for this CXSBgCtrl object.

```
// ---------------------------------------------------------------
// Function  :
//   CXSBgCtrl::GetButtonBorder
// Purpose   :
//   Returns the BOOL determing if ButtonBorder is in use.
// Parameters:
//   None
```

III

7

```
// Returns   :
//   BOOL - TRUE if use button border is turned on
//        - FALSE if button border is off
// ------------------------------------------------------------
BOOL
CXSBgCtrl::GetButtonBorder()
{
    return m_bButtonBorder;
}
```

CXSBgCtrl::DoCreateBackgroundBmp

When the virtual function DoCreateBackgroundBmp is called, it uses stored information to determine which type of background bitmap is to be created and then calls the appropriate function. This gives us a single-point-of-creation function so we don't have to deal with the logic that determines which function is called to paint the desired bitmaps in several places throughout the code.

```
// ------------------------------------------------------------
// Function  :
//     CXSBgCtrl::DoCreateBackgroundBmp
// Purpose   :
//     Creates the background bitmap by calling the appropriate
//     function to create the background type.
// Parameters:
//     CDC* pDC - DC to use for painting
//     BOOL bActive - determines which active state to draw.
//      0 for inactive state, 1 for active state
//     CXSBitmap& bmp - The bitmap to receive the end result of
//      the paint
//     CRect& rcDim - the dimensions of what to paint
// Returns   :
//     TRUE on success, FALSE on failure
// ------------------------------------------------------------
BOOL
CXSBgCtrl::DoCreateBackgroundBmp(CDC* pDC, BOOL bActive,
                                 CXSBitmap& bmp, CRect& rcDim)
```

```
{
    switch(m_nBackgroundType)
    {
    case BackgroundNormal:
    case BackgroundColor:
    case BackgroundGradient:
        return CreateGradientBmp(pDC, bActive, bmp, rcDim);
    case BackgroundBitmap:
        return CreateBitmapBmp(pDC, bActive, bmp, rcDim);
    case BackgroundCustom:
        return DoCreateCustomBmp(pDC, bActive, bmp, rcDim);
    }

    return FALSE;
}
```

CXSBgCtrl::CreateGradientBmp

The CreateGradientBmp function is used to paint a gradient background onto the passed bitmap. You may have noticed that a BackgroundType of BackgroundColor also uses CreateGradientBmp. This is because a solid color is really a gradient with one step. The function used to create the gradient, XSPaint_Gradient, checks how many steps are needed. If it is one, then it paints a solid color.

```
// -----------------------------------------------------------
// Function  :
//    CXSBgCtrl::CreateGradientBmp
// Purpose   :
//    Paints a bitmap with a gradient.  If m_nGradFills == 1,
//    then the color will be solid.
// Parameters:
//    CDC* pDC - DC to use for painting
//    BOOL bActive - determines which active state to draw.
//     0 for inactive state, 1 for active state
//    CXSBitmap& bmp - The bitmap to receive the end result of
//     the paint
//    CRect& rcDim - the dimensions of what to paint
```

```
// Returns   :
//    TRUE on success, FALSE on failure
// -------------------------------------------------------------
BOOL
CXSBgCtrl::CreateGradientBmp(CDC* pDC, BOOL bActive,
                                 CXSBitmap& bmp, CRect& rcDim)
{
    ASSERT(bmp.GetSafeHandle());
    ASSERT(m_nGradFills >= 1);
    ASSERT(pDC);


    BOOL bResult;

    // Select the bitmap into the DC so it gets painted on
    CBitmap* pOldBitmap = pDC->SelectObject(&bmp);

    // Select the main color to be used for the caption
    COLORREF crBG = m_crColor[0 != bActive];

    // Paint the bitmap
    bResult = ::XSPaint_Gradient(pDC, rcDim, crBG, m_nGradFills);

    // Select old bitmap back into DC
    pDC->SelectObject(pOldBitmap);


    return bResult;
}
```

CXSBgCtrl::CreateBitmapBmp

The function CreateBitmapBmp is used to paint a bitmapped image background onto the passed bitmap object.

```
// -------------------------------------------------------------
// Function  :
//    CXSBgCtrl::CreateBitmapBmp
// Purpose   :
//    Creates the background bitmap by using a DDB.  If the DDB
```

```
//    is smaller than rcDim and m_bTile == TRUE, the bitmap is
//    tiled, otherwise it is stretched.
// Parameters:
//    CDC* pDC - DC to use for painting
//    BOOL bActive - determines which active state to draw.
//     0 for inactive state, 1 for active state
//    CXSBitmap& bmp - The bitmap to receive the end result of
//     the paint
//    CRect& rcDim - the dimensions of what to paint
// Returns   :
//    TRUE on success, FALSE on failure
// -------------------------------------------------------------
BOOL
CXSBgCtrl::CreateBitmapBmp(CDC* pDC, BOOL bActive,
                           CXSBitmap& bmp, CRect& rcDim)
{
    ASSERT(pDC);
    ASSERT(bmp.GetSafeHandle());

    // Make sure the bitmaps are available
    ASSERT(m_bmp[0].GetSafeHandle() &&
        m_bmp[1].GetSafeHandle());

    // Draw the holder bitmaps to the caption bitmaps
    CDC dc;
    dc.CreateCompatibleDC(pDC);
    CBitmap* pOldBitmap = dc.SelectObject(&bmp);

    // Paint the bitmap
    m_bmp[bActive].DoPaintNormal(&dc, CRect(0, 0, rcDim.Width(),
        rcDim.Height()), m_bTile);

    // Select old bitmap back into DC
    dc.SelectObject(pOldBitmap);

    return TRUE;
}
```

III

7

CXSBgCtrl::DoCreateCustomBmp

The DoCreateCustomBmp function exists so that derived classes can paint a custom background bitmap.

```
// -------------------------------------------------------------
// Function  :
//     CXSBgCtrl::CreateCustomBmp
// Purpose   :
//     Virtual function that allows a derived class to paint a
//     custom background bitmap.
// Parameters:
//     CDC* pDC - DC to use in painting the border
//     BOOL bState -
//     CXSBitmap& bmp - The bitmap to receive the end result of
//      the paint
//     CRect rcDim - dimensions of where to paint the bitmap
//      within the DC
// Returns   :
//     Nothing
// -------------------------------------------------------------
BOOL
CXSBgCtrl::DoCreateCustomBmp(CDC* pDC, BOOL bState,
                             CXSBitmap& bmp, CRect& rcDim)
{
    return FALSE;
}
```

CXSBgCtrl::DoDrawButtonBorder

The virtual function DoDrawButtonBorder draws a button border using the Windows API function Draw3dRect. The colors it uses are hard-coded and may not be quite what you want if you need this function. If this is the case, then simply override this virtual function and provide your own button border colors.

```
// -------------------------------------------------------------
// Function  :
//     CXSBgCtrl::DoDrawButtonBorder
// Purpose   :
```

```
//    Virtual function that paints a border to create a 3D or
//    button-type look.  Uses white for the top and left, black
//    for the bottom and right.
// Parameters:
//    CDC* pDC - DC to use in painting the border
//    CXSBitmap& bmp - The bitmap to receive the end result of
//     the paint
//    CRect rect - dimensions of where to paint the border
//     within the DC
// Returns   :
//    Nothing
// -------------------------------------------------------------
void
CXSBgCtrl::DoDrawButtonBorder(CDC* pDC, CXSBitmap& bmp,
                                CRect rcDim)
{
    ASSERT_VALID(pDC);

    // Select the bitmap into the DC so it gets painted on
    CBitmap* pOldBitmap = pDC->SelectObject(&bmp);

    // Paint the Border
    pDC->Draw3dRect(rcDim, RGB(255,255,255), RGB(0,0,0));

    // Select old bitmap back into DC
    pDC->SelectObject(pOldBitmap);
}
```

CXSBgCtrl::DoPaint

The virtual function DoPaint simply calls the CXSBitmap object that contains the desired background image to do all the actual painting for us.

```
// -------------------------------------------------------------
// Function  :
//    CXSBgCtrl::DoPaint
// Purpose   :
//    Paints the background to the window
```

```
// Parameters:
//    CDC* pDC - DC to use in painting the border
//    CXSBitmap& bmp - The bitmap to receive the end result of
//     the paint
//    CRect rect - dimensions of where to paint the border
//     within the DC
// Returns   :
//    Nothing
// -------------------------------------------------------------
BOOL
CXSBgCtrl::DoPaint(CDC* pDC, CXSBitmap& bmp, CRect rcDim)
{
    return bmp.DoPaintNormal(pDC, rcDim, FALSE);
}
```

CXSBgCtrl::DoGetBitmapRect

The virtual function DoGetBitmapRect returns the required dimensions needed by the bitmap object when it is created.

```
// -------------------------------------------------------------
// Function  :
//    CXSBgCtrl::DoGetBitmapRect
// Purpose   :
//    Virtual function that returns the dimensions of the needed
//     bitmap dimensions.
// Parameters:
//    CWnd& wnd - Reference to a CWnd
// Returns   :
//    CRect - The dimensions of the needed bitmap size
// -------------------------------------------------------------
CRect
CXSBgCtrl::DoGetBitmapRect(CWnd& wnd)
{
    return CXSClientRect(wnd);
}
```

CXSBgCtrl::DoGetPaintRect

The virtual function DoGetPaintRect returns the required dimensions in client coordinates of the location at which the painting needs to take place.

```
// -----------------------------------------------------------
// Function :
//     CXSBgCtrl::DoGetPaintRect
// Purpose  :
//     Virtual function that returns the dimensions in client
//     coordinates of where to paint.
// Parameters:
//     CWnd& wnd - Reference to a CWnd
// Returns   :
//     CRect - The dimensions in client coordinates within the
//     CWnd to use for painting.
// -----------------------------------------------------------
CRect
CXSBgCtrl::DoGetPaintRect(CWnd& wnd)
{
    return CXSClientRect(wnd);
}
```

CXSBgCtrl::DoGetDC

The virtual function DoGetDC returns the desired device context of the location at which the painting should take place. When CXSBgCtrl is done painting with this DC pointer, it will call delete to clean it up.

```
// -----------------------------------------------------------
// Function :
//   CXSBgCtrl::DoGetDC
// Purpose  :
//   Virtual function to return the DC for painting
// Parameters:
//   CWnd& wnd - reference to the window that will be used for
//   painting operations
// Returns   :
//   CDC* - pointer to the requested device context
// -----------------------------------------------------------
```

III

7

```
CDC*
CXSBgCtrl::DoGetDC(CWnd& wnd)
{
    CPaintDC* pDC = new CPaintDC(&wnd);
    return pDC;
}
```

CXSBgCtrl::DoGetState

The virtual function DoGetState returns the state of the subclassed window. It will return zero (0) for inactive/no focus and one (1) for active/has focus.

```
// -------------------------------------------------------------
// Function  :
//   CXSBgCtrl::DoGetState
// Purpose   :
//   Returns the state of the passed CWnd
// Parameters:
//   CWnd& wnd - reference to the window that needs the state
//   reported
// Returns   :
//   BOOL - TRUE if the state is active
//        - FALSE if the state is inactive
// -------------------------------------------------------------
BOOL
CXSBgCtrl::DoGetState(CWnd& wnd)
{
    BOOL bState = 1;

    // Find out what state the CWnd is in.  For a CWnd that is
    // the active window, or has focus, the state = 1,
    // otherwise state = 0
    CWnd* pWnd = DoGetWnd()->GetFocus();
    if (pWnd->GetSafeHwnd() == DoGetWnd()->GetSafeHwnd())
        bState = 1;
    else
    {
        // It didn't have focus, so check to see if this CWnd
```

```
        // is the active window
        pWnd = DoGetWnd()->GetActiveWindow();

        if (pWnd->GetSafeHwnd() == DoGetWnd()->GetSafeHwnd())
            bState = 1;
        else
            bState = 0;
    }


    return bState;
}
```

CXSBgCtrl::DoCheckIconic

The virtual function DoCheckIconic checks the iconic state of the subclassed window. If the window is iconic, it returns FALSE; otherwise, it returns TRUE.

```
// ------------------------------------------------------------
// Function :
//   CXSBgCtrl::DoCheckIconic
// Purpose  :
//   Checks to see if the passed CWnd is in an iconic state.
//   There is no need to draw the background bitmaps if the CWnd
//   is in an iconic state.
// Parameters:
//   CWnd& wnd - reference to the window that needs the iconic
//   state reported
// Returns  :
//   BOOL - TRUE if the window is in an iconic state
//        - FALSE if the window is not in an iconic state
// ------------------------------------------------------------
BOOL
CXSBgCtrl::DoCheckIconic(CWnd& wnd)
{
    if (DoGetWnd()->IsIconic())
    {
        return FALSE;
```

```
        }

        return TRUE;
    }
```

Using `CXSBgCtrl`

Now that we have created the code that will be used as our background control, we can start to use it. I created a small AppWizard dialog-based program to display the capabilities of the `CXSBgCtrl` in relationship to a dialog's background.

Figure 7.1   The dialog displayed with a normal background.

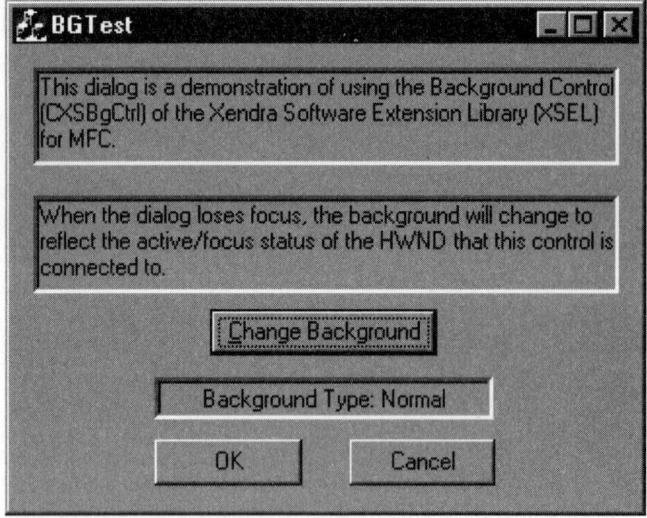

Figure 7.1 is the dialog when the background is set to `BackgroundNormal`. This is the Windows default background. I would show you the dialog changed for when the background is set to `BackgroundColor`, but it looks just the same as the `BackgroundNormal` when displayed on back and white pages.

Figure 7.2   The dialog displayed with a gradient color background.

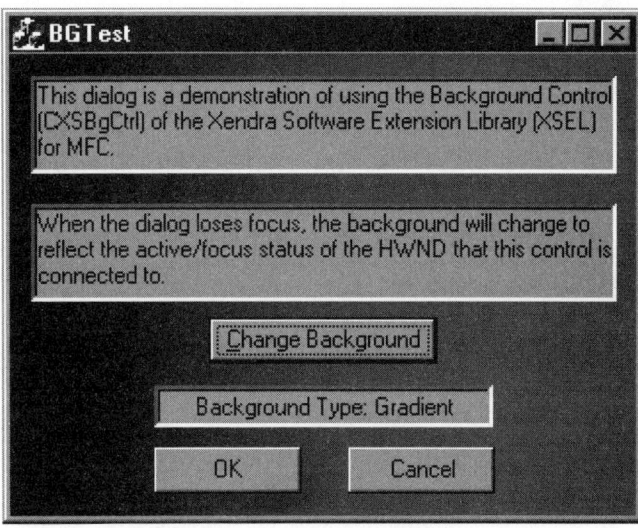

Figure 7.3   The dialog displayed with a tiled bitmap background.

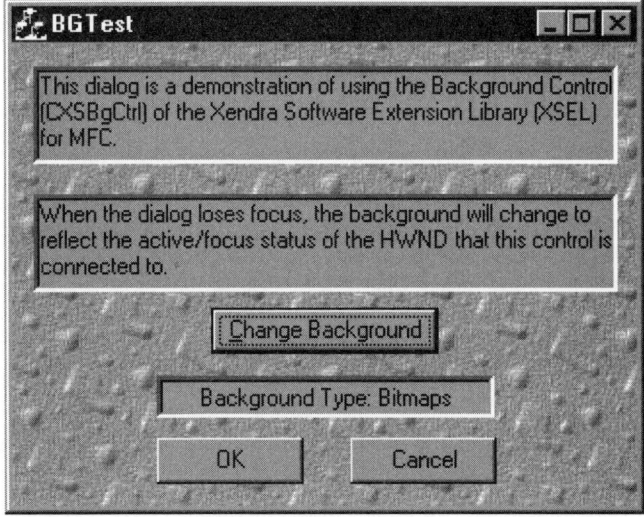

III

7

As you can see, the main item I added to the dialog is a button to allow the background type to be changed. Clicking this button rotates us to the next background type. A static display tells us which background type is currently in use.

The following code was used to create the example program. The important areas that show how the CXSBgCtrl class was used are displayed with a border.

```
// BGTestDlg.h : header file
//


/////////////////////////////////////////////////////////////////
// CBGTestDlg dialog

class CBGTestDlg : public CDialog
{
// Construction
public:
    CBGTestDlg(CWnd* pParent = NULL);    // standard constructor

    CXSBgCtrl m_BgCtrl;

// Dialog Data
    //{{AFX_DATA(CBGTestDlg)
    enum { IDD = IDD_BGTEST_DIALOG };
    CString     m_strBgType;
    //}}AFX_DATA

    // ClassWizard generated virtual function overrides
    //{{AFX_VIRTUAL(CBGTestDlg)
    protected:
    virtual void DoDataExchange(CDataExchange* pDX);
    //}}AFX_VIRTUAL

// Implementation
protected:
    HICON m_hIcon;

    // Generated message map functions
    //{{AFX_MSG(CBGTestDlg)
```

```
        virtual BOOL OnInitDialog();
        afx_msg void OnSysCommand(UINT nID, LPARAM lParam);
        afx_msg void OnPaint();
        afx_msg HCURSOR OnQueryDragIcon();
        afx_msg void OnChange();
        //}}AFX_MSG
        DECLARE_MESSAGE_MAP()
};


#endif


// BGTestDlg.cpp : implementation file
//

#include "stdafx.h"
#include "BGTest.h"
#include "BGTestDlg.h"

#ifdef _DEBUG
#define new DEBUG_NEW
#undef THIS_FILE
static char THIS_FILE[] = __FILE__;
#endif


/////////////////////////////////////////////////////////////////
// CAboutDlg dialog used for App About

class CAboutDlg : public CDialog
{
public:
    CAboutDlg();

// Dialog Data
    //{{AFX_DATA(CAboutDlg)
    enum { IDD = IDD_ABOUTBOX };
    //}}AFX_DATA
```

```
    // ClassWizard generated virtual function overrides
    //{{AFX_VIRTUAL(CAboutDlg)
    protected:
    virtual void DoDataExchange(CDataExchange* pDX);
    //}}AFX_VIRTUAL

// Implementation
protected:
    //{{AFX_MSG(CAboutDlg)
    //}}AFX_MSG
    DECLARE_MESSAGE_MAP()
};

CAboutDlg::CAboutDlg() : CDialog(CAboutDlg::IDD)
{
    //{{AFX_DATA_INIT(CAboutDlg)
    //}}AFX_DATA_INIT
}

void CAboutDlg::DoDataExchange(CDataExchange* pDX)
{
    CDialog::DoDataExchange(pDX);
    //{{AFX_DATA_MAP(CAboutDlg)
    //}}AFX_DATA_MAP
}

BEGIN_MESSAGE_MAP(CAboutDlg, CDialog)
    //{{AFX_MSG_MAP(CAboutDlg)
        // No message handlers
    //}}AFX_MSG_MAP
END_MESSAGE_MAP()


/////////////////////////////////////////////////////////////
// CBGTestDlg dialog

CBGTestDlg::CBGTestDlg(CWnd* pParent /*=NULL*/)
    : CDialog(CBGTestDlg::IDD, pParent)
```

```
{
    //{{AFX_DATA_INIT(CBGTestDlg)
    m_strBgType = _T("");
    //}}AFX_DATA_INIT
    // Note that LoadIcon does not require a subsequent
    // DestroyIcon in Win32
    m_hIcon = AfxGetApp()->LoadIcon(IDR_MAINFRAME);
}

void CBGTestDlg::DoDataExchange(CDataExchange* pDX)
{
    CDialog::DoDataExchange(pDX);
    //{{AFX_DATA_MAP(CBGTestDlg)
    DDX_Text(pDX, IDC_BGTYPE, m_strBgType);
    //}}AFX_DATA_MAP
}

BEGIN_MESSAGE_MAP(CBGTestDlg, CDialog)
    //{{AFX_MSG_MAP(CBGTestDlg)
    ON_WM_SYSCOMMAND()
    ON_WM_PAINT()
    ON_WM_QUERYDRAGICON()
    ON_BN_CLICKED(IDC_CHANGE, OnChange)
    //}}AFX_MSG_MAP
END_MESSAGE_MAP()


/////////////////////////////////////////////////////////////
// CBGTestDlg message handlers

BOOL CBGTestDlg::OnInitDialog()
{
    CDialog::OnInitDialog();

    // Add "About..." menu item to system menu.

    // IDM_ABOUTBOX must be in the system command range.
    ASSERT((IDM_ABOUTBOX & 0xFFF0) == IDM_ABOUTBOX);
```

III

7

```
    ASSERT(IDM_ABOUTBOX < 0xF000);

    CMenu* pSysMenu = GetSystemMenu(FALSE);
    if (pSysMenu != NULL)
    {
        CString strAboutMenu;
        strAboutMenu.LoadString(IDS_ABOUTBOX);
        if (!strAboutMenu.IsEmpty())
        {
            pSysMenu->AppendMenu(MF_SEPARATOR);
            pSysMenu->AppendMenu(MF_STRING, IDM_ABOUTBOX,
                strAboutMenu);
        }
    }

    // Set the icon for this dialog.
    // The framework does this automatically
    //  when the application's main window is not a dialog
    SetIcon(m_hIcon, TRUE);            // Set big icon
    SetIcon(m_hIcon, FALSE);           // Set small icon
```
```
    // Install and set up the background control
    m_BgCtrl.DoInstall(this);
    m_BgCtrl.SetBitmaps(AfxGetResourceHandle(),
        IDB_ACTIVE, IDB_INACTIVE);
    m_strBgType = _T("Background Type: Bitmaps");
    UpdateData(FALSE);
```
```
    return TRUE;  // return TRUE  unless you set the focus to a control
}

void CBGTestDlg::OnSysCommand(UINT nID, LPARAM lParam)
{
    if ((nID & 0xFFF0) == IDM_ABOUTBOX)
    {
        CAboutDlg dlgAbout;
        dlgAbout.DoModal();
```

```
    }
    else
    {
        CDialog::OnSysCommand(nID, lParam);
    }
}


// If you add a minimize button to your dialog, you will
// need the code below to draw the icon.  For MFC
// applications using the document/view model,
//  this is automatically done for you by the framework.

void CBGTestDlg::OnPaint()
{
    if (IsIconic())
    {
        CPaintDC dc(this); // device context for painting

        SendMessage(WM_ICONERASEBKGND, (WPARAM) dc.GetSafeHdc(), 0);

        // Center icon in client rectangle
        int cxIcon = GetSystemMetrics(SM_CXICON);
        int cyIcon = GetSystemMetrics(SM_CYICON);
        CRect rect;
        GetClientRect(&rect);
        int x = (rect.Width() - cxIcon + 1) / 2;
        int y = (rect.Height() - cyIcon + 1) / 2;

        // Draw the icon
        dc.DrawIcon(x, y, m_hIcon);
    }
    else
    {
        CDialog::OnPaint();
    }
}
```

III

7

```
// The system calls this to obtain the cursor to display while the user drags
//   the minimized window.
HCURSOR CBGTestDlg::OnQueryDragIcon()
{
    return (HCURSOR) m_hIcon;
}
```

```
void CBGTestDlg::OnChange()
{
    static int nPos = 0;

    nPos++;
    if (nPos > 3)
        nPos = 0;

    m_strBgType = _T("Background Type: ");

    switch(nPos)
    {
    case 0:
        m_BgCtrl.SetBitmaps(AfxGetResourceHandle(),
            IDB_ACTIVE, IDB_INACTIVE);
        m_strBgType += _T("Bitmaps");
        break;

    case 1:
        m_BgCtrl.SetColor(RGB(55,110,220), RGB(0,55,110));
        m_strBgType += _T("Color");
        break;

    case 2:
        m_BgCtrl.SetGradient(RGB(55,110,220), RGB(0,55,110), 100);
        m_strBgType += _T("Gradient");
        break;

    case 3:
        m_BgCtrl.SetNormal();
```

```
        m_strBgType += _T("Normal");
        break;
    }


    UpdateData(FALSE);
    Invalidate();
}
```

Summary

In this chapter, we created a background control, CXSBgCtrl, for handling different variations of desired backgrounds within a window. This control can be used with any type of window. However, you may have to derive a class and add specific code for different window types. In the future, you should be able to find these derived classes on the http://www.xendra.com web site.

III

7

Chapter 8

Creating a Caption Control

Introduction

In this chapter, we are going to derive from the `CXSBgCtrl` class (the Background Control class we created in the previous chapter) and create a Caption Control class. Our newly derived `CXSCaption` class will have an effect similar to the `CXSBgCtrl` class, except this time, we'll redirect our painting from the client area to the nonclient area of the caption area. The purpose of this chapter is to show you how easy it is to derive from the classes within the framework presented in this book by overriding the appropriate virtual functions.

A Caption Control is an object whereby we can redefine the way the caption area of a window looks and behaves. As I mentioned earlier, most of the functionality for how the caption control looks is derived from the `CXSBgCtrl` class. It should work with any window that has the `WS_CAPTION` window style, including dialogs and MDI (multiple document interface) child windows.

XSCAPTION.H

CXSCaption **Class Declaration**

Aside from the functionality inherited from the CXSBgCtrl class, like resizing windows and maintaining the bitmaps, we have to think of what affects the caption bar. For one thing, we really don't have to draw the caption bar if the window is in an iconic state. Or do we? Run a regular Windows program that has MDI child windows. Minimize one of the child windows. Notice that what you are left with is the caption bar down towards the bottom left of the parent window. So, for MDI child windows, we have to make sure that we continue to paint the caption area, even if it is in an iconic state. You will see a new virtual function, DoCheckIconic, that returns TRUE if the window is in an iconic state. However, for a window with an extended style of WS_EX_MDICHILD, it always returns TRUE, with one exception. If you maximize a child window within its parent frame, you will see that there is no longer a caption to paint. So, in this case, we return FALSE.

When we work with the caption area of a window, we also have to deal with all objects that are contained within the caption area. This means dealing with the text, the caption icon, and the caption buttons. We also have to think about handling these objects if the extended window style is of type WS_EX_TOOLWINDOW. If this style is applied, the caption bar and caption objects become thinner.

We can change the attributes of the text in the caption area. We can change the font type, make it bold or italic, change its color, and the list goes on.

The CXSCaption class that we're going to create in this chapter works with any window that has the WS_CAPTION style applied to it, including regular dialogs. In the sample program at the end of this chapter, we'll apply this class to an MDI application. The dialog box will have a red caption to indicate an error. This is an excellent example of using color to convey a message to the user. Of course, this class has many more uses, but now that you have some ideas, let's get onto the implementation details.

```
class XSCLASS
CXSCaption : public CXSBgCtrl
{
// Construction
```

```
public:
                CXSCaption();
    virtual     ~CXSCaption();

    virtual BOOL DoInstall(CWnd* pWnd, BOOL bNotify = FALSE);
    virtual void DoInvalidate();

protected:
    virtual BOOL OnNcPaint(WPARAM wParam, LPARAM lParam);
    virtual BOOL OnNcActivate(WPARAM wParam, LPARAM lParam,
        LRESULT& lResult);
    virtual BOOL OnNcHitTest(WPARAM wParam, LPARAM lParam,
        LRESULT& lResult);
    virtual BOOL OnSetText(WPARAM wParam, LPARAM lParam,
        LRESULT& lResult);
    virtual BOOL OnSysColorChange(WPARAM wParam, LPARAM lParam);
    virtual BOOL OnPaletteChanged(WPARAM wParam, LPARAM lParam);
    virtual BOOL OnEraseBkgnd(WPARAM wParam, LPARAM lParam,
        LRESULT& lResult);
    virtual BOOL OnPaint(WPARAM wParam, LPARAM lParam);

    // font info
    struct _fontInfo
    {
        CFont       m_fntCap;
        COLORREF    m_crCap;
        BOOL        m_bBold;
        BOOL        m_bItalic;
        LOGFONT     m_lf;
        CString     m_str;
    } m_FontInfo[2];   // (inactive/active state)
```

III

8

```
public:
    virtual BOOL DoSetFonts(CString strActiveFontName = _T(""),
                            CString strInactiveFontName = _T(""));

protected:
    virtual void DoResetFontInfo();
    virtual void DoResetBitmaps();
    virtual void DoResetAll();

    virtual CRect DoGetBitmapRect(CWnd& wnd);
    virtual CRect DoGetPaintRect(CWnd& wnd);
    virtual CDC*  DoGetDC(CWnd& wnd);
    virtual BOOL  DoGetState(CWnd& wnd);
    virtual BOOL  DoCheckIconic(CWnd& cwnd);

    virtual BOOL DoDrawBackground(CDC* pDC, CXSBitmap& bmp,
        CRect& rcDim);
    virtual BOOL DoDrawIcon(CDC* pDC);
    virtual BOOL DoDrawButtons(CDC* pDC);
    virtual BOOL DoPreCreateFonts();
    virtual BOOL DoDrawText(CDC* pDC);
    virtual BOOL DoGetCaptionText();

    // create from serialization only
    DECLARE_DYNCREATE(CXSCaption);
};
```

XSCAPTION.CPP

Header Files

The following header files are needed for the CXSCaption class.

```
#include "stdafx.h"
#include "XSMisc.h"
#include "XSRect.h"
#include "XSPalette.h"
#include "XSDibApi.h"
#include "XSBitmap.h"
#include "XSSubWndCtrl.h"
#include "XSNotify.h"
#include "XSObject.h"
#include "XSBgCtrl.h"
#include "XSCaption.h"


IMPLEMENT_DYNCREATE(CXSCaption, CXSBgCtrl)
```

CXSCaption::CXSCaption

In the constructor, we call DoResetAll to initialize all pertinent variables. It is called in DoResetAll so that the code can be localized into one function. This allows us to call it during tasks other than initialization.

```
// --------------------------------------------------------------
// Function :
//     CXSCaption::CXSCaption
// Purpose  :
//     Constructor, initializes memory
// --------------------------------------------------------------
CXSCaption::CXSCaption()
{
    // Initialize
    DoResetAll();
```

III

8

```
}
CXSCaption::~CXSCaption
There are no dynamic allocations in this class so we don't
really have anything to clean up.


// --------------------------------------------------------------
// Function  :
//      CXSCaption::~CXSCaption
// Purpose   :
//      Destructor, cleans up memory
// --------------------------------------------------------------
CXSCaption::~CXSCaption()
{
}
```

CXSCaption::DoInstall

If you have been following along from previous chapters, then you know that the DoInstall function installs the subclass handler for the passed window. This particular rendition of DoInstall verifies that the passed window is of a certain type (i.e., a CWnd) before proceeding. We only want to subclass windows that may have the WS_CAPTION window style set, but this flag could be turned on and off programmatically. Therefore, we don't use this flag for verification purposes. Instead, we use the MFC Runtime Class information and the IsKindOf function to make sure our window is derived from one of the three classes: CWnd, CFrameWnd, or CDialog. If the subclassed window does not inherit from one of these window types, then we return FALSE and the subclassing does not take place. We need to do this for all classes that eventually inherit from the CXSObject class. Especially if the inherited class is not generic enough to work with all windows types.

```
// --------------------------------------------------------------
// Function  :
//      CXSCaption::DoInstall
// Purpose   :
//      Installs the CXSCaption instance as the handler for the
//      passed CWnd pointer
```

```
// Parameters:
//     CWnd* pWnd - The CWnd to attach to
// Returns    :
//     TRUE on success, FALSE on failure
// -------------------------------------------------------------
BOOL
CXSCaption::DoInstall(CWnd* pWnd, BOOL bNotify)
{
    ASSERT(pWnd);

    // Types this class can into install into
    if (!pWnd->IsKindOf(RUNTIME_CLASS(CWnd)) &&
        !pWnd->IsKindOf(RUNTIME_CLASS(CFrameWnd)) &&
        !pWnd->IsKindOf(RUNTIME_CLASS(CDialog)))
    {
        // You are trying to install the wrong type!
        ASSERT(FALSE);
        return FALSE;
    }

    return CXSBgCtrl::DoInstall(pWnd, bNotify);
}
```

CXSCaption::DoInvalidate

The virtual function DoInvalidate from the CXSBgCtrl class is overridden so a WM_NCPAINT message can be sent. This is important because the nonclient areas are not normally updated as much as the client areas. By calling DoInvalidate, we can ensure that the update takes place.

```
// -------------------------------------------------------------
// Function  :
//     CXSCaption::DoInvalidate
// Purpose   :
//     Invalidates the CXSCaption so that the bitmaps are
//     recreated and they are redrawn
```

III

8

```
// Parameters:
//    None
// Returns   :
//    Nothing
// -----------------------------------------------------------
void
CXSCaption::DoInvalidate()
{
    m_szBackground = CSize(0,0);
    DoGetWnd()->SendMessage(WM_NCPAINT);
}


// -----------------------------------------------------------
// Windows Message Handlers
// -----------------------------------------------------------
```

CXSCaption::OnNcPaint

You will notice that although the caption area is in the nonclient area, the painting is actually done in the WM_PAINT message handler, OnPaint. The OnNcPaint function determines if the caption area is inside the invalidated region to be updated. If it isn't, this function returns FALSE and allows Windows to do its default handling. If it is, the default functionality is called through the function Default and then a SendMessage sends a WM_PAINT message to make sure the caption bar is painted correctly.

```
// -----------------------------------------------------------
// Function  :
//    CXSCaption::OnNcPaint
// Purpose   :
//    Called when Windows asks for the non-client areas  to be
//    painted.
// Parameters:
//    HRGN hRgn - region that needs repainting
// Returns   :
//    Nothing
```

```
// -------------------------------------------------------------
BOOL
CXSCaption::OnNcPaint(WPARAM wParam, LPARAM lParam)
{
    // If we're normal, then let Windows/MFC
    // do all of the work
    if (BackgroundNormal == m_nBackgroundType)
        return FALSE;

    HRGN hRgn = (HRGN)wParam;

    // caption rect
    CXSCaptionRect rcDim(*DoGetWnd());

    // Get window cordinates
    CRect rcWin = CXSWindowRect(*DoGetWnd());

    // convert to screen coordinates
    rcDim += rcWin.TopLeft();

    // Don't paint if caption isn't within region to be
    // updated, just do the Default
    if ((WORD)hRgn > 1 && !::RectInRegion(hRgn, &rcDim))
        return FALSE;

    // Exclude caption from update region
    HRGN hRgnCaption = ::CreateRectRgnIndirect(&rcDim);
    HRGN hRgnNew = ::CreateRectRgnIndirect(&rcDim);
    if ((WORD)hRgn > 1)
    {
        // wParam is a valid region - subtract caption bar
        // from it
        ::CombineRgn(hRgnNew, hRgn, hRgnCaption, RGN_DIFF);
    }
```

III

8

```
    else
    {
        // wParam is not a valid region
        // create a region containing the whole window
        // minus the caption bar
        HRGN hRgnAll = ::CreateRectRgnIndirect(&rcWin);
        ::CombineRgn(hRgnNew, hRgnAll, hRgnCaption, RGN_DIFF);
        ::DeleteObject(hRgnAll);
    }

    // Call windows to do WM_NCPAINT with altered update region
    MSG& msg = AfxGetThreadState()->m_lastSentMsg;
    WPARAM wpSave = msg.wParam;         // save original wParam
    msg.wParam = (WPARAM)hRgnNew;       // set new region
    Default();                          // call normal WM_NCPAINT
    msg.wParam = wpSave;                // restore original wParam

    ::DeleteObject(hRgnCaption);
    ::DeleteObject(hRgnNew);

    DoGetWnd()->SendMessage(WM_PAINT, 0, 0);

    return TRUE;
}
```

CXSCaption::OnNcActivate

The OnNcActivate function determines if the caption bar needs to be repainted as a result of the window being made active. The determination of the active state is stored in a local boolean variable, bState. The first thing OnNcActivate checks is the WF_STAYACTIVE flag, which MFC uses to make a window look active, although it is not.

OnNcActivate must also determine if the window is derived from the CMDIFrameWnd class because child frames are not updated properly. We have to get the active frame using GetActiveFrame and then send the appropriate messages to ensure that everything is taken care of properly.

Next, we'll allow the default handling to take place. However, we want to avoid flicker when this happens, so the WS_VISIBLE flag is turned off. Then we allow the handling to take place by calling Default. Then, the WS_VISIBLE flag is turned back on.

Finally, a WM_NCPAINT message is sent to the window so that the caption will be painted.

```cpp
// ----------------------------------------------------------
// Function  :
//     CXSCaption::OnNcActivate
// Purpose   :
//     Determines if caption needs to be repainted
// Parameters:
//     BOOL bState - if this is 1, then it is the active state,
//        otherwise if it is 0, then it is the inactive state.
// Returns   :
//     BOOL - TRUE on success, FALSE on failure
// ----------------------------------------------------------
BOOL
CXSCaption::OnNcActivate(WPARAM wParam, LPARAM lParam,
                         LRESULT& lResult)
{
    // If we're normal, then let Windows/MFC
    // do all of the work
    if (BackgroundNormal == m_nBackgroundType)
        return FALSE;

    BOOL bState = (BOOL)wParam;
    lResult = TRUE;

    // Mimic MFC to stay active if WM_STAYACTIVE bit is on
    if (DoGetWnd()->m_nFlags & WF_STAYACTIVE)
        bState = TRUE;

    // Check to see if window is in inactive state
    if (!DoGetWnd()->IsWindowEnabled())
```

III

8

```
        bState = FALSE;

    // If this is an MDI app, manually activate/paint active
    // MDI child window, because windows won't do it if parent
    // frame is invisible. MUST do this before calling Default
    // or it will not work.
    if (DoGetWnd()->IsKindOf(RUNTIME_CLASS(CMDIFrameWnd)))
    {
        CMDIFrameWnd* pMDIFrame = (CMDIFrameWnd*)m_pWnd;
        CFrameWnd* pFrame = pMDIFrame->GetActiveFrame();
        if (pFrame != pMDIFrame)
        {
            pFrame->SendMessage(WM_NCACTIVATE, bState);
            pFrame->SendMessage(WM_NCPAINT);
        }
    }


    // Turn WS_VISIBLE off before calling DefWindowProc,
    // so DefWindowProc won't paint and thereby cause flicker
    DWORD dwStyle = DoGetWnd()->GetStyle();
    if (dwStyle & WS_VISIBLE)
        ::SetWindowLong(*DoGetWnd(), GWL_STYLE,
            (dwStyle & ~WS_VISIBLE));

    MSG& msg = AfxGetThreadState()->m_lastSentMsg;
    msg.wParam = bState;
    Default();
    if (dwStyle & WS_VISIBLE)
        ::SetWindowLong(*DoGetWnd(), GWL_STYLE, dwStyle);


    // Nothing has happened yet because WS_VISIBLE was
    // turned off.
    // Now it's time to rock'n'roll
    m_bState = bState;                    // update the state
```

```
    DoGetWnd()->SendMessage(WM_NCPAINT);   // do paint


    return TRUE;
}
```

CXSCaption::OnNcHitTest

The OnNcHitTest function is used to help solve a bug in the Windows caption bar handling. Although this is not a perfect solution, it does work somewhat. I am looking for a better alternative, so if anyone finds one, please let me know.

Here's a rundown of the bug. If you paint a window caption area, Windows will occasionally redraw the caption buttons along with the border around them in the default caption color. If you have not changed the default colors, this border will be blue. It looks ugly. This behavior happens when you drag the mouse over a nonclient area, such as the border, or click and drag the window using the caption bar.

This bug may be caused by some code in the default WM_NCHITTEST handler calling a function directly to paint the caption buttons. If this is true, it goes against the message passing methodology of the Windows operating system. There are several places in this class that could have called its handlers directly, but messages are sent instead. This is the correct method so that developers are not limited or boxed into the decisions that others make. I cannot see the logic in painting the caption buttons on every WM_NCHITTEST message, either.

The best we can do with this problem is to repaint the caption bar every time there is a WM_NCHITTEST message so that the border around the caption buttons is not permanent.

This problem is visible on all frames and dialogs. However, it is not visible on child windows of an MDI frame.

```
// ------------------------------------------------------------
// Function  :
//   CXSCaption::OnNcHitTest
// Purpose   :
//   To correct a bug in Windows that repaints the caption
//   buttons directly when a WM_NCHITTEST is detected.
// Parameters:
// ------------------------------------------------------------
```

III

8

```
BOOL
CXSCaption::OnNcHitTest(WPARAM wParam, LPARAM lParam,
                        LRESULT& lResult)
{
    // If we're normal, then let Windows/MFC
    // do all of the work
    if (BackgroundNormal == m_nBackgroundType)
        return FALSE;

    // Call Default handling
    lResult = Default();

    // Repaint caption because of bug
    DoInvalidate();

    return TRUE;
}
```

CXSCaption::OnSetText

Windows keeps an internal buffer for the text in the caption area. Whenever this text changes, Windows will send the appropriate messages to repaint the caption bar. We do not want Windows to do our caption painting, but we do want the text buffer to be updated. In Section I, Building Blocks, we discussed a function called XSCaption_SetText. This function turns the WS_VISIBLE window style flag off before actually setting the text of the window. The end result is that Windows first verifies whether the window is visible; if not, it doesn't force a repaint on the caption area. This achieves our goal of handling the update to the caption bar, without Windows meddling and messing it up.

Now that the text to the windows internal buffer has been updated, we need to recreate our bitmaps with the new text information. We invalidate our internal bitmaps, invalidate the Windows window, and send a WM_PAINT message.

```
// --------------------------------------------------------------
// Function   :
//  CXSCaption::OnSetText
// Purpose    :
//  Changes the text of the caption for this dialog
// Parameters:
// --------------------------------------------------------------
BOOL
CXSCaption::OnSetText(WPARAM wParam, LPARAM lParam,
                      LRESULT& lResult)
{
    // If we're normal, then let Windows/MFC
    // do all of the work
    if (BackgroundNormal == m_nBackgroundType)
        return FALSE;

    LPCTSTR lpText = (LPCTSTR)lParam;

    // Turn WS_VISIBLE off before calling windows to set the
    // text then turn it back on again
    ::XSCaption_SetText(*DoGetWnd(), lpText, FALSE);

    DoInvalidate();   // Set repaint flag

    lResult = TRUE;

    InvalidateWindow();
    DoGetWnd()->SendMessage(WM_PAINT, 0, 0);

    return TRUE;
}
```

III

8

CXSCaption::DoGetCaptionText

The DoGetCaptionText function retrieves the text from the window buffer and assigns it into our font structure. This function is virtual so that classes that inherit from this one can override this function and change the behavior of what is displayed for the caption text.

```
// ------------------------------------------------------------
// Function  :
//   CXSCaption::DoGetCaptionText
// Purpose   :
//   Gets the text of the current caption
// Returns   :
//   BOOL - TRUE on success
//        - FALSE on failure
// ------------------------------------------------------------
BOOL
CXSCaption::DoGetCaptionText()
{
    CString str;

    // Get the text from the window
    DoGetWnd()->GetWindowText(str);

    m_FontInfo[0].m_str = str;
    m_FontInfo[1].m_str = str;

    // Returning FALSE calls Default()
    return FALSE;
}
```

CXSCaption::DoResetBitmaps

We override the virtual function DoResetBitmap from the base class CXSBgCtrl because the default colors for a background control differ from a caption control. Here, for the caption control, we need to set

COLOR_INACTIVECAPTION as the inactive color and COLOR_ACTIVECAPTION as the active color.

```
// --------------------------------------------------------------
// Function  :
//     CXSCaption::DoResetBitmaps
// Purpose   :
//     Sets the bitmaps back to the default.  Uses system colors
//     COLOR_INACTIVECAPTION and COLOR_ACTIVECAPTION.
// Parameters:
//     None
// Returns   :
//     Nothing
// --------------------------------------------------------------
void
CXSCaption::DoResetBitmaps()
{
    // re-initialize attribute info
    m_nBackgroundType   = BackgroundNormal;
    m_crColor[0] = ::GetSysColor(COLOR_INACTIVECAPTION);
    m_crColor[1] = ::GetSysColor(COLOR_ACTIVECAPTION);
    m_nGradFills = 1;

    // initialize bitmaps
    for( int x = 0; x < 2; x++)
        m_bmp[x].DeleteObject();
}
```

III

8

CXSCaption::DoResetFontInfo

Because of the text information that we need to store in this control, we also have to maintain information about the text. This information is kept in a structure, or more accurately, in an array of structures. The first element of this array keeps information about the inactive attributes of the text information. The first element keeps information about the active attributes.

```
// -------------------------------------------------------------
// Function :
//    CXSCaption::DoResetFontInfo
// Purpose  :
//    Sets the font info back to the default.
// Parameters:
//    None
// Returns  :
//    Nothing
// -------------------------------------------------------------
void
CXSCaption::DoResetFontInfo()
{
    // initialize font attributes
    for( int x = 0; x < 2; x++)
    {
        m_FontInfo[x].m_fntCap.DeleteObject();
        m_FontInfo[x].m_crCap = (COLORREF)-1;
        m_FontInfo[x].m_bBold = TRUE;
        m_FontInfo[x].m_bItalic = FALSE;
        memset(&m_FontInfo[x].m_lf, 0, sizeof(LOGFONT));
        m_FontInfo[x].m_str = _T("");
    }
}
```

CXSCaption::DoResetAll

The DoResetAll function is a utility function for calling any other functions that reset variable data.

```
// -------------------------------------------------------------
// Function :
//    CXSCaption::ResetAll
// Purpose  :
```

```
//    Calls all appropriate reset functions.
// Parameters:
//    None
// Returns  :
//    Nothing
// -------------------------------------------------------------
void
CXSCaption::DoResetAll()
{
    DoResetFontInfo();
    DoResetBitmaps();
}
```

CXSCaption::DoSetFonts

The `DoSetFonts` function is used to set the fonts to be used for the active and inactive states of the caption bar. The string names of the fonts to be used are passed as arguments to this function. The strings may be empty, in which case, the default font for captions will be used. The color is set using the system `COLOR_INACTIVECAPTIONTEXT` and `COLOR_CAPTIONTEXT` definitions. The text is then set to `Bold` as a default. Finally, before the fonts are actually created, the virtual function `DoPreCreateFonts` is called. This allows the programmer to make any changes to the font other than the default values created in this function. After returning from `DoPreCreate-Fonts`, the font size is adjusted based on the caption bar height. Then, the fonts are created.

III

8

```
// -------------------------------------------------------------
// Function  :
//    CXSCaption::DoSetFonts
// Purpose   :
//    Sets the fonts to be used when painting the caption
// Parameters:
//    CString strActiveFontName - face name of the active font
//    CString strInactiveFontName - face name of the inactive
//       font
// Returns  :
```

```
//    TRUE on success, FALSE on failure
// -------------------------------------------------------------
BOOL
CXSCaption::DoSetFonts(CString strActiveFontName,
                       CString strInactiveFontName)
{
    // Rest the font information
    DoResetFontInfo();

    // Get current system caption font, just to get its size
    NONCLIENTMETRICS ncm;
    ncm.cbSize = sizeof(ncm);
    VERIFY(SystemParametersInfo(SPI_GETNONCLIENTMETRICS, 0,
                                &ncm, 0));

    // See if the strings are empty.  If they are, use
    // the default system font for captions
    if (strActiveFontName.IsEmpty())
        strActiveFontName = ncm.lfCaptionFont.lfFaceName;

    if (strInactiveFontName.IsEmpty())
        strInactiveFontName = ncm.lfCaptionFont.lfFaceName;

    // used for getting installed font information
    CFont fnt;

    // Create fonts the same size as caption
    // font, but use passed font name
    fnt.CreatePointFont(120, strInactiveFontName);
    fnt.GetLogFont(&m_FontInfo[0].m_lf);
    fnt.DeleteObject();

    fnt.CreatePointFont(120, strActiveFontName);
    fnt.GetLogFont(&m_FontInfo[1].m_lf);
    fnt.DeleteObject();
```

```
// Set up the default colors for the fonts
m_FontInfo[0].m_crCap =
    ::GetSysColor(COLOR_INACTIVECAPTIONTEXT);
m_FontInfo[1].m_crCap =
    ::GetSysColor(COLOR_CAPTIONTEXT);

// Default caption fonts are bold
m_FontInfo[0].m_bBold = TRUE;
m_FontInfo[1].m_bBold = TRUE;

// Call virtual function so attributes can be changed
// before font creation by any derived classes
DoPreCreateFonts();

// Make the fonts are the same height as caption font
m_FontInfo[0].m_lf.lfHeight = ncm.lfCaptionFont.lfHeight;
m_FontInfo[1].m_lf.lfHeight = ncm.lfCaptionFont.lfHeight;

// Create the fonts
m_FontInfo[0].m_fntCap.
    CreateFontIndirect(&m_FontInfo[0].m_lf);
m_FontInfo[1].m_fntCap.
    CreateFontIndirect(&m_FontInfo[1].m_lf);

return TRUE;
}
```

III

8

CXSCaption::DoPreCreateFonts

The DoPreCreateFonts function is called by the DoSetFonts function before the actual fonts are created. This gives the developer a chance to change the default behavior of the fonts before they are created.

```
// ----------------------------------------------------------------
// Function  :
//     CXSCaption::DoPreCreateFonts
// Purpose   :
//     Creates the fonts to be used for painting the screen.
//     This is a virtual function that allows a derived class
//     to modify the defaults.
// Parameters:
//     None
// Returns   :
//     BOOL - TRUE on success, FALSE on failure
// ----------------------------------------------------------------
BOOL
CXSCaption::DoPreCreateFonts()
{
    // Check for bold attribute
    if (m_FontInfo[0].m_bBold)
        m_FontInfo[0].m_lf.lfWeight |= FW_BOLD;

    if (m_FontInfo[1].m_bBold)
        m_FontInfo[1].m_lf.lfWeight |= FW_BOLD;

    // Check for italic attribute
    m_FontInfo[0].m_lf.lfItalic = m_FontInfo[0].m_bItalic;
    m_FontInfo[1].m_lf.lfItalic = m_FontInfo[1].m_bItalic;

    return TRUE;
}
```

CXSCaption::DoDrawBackground

As the following comments mention, the `DoDrawBackground` function acts like a director, calling the appropriate functions to get the job of painting the caption bar completed. This function calls `DoDrawIcon`, `DoDrawButtons`, and `DoDrawText` to take care of the objects that are to be painted on top of the bitmap that will eventually be used for the caption bar.

```cpp
// --------------------------------------------------------------
// Function  :
//   CXSCaption::DoDrawBackground
// Purpose   :
//   This is the actual function that processes the painting of
//   the caption.  It works as a director, calling the
//   appropriate functions.  To change the default behavior,
//   derive this class and provide the appropriate virtual
//   functions. handler for the passed caption pointer.
// Parameters:
//   CDC* pDC - Device context to draw on
//   const CRect& rcDim - RECT of where to paint
//   CXSBitmap& bmp - Bitmap to paint in to
// Returns   : TRUE on success
//             FALSE on failure
// --------------------------------------------------------------
BOOL
CXSCaption::DoDrawBackground(CDC* pDC, CXSBitmap& bmp,
                             CRect& rcDim)
{
    // Select bitmap to draw on to
    CBitmap* pOldBitmap;
    pOldBitmap = pDC->SelectObject(&bmp);

    // Draw onto the bitmap
    DoDrawIcon(pDC);
    DoDrawButtons(pDC);
    DoDrawText(pDC);
```

III

8

```
    // Done drawing
    pDC->SelectObject(pOldBitmap);


    return TRUE;
}
```

CXSCaption::DoDrawIcon

The DoDrawIcon function takes care of the work needed to draw the icon sometimes found in the upper-left of the caption bar. If there is no icon associated with this window, the function returns FALSE. The size of the icon is determined by calling the API function GetSystemMetrics with the appropriate value. The appropriate value is different if this window has the WS_EX_TOOLWINDOW window style applied. The output is accomplished by calling the API function DrawIconEx.

```
// -----------------------------------------------------------------
// Function :
//   CXSCaption::DoDrawIcon
// Purpose  :
//   Draws the Icon on the caption of the specified device
//   context
// Parameters:
//   CDC* pDC - Device context to draw on
// Returns  : TRUE on success
//             FALSE on failure
// -----------------------------------------------------------------
BOOL
CXSCaption::DoDrawIcon(CDC* pDC)
{
    ASSERT(pDC);

    HICON hIcon;
    hIcon = (HICON)::GetClassLong(DoGetWnd()->m_hWnd,
        GCL_HICONSM);
```

```
if (!hIcon)
    return FALSE;

DWORD dwExStyle = DoGetWnd()->GetExStyle();
BOOL bToolWindow = (dwExStyle & WS_EX_TOOLWINDOW);

// Get caption rect
CRect rcDim = DoGetBitmapRect(*DoGetWnd());

// Within the basic button rectangle, Windows 95 uses
// a 1 or 2 pixel border.  The Icon has 2 pixel border
// on left, 1 pixel on top/bottom, 0 on the right
int cxIcon = bToolWindow - ::GetSystemMetrics(SM_CXSMSIZE)
    ::GetSystemMetrics(SM_CXSIZE);
    int cyIcon = bToolWindow -
        ::GetSystemMetrics(SM_CYSMSIZE) :
        ::GetSystemMetrics(SM_CYSIZE);

CRect rc(rcDim.left, rcDim.top, rcDim.left + cxIcon,
    rcDim.top + cyIcon);
rc.DeflateRect(0,1);
rc.left += 2;

// Get the registered icon and display it
return ::DrawIconEx(pDC->m_hDC, rc.left, rc.top,
        hIcon, rc.Width(), rc.Height(), 0, NULL,
        DI_NORMAL);
}
```

III

8

CXSCaption::DoDrawButtons

The DoDrawButtons function takes care of drawing the caption buttons in the correct area of the caption bar. Several conditions apply for making this work properly. The size of the buttons is determined by finding out if this window has the WS_EX_TOOLWINDOW window style applied. If the window is an MDI child window in its iconic state, the buttons are drawn a bit differently than in its non-iconic state. All buttons are drawn using the API function DrawFrameControl. The style associated with the window is tested for each type of caption button before it is drawn. The DFCS_CAPTIONRESTORE and DFCS_CAPTIONMAX reside in the same area, so some logic has to be used in determining which one is drawn. For instance, if the window is maximized, the DFCS_CAPTIONRESTORE is used; otherwise, the DFCS_CAPTIONMAX button is used. Other styles that are observed, besides WS_MAXIMIZEBOX, are WS_EX_CONTEXTHELP and WS_MINIMIZEBOX.

```
// --------------------------------------------------------------
// Function  :
//   CXSCaption::DoDrawButtons
// Purpose   :
//   Draws the standard Windows 95 button (minimize, restore, and
//   close) on the passes device context
// Parameters:
//   CDC* pDC - Device context to draw on
// Returns   : TRUE on success
//             FALSE on failure
// --------------------------------------------------------------
BOOL
CXSCaption::DoDrawButtons(CDC* pDC)
{
    ASSERT(pDC);

    // Get the window style
    DWORD dwStyle = DoGetWnd()->GetStyle();
    DWORD dwExStyle = DoGetWnd()->GetExStyle();
    BOOL bMdiChild = (dwExStyle & WS_EX_MDICHILD);
    BOOL bToolWindow = (dwExStyle & WS_EX_TOOLWINDOW);

    // Get system icon sizes
    int cxIcon = bToolWindow - ::GetSystemMetrics(SM_CXSMSIZE) :
        ::GetSystemMetrics(SM_CXSIZE);
    int cyIcon = bToolWindow - ::GetSystemMetrics(SM_CYSMSIZE) :
        ::GetSystemMetrics(SM_CYSIZE);
```

```
    // Get caption rect
    CRect rcDim = DoGetBitmapRect(*DoGetWnd());

    // Draw caption buttons. These are all drawn inside a
    // rectangle of dimensions SM_CXSIZE by SM_CYSIZE
    CRect rc(rcDim.right - cxIcon, rcDim.top,
        rcDim.right, rcDim.top + cyIcon);

    // If the window is a MDI child window in it's iconic
    // state, then the buttons are drawn different then
    // a regular window with a caption
    if (DoGetWnd()->IsIconic() && bMdiChild)
        rc.DeflateRect(1, 1, 1, 3);  // iconic MDI child
    else
        rc.DeflateRect(0, 2, 2, 2);  // regular caption window


    pDC->DrawFrameControl(&rc, DFC_CAPTION, DFCS_CAPTIONCLOSE);

    // Max/restore button is like close box; just shift
    // rectangle left.  Also does help button, if any.
    BOOL bMaxBox = dwStyle & WS_MAXIMIZEBOX;
    if (bMaxBox || (dwExStyle & WS_EX_CONTEXTHELP))
    {
        rc -= CPoint(cxIcon, 0);
        if (DoGetWnd()->IsIconic() && bMdiChild)
        {
            pDC->DrawFrameControl(&rc, DFC_CAPTION,
                bMaxBox - (DoGetWnd()->IsZoomed() -
                DFCS_CAPTIONRESTORE : DFCS_CAPTIONMAX) :
                DFCS_CAPTIONHELP);
        }
        else
```

III

8

```
    {
        pDC->DrawFrameControl(&rc, DFC_CAPTION,
            bMaxBox - (DoGetWnd()->IsZoomed() -
            DFCS_CAPTIONRESTORE : DFCS_CAPTIONMAX) :
            DFCS_CAPTIONHELP);
    }
}


// Minimize button has 2 pixel border on all sides but right.
if (dwStyle & WS_MINIMIZEBOX)
{
    rc -= CPoint(cxIcon-2,0);
    if (DoGetWnd()->IsIconic() && bMdiChild)
        pDC->DrawFrameControl(&rc, DFC_CAPTION,
        DFCS_CAPTIONRESTORE);
    else
        pDC->DrawFrameControl(&rc, DFC_CAPTION,
        DFCS_CAPTIONMIN);
}

return TRUE;
}
```

CXSCaption::DoDrawText

DoDrawText paints the text that will be displayed in the caption area. If no font has been set up, this function calls DoSetFonts to set up the default system caption fonts. The function then calls DoGetCaptionText to get the text to be used for painting. By default, the DoGetCaptionText accesses the window's internal buffer that contains the default text. The DoGetCaptionText is virtual so a developer can override the function to provide alternative text.

Before actually painting the text onto the bitmap that will be placed into the caption area, DoDrawText checks whether this window has an associated icon by calling the Windows API function GetClassLong with the GCL_HICONSM flag. If the window does have an icon, the text will be shifted

to make room. To find out the width of the icon, we call the API function
GetSystemMetrics with the SM_CXSIZE flag.

Just before painting the text, the background mode is set to TRANSPARENT
using the SetBkMode member function of the passed CDC. Then, the text
color is set with the SetTextColor member function of the CDC. The font
object is then selected into the CDC and we paint the text with a call to Draw-
Text. The DT_END_ELLIPSIS flag is used when painting the text in case the
text exceeds the width of the window. If the text does exceed the window
width, it is painted to the width of the window ending with an ellipsis
("..."). This shows the user that there is more text available than they can
see right now. Finally, we clean up by selecting the old font object back into
the CDC.

```
// -----------------------------------------------------------------
// Function  :
//   CXSCaption::DoDrawText
// Purpose   :
//   Draws the text to be used on the internal bitmaps before
//   painting them to the caption
// Parameters:
//   CDC* pDC - The device context on which to draw
// Returns   : TRUE on success
//             FALSE on failure
// -----------------------------------------------------------------
BOOL
CXSCaption::DoDrawText(CDC* pDC)
{
    ASSERT(pDC);

    // If one is set, they are all set
    if (!m_FontInfo[0].m_fntCap.GetSafeHandle())
        DoSetFonts(); // create default fonts


    // Call virtual function to retrieve text
    // Default function gets regular text
    // Programmer can change this by deriving from virtual
    // function
```

III

8

```
    DoGetCaptionText();

    // Get caption rect
    CRect rcDim = DoGetBitmapRect(*DoGetWnd());

    // Shift away from the border
    rcDim.left += 3;

    HICON hIcon;
    hIcon = (HICON)GetClassLong(DoGetWnd()->m_hWnd, GCL_HICONSM);
    if (hIcon)
    {
        // We want to draw to the right of the icon, not on it
        int cxIcon = GetSystemMetrics(SM_CXSIZE);
        rcDim.left += cxIcon;
    }

    // Now, let's draw the text
    CFont* pOldFont;

    // draw on top of our background
    pDC->SetBkMode(TRANSPARENT);
    pDC->SetTextColor(m_FontInfo[m_bState].m_crCap);
    pOldFont = pDC->SelectObject(&m_FontInfo[m_bState].
                                  m_fntCap);
    pDC->DrawText(m_FontInfo[m_bState].m_str, &rcDim,
        DT_LEFT|DT_VCENTER|DT_SINGLELINE|DT_END_ELLIPSIS);

    pDC->SelectObject(pOldFont);

    return TRUE;
}
```

CXSCaption::DoGetBitmapRect

DoGetBitmapRect is a utility function for retrieving the rectangular area of the bitmap needed for painting to the caption area.

```
// ------------------------------------------------------------
// Function  :
//   CXSBgCtrl::DoGetBitmapRect
// Purpose   :
//   Gets the dimensions of the needed bitmap
// Parameters:
//   CWnd& wnd - Reference to a CWnd
// Returns   :
// ------------------------------------------------------------
CRect
CXSCaption::DoGetBitmapRect(CWnd& wnd)
{
    CXSCaptionRect rcDim(wnd);

    // Normalize the CRect to 0,0 coordinates
    CRect rcTemp = rcDim;
    rcTemp.left -= rcDim.left;
    rcTemp.right -= rcDim.left;
    rcTemp.top -= rcDim.top;
    rcTemp.bottom -= rcDim.top;

    return rcTemp;
}
```

III

8

CXSCaption::DoGetPaintRect

DoGetPaintRect is also a utility function for retrieving the client dimensions of where the painting will take place.

```
// ------------------------------------------------------------
// Function  :
//     CXSBgCtrl::DoGetPaintRect
// Purpose   :
```

```
//     Virtual function that returns the dimensions in client
//       coordinates of where to paint.
// Parameters:
//     CWnd& wnd - Reference to a CWnd
// Returns   :
//     CRect - The dimensions in client coordinates within the
//       CWnd to use for painting.
// --------------------------------------------------------------
CRect
CXSCaption::DoGetPaintRect(CWnd& wnd)
{
    return CXSCaptionRect(wnd);
}
```

CXSCaption::DoGetDC

DoGetDC is another utility function for retrieving the device context needed for painting operations.

```
// --------------------------------------------------------------
// Function :
//   CXSCaption::DoGetDC
// Purpose  :
//   Gets the DC to paint on to
// Parameters:
//   CWnd& wnd - window to get DC from
// Returns   :
//   CDC* - pointer to the needed DC.
// Comments  :
//   Remember to release this DC when you are done with it.
// --------------------------------------------------------------
CDC*
CXSCaption::DoGetDC(CWnd& wnd)
```

```
{
    CWindowDC* pDC = new CWindowDC(&wnd);
    return pDC;
}
```

CXSCaption::DoGetState

The DoGetState function returns the active state of the passed CWnd. If the window is derived from CMDIChildWnd, we get a CMDIFrameWnd pointer to the parent. This pointer is then used by calling GetActiveFrame to get the CFrameWnd pointer to the active child frame. If the CFrameWnd pointer matches the address of the passed window, then we know it is the active child frame. If it is the active child frame, the parent frame is then tested to see if it is active by calling GetForegroundWindow. If the parent is the foreground window, then we know the active state is TRUE; otherwise, it is not active. If our passed window is not a child frame, then the default handler in our base class, CXSBgCtrl::DoGetState, is called.

```
// -------------------------------------------------------------
// Function  :
//   CXSCaption::DoGetState
// Purpose   :
//   Returns the state of the passed CWnd
// Parameters:
//   CWnd& wnd - reference to the window that needs the state
//   reported
// Returns   :
//   BOOL - TRUE if the state is active
//        - FALSE if the state is inactive
// -------------------------------------------------------------
BOOL
CXSCaption::DoGetState(CWnd& wnd)
{
    BOOL bState = 1;  // Assume active

    // Child Frames in an MDI app need help knowing what state
    // they are in...
```

III

8

```
if (DoGetWnd()->IsKindOf(RUNTIME_CLASS(CMDIChildWnd)))
{
    CMDIFrameWnd* pMDIFrame =
        (CMDIFrameWnd*)((CMDIChildWnd*)DoGetWnd())->
        GetParentFrame();
    if (pMDIFrame)
    {
        CFrameWnd* pFrame = pMDIFrame->GetActiveFrame();
        if (pFrame && pFrame == m_pWnd)
        {
            // This is the active frame, but is the
            // parent frame
            if (pFrame->GetForegroundWindow() == pMDIFrame)
            {
                bState = 1;
            }
            else
            {
                bState = 0;
            }
        }
    }
}
else
{
    bState = CXSBgCtrl::DoGetState(wnd);
}

return bState;
}
```

CXSCaption::DoCheckIconic

The DoCheckIconic function is a critical component to the CXSCaption class. Normally, if the window is in its iconic state, we do have to worry about painting the caption because there is none. The exception to this rule is a child window of an MDI frame. In this case, the caption is drawn along with the associated icon and caption buttons. The other prevalent rule we have to observe is if the window is a child frame and it is in its zoomed, or maximized, state. In this case, the window has no caption to paint.

```cpp
// -------------------------------------------------------------
// Function  :
//   CXSCaption::DoCheckIconic
// Purpose   :
//   Checks to see if the passed CWnd is in an iconic state.
//   There is no need to draw the background bitmaps if the CWnd
//   is in an iconic state.
// Parameters:
//   CWnd& wnd - reference to the window that needs the iconic
//   state reported
// Returns   :
//   BOOL - TRUE if the window is in an iconic state
//        - FALSE if the window is not in an iconic state
// -------------------------------------------------------------
BOOL
CXSCaption::DoCheckIconic(CWnd& cwnd)
{
    if (DoGetWnd()->IsIconic())
    {
        // EXCEPTION: If it is a MDI child window,
        // then we do draw it
        if (!(DoGetWnd()->GetExStyle() & WS_EX_MDICHILD))
            return TRUE;
        else
        {
            // Don't draw caption if MDI child is zoomed
            if (DoGetWnd()->IsZoomed())
                return TRUE;
            else
                return FALSE;
```

III

8

```
        }
    }


    return TRUE;
}
```

CXSCaption::OnPaint

The painting operations of the CXSCaption class are administered by calling the base class function CXSBgCtrl::OnPaint and using virtual functions to redirect the caption painting. However, if we returned TRUE from the OnPaint function, then no other painting operations would occur by other subclass handlers or the default processing. Because we only paint the caption bar, it is conceivable that some other handler will need to paint the rest of the client area. For this reason, we return FALSE to indicate that the subclass handler manager should continue with further processing.

```
// ----------------------------------------------------------------
// Function :
//   CXSCaption::OnPaint
// Purpose  :
//   Calls CXSBgCtrl::Paint in case other painting is needed.
// Parameters:
// Returns  :
// Comments :
//   This function exists in this class because there
//   are really two painting operations happening here.  The
//   appropriate variables have been set up so that only the
//   caption (title bar) is painted by calling the base class
//   CXSBgCtrl::OnPaint.  However, if we left it at this, then
//   the rest of the client area of the window would not get
//   painted.  So, we then return FALSE so that default
//   processing can finish up what is needed.
// ----------------------------------------------------------------
BOOL
CXSCaption::OnPaint(WPARAM wParam, LPARAM lParam)
```

```
{
    CXSBgCtrl::OnPaint(wParam, lParam);

    // Provide default processing for client area
    return FALSE;
}
```

Using CXSCaption

Now that the CXSCaption code is complete, I'm sure you'd like to see it in action. The sample program, FrameTest, will be used to display an MDI application with child frames and a dialog. The main frame, the child frame, and the dialog will all have their captions modified using the CXSCaption class.

To apply the CXSCaption changes to a particular frame, you select the menu item Caption, then Normal, Color or Bitmap. One rule to remember with this sample program is that the changes apply to the active frame. If you have any child frames visible, you will not be able to change the main frame window. You can also create several child frames by selecting the menu item File/ New. You can activate each child frame by selecting it and then making changes to it.

Finally, you can also select the menu item Caption, then Dialog to see a sample dialog with a changed caption bar. The sample program has not been programmed to allow you to change the properties of the dialog. The default color of the dialog's caption bar has been set to red to indicate an error condition.

One thing you should do after setting the properties of a frame is test its active and inactive states and notice how the caption changes to reflect this state.

In Figures 8.1 and 8.2, you will see some images of the expected output.

III

8

Figure 8.1   The main frame using a gradient color.

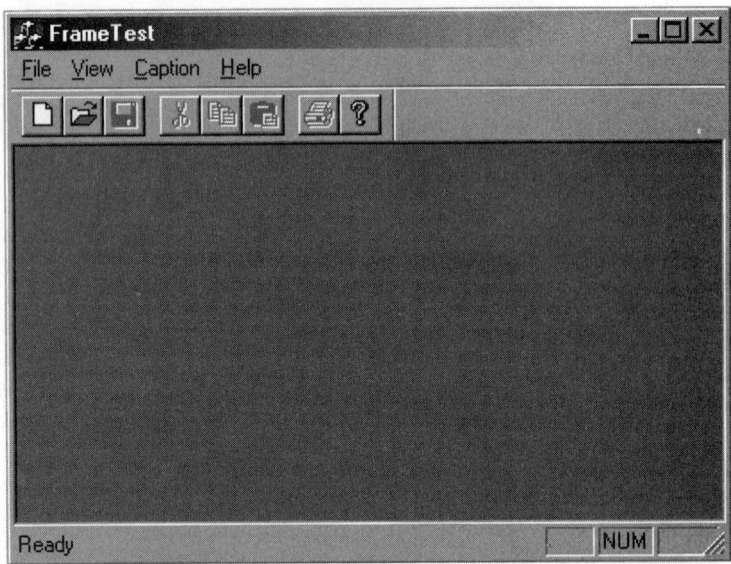

Figure 8.2   The child frame using a tiled bitmap.

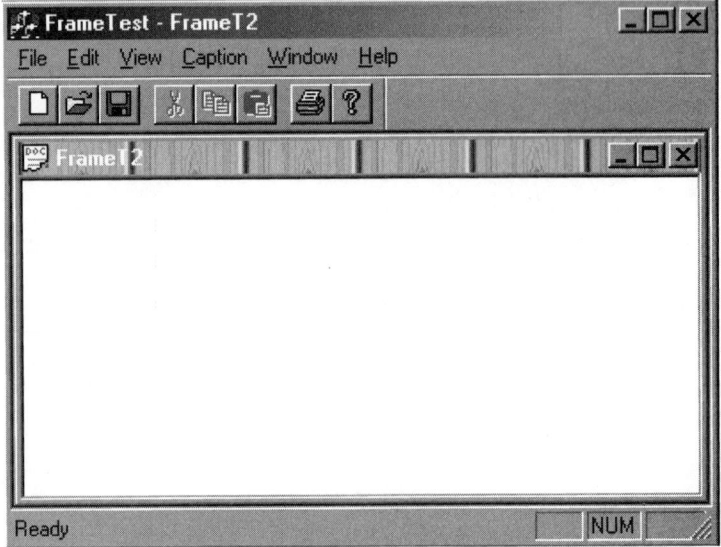

Not all the code from the sample program is displayed in the following fragment. The important areas of the code have been emphasized with a border to show code that has been modified for the sample program.

```
// FrameStatic.h : header file

/////////////////////////////////////////////////////////////////////
// CFrameStatic window

class CFrameStatic : public CStatic
{
// Construction
public:
    CFrameStatic();

// Attributes
public:

private:
    COLORREF    m_crColor;

// Operations
public:
    void SetColor(COLORREF cr);

// Overrides
    // ClassWizard generated virtual function overrides
    //{{AFX_VIRTUAL(CFrameStatic)
    //}}AFX_VIRTUAL

// Implementation
public:
    virtual ~CFrameStatic();

    // Generated message map functions
protected:
    //{{AFX_MSG(CFrameStatic)
    afx_msg void OnPaint();
    //}}AFX_MSG
```

III

8

```
    DECLARE_MESSAGE_MAP()
};


#endif
```

```
// FrameStatic.cpp : implementation file

#include "stdafx.h"
#include "FrameTest.h"
#include "FrameStatic.h"

#ifdef _DEBUG
#define new DEBUG_NEW
#undef THIS_FILE
static char THIS_FILE[] = __FILE__:
#endif

/////////////////////////////////////////////////////////////////
// CFrameStatic

CFrameStatic::CFrameStatic()
{
    // Initial color
    m_crColor = ::GetSysColor(COLOR_3DFACE);
}

CFrameStatic::~CFrameStatic()
{
}

BEGIN_MESSAGE_MAP(CFrameStatic, CStatic)
    //{{AFX_MSG_MAP(CFrameStatic)
    ON_WM_PAINT()
    //}}AFX_MSG_MAP
END_MESSAGE_MAP()


/////////////////////////////////////////////////////////////////
```

```
// CFrameStatic message handlers

void CFrameStatic::SetColor(COLORREF cr)
{
    m_crColor = cr;
}

void CFrameStatic::OnPaint()
{
    CPaintDC dc(this); // device context for painting

    CRect rect;
    GetClientRect(&rect);

    ::XSPaint_Rect(&dc, 0, 0, rect.Width(), rect.Height(), m_crColor);
    dc.Draw3dRect(0, 0, rect.Width(), rect.Height(),
        RGB(255,255,255), RGB(0,0,0));
}
```

```
// SelectColors.h : header file

#include "resource.h"
#include "FrameStatic.h"

/////////////////////////////////////////////////////////////////
// CSelectColors dialog

class CSelectColors : public CDialog
{
// Construction
public:
    CSelectColors(CWnd* pParent = NULL);   // standard constructor
    virtual ~CSelectColors();

// Dialog Data
    //{{AFX_DATA(CSelectColors)
    enum { IDD = IDD_COLOR_SELECT };
```

```
    CFrameStatic    m_stInactiveColor;
    CFrameStatic    m_stActiveColor;
    int        m_nGradients;
    //}}AFX_DATA


// Overrides
    // ClassWizard generated virtual function overrides
    //{{AFX_VIRTUAL(CSelectColors)
    protected:
    virtual void DoDataExchange(CDataExchange* pDX);
    //}}AFX_VIRTUAL

// Implementation
protected:

    // Generated message map functions
    //{{AFX_MSG(CSelectColors)
    afx_msg void OnActiveColor();
    afx_msg void OnInactiveColor();
    virtual void OnOK();
    virtual BOOL OnInitDialog();
    //}}AFX_MSG
    DECLARE_MESSAGE_MAP()

protected:
    COLORREF    m_crActive;
    COLORREF    m_crInactive;

    void ColorStatics(COLORREF crActive, COLORREF crInactive);
    void ShowColorDialog(COLORREF& cr);

public:
    COLORREF    GetActiveColor(){ return m_crActive; }
    COLORREF    GetInactiveColor(){ return m_crInactive; }
    int        GetGradientNum(){ return m_nGradients; }
};
```

```
#endif
```

```
// SelectColors.cpp : implementation file

#include "stdafx.h"
#include "FrameTest.h"
#include "SelectColors.h"

#ifdef _DEBUG
#define new DEBUG_NEW
#undef THIS_FILE
static char THIS_FILE[] = __FILE__;
#endif


/////////////////////////////////////////////////////////////////
// CSelectColors dialog
```

```
CSelectColors::CSelectColors(CWnd* pParent /*=NULL*/)
    : CDialog(CSelectColors::IDD, pParent)
{
    //{{AFX_DATA_INIT(CSelectColors)
    m_nGradients = 1;
    //}}AFX_DATA_INIT

    // Initialize members
    m_crActive = ::GetSysColor(COLOR_ACTIVECAPTION);
    m_crInactive = ::GetSysColor(COLOR_INACTIVECAPTION);
}
```

```
CSelectColors::~CSelectColors()
{
}
```

```
void CSelectColors::DoDataExchange(CDataExchange* pDX)
{
    CDialog::DoDataExchange(pDX);
```

III

8

```
    //{{AFX_DATA_MAP(CSelectColors)
    DDX_Control(pDX, IDC_INACTIVE_COLOR_STATIC, m_stInactiveColor);
    DDX_Control(pDX, IDC_ACTIVE_COLOR_STATIC, m_stActiveColor);
    DDX_Text(pDX, IDC_EDIT_GRADIENTS, m_nGradients);
    DDV_MinMaxInt(pDX, m_nGradients, 1, 100);
    //}}AFX_DATA_MAP
}
```

```
BEGIN_MESSAGE_MAP(CSelectColors, CDialog)
    //{{AFX_MSG_MAP(CSelectColors)
    ON_BN_CLICKED(IDC_ACTIVE_COLOR, OnActiveColor)
    ON_BN_CLICKED(IDC_INACTIVE_COLOR, OnInactiveColor)
    //}}AFX_MSG_MAP
END_MESSAGE_MAP()
```

```
//////////////////////////////////////////////////////////
// CSelectColors message handlers
```

```
void CSelectColors::OnActiveColor()
{
    ShowColorDialog(m_crActive);
}
```

```
void CSelectColors::OnInactiveColor()
{
    ShowColorDialog(m_crInactive);
}
```

```
void CSelectColors::OnOK()
{
    // TODO: Add extra validation here

    CDialog::OnOK();
}
```

```
BOOL CSelectColors::OnInitDialog()
{
```

```
    CDialog::OnInitDialog();

    // Set the statics to normal color initially
    ColorStatics(m_crActive, m_crInactive);

    return TRUE;  // return TRUE unless you set the focus to a control
                  // EXCEPTION: OCX Property Pages should return FALSE
}
```

```
void
CSelectColors::ColorStatics(COLORREF crActive, COLORREF crInactive)
{
    m_crActive = crActive;
    m_stActiveColor.SetColor(m_crActive);
    m_stActiveColor.Invalidate();
    m_crInactive = crInactive;
    m_stInactiveColor.SetColor(m_crInactive);
    m_stInactiveColor.Invalidate();
}
```

```
void
CSelectColors::ShowColorDialog(COLORREF& cr)
{
    CColorDialog dlgColor;

    dlgColor.m_cc.Flags |= CC_RGBINIT;
    dlgColor.m_cc.rgbResult = cr;

    if (IDCANCEL == dlgColor.DoModal())
        return;

    cr = dlgColor.GetColor();
    ColorStatics(m_crActive, m_crInactive);
}
```

III

8

```
// ErrorDlg.h : header file
```

```
///////////////////////////////////////////////////////////
// CErrorDlg dialog

class CErrorDlg : public CDialog
{
// Construction
public:
    CErrorDlg(CWnd* pParent = NULL);   // standard constructor

// Dialog Data
    //{{AFX_DATA(CErrorDlg)
    enum { IDD = IDD_ERROR_DLG };
        // NOTE: the ClassWizard will add data members here
    //}}AFX_DATA

// Overrides
    // ClassWizard generated virtual function overrides
    //{{AFX_VIRTUAL(CErrorDlg)
    protected:
    virtual void DoDataExchange(CDataExchange* pDX);
    //}}AFX_VIRTUAL

public:
    CXSCaption      m_dlgCaption;

// Implementation
protected:

    // Generated message map functions
    //{{AFX_MSG(CErrorDlg)
    afx_msg int OnCreate(LPCREATESTRUCT lpCreateStruct);
    virtual BOOL OnInitDialog();
    //}}AFX_MSG
    DECLARE_MESSAGE_MAP()
};

#endif
```

```
// ErrorDlg.cpp : implementation file

#include "stdafx.h"
#include "FrameTest.h"
#include "ErrorDlg.h"

#ifdef _DEBUG
#define new DEBUG_NEW
#undef THIS_FILE
static char THIS_FILE[] = __FILE__;
#endif

/////////////////////////////////////////////////////////////////
// CErrorDlg dialog


CErrorDlg::CErrorDlg(CWnd* pParent /*=NULL*/)
    : CDialog(CErrorDlg::IDD, pParent)
{
    //{{AFX_DATA_INIT(CErrorDlg)
        // NOTE: the ClassWizard will add member initialization here
    //}}AFX_DATA_INIT
}

void CErrorDlg::DoDataExchange(CDataExchange* pDX)
{
    CDialog::DoDataExchange(pDX);
    //{{AFX_DATA_MAP(CErrorDlg)
        // NOTE: the ClassWizard will add DDX and DDV calls here
    //}}AFX_DATA_MAP
}

BEGIN_MESSAGE_MAP(CErrorDlg, CDialog)
    //{{AFX_MSG_MAP(CErrorDlg)
    ON_WM_CREATE()
    //}}AFX_MSG_MAP
```

III

8

```
END_MESSAGE_MAP()

/////////////////////////////////////////////////////////////////
// CErrorDlg message handlers

int CErrorDlg::OnCreate(LPCREATESTRUCT lpCreateStruct)
{
if (CDialog::OnCreate(lpCreateStruct) == -1)
        return -1;

    // Subclass the Child window frame
    m_dlgCaption.DoInstall(this);


    return 0;
}

BOOL CErrorDlg::OnInitDialog()
{
    CDialog::OnInitDialog();

    m_dlgCaption.SetColor(RGB(255,0,0), RGB(255,100,100));

    return TRUE;  // return TRUE unless you set the focus to a control
                  // EXCEPTION: OCX Property Pages should return FALSE
}

// MainFrm.h : interface of the CMainFrame class
//
/////////////////////////////////////////////////////////////////

class CMainFrame : public CMDIFrameWnd
{
    DECLARE_DYNAMIC(CMainFrame)
public:
    CMainFrame();

// Attributes
```

```
public:
    CXSCaption     m_frmCaption;  // class for changing the caption

// Operations
public:

// Overrides
    // ClassWizard generated virtual function overrides
    //{{AFX_VIRTUAL(CMainFrame)
    virtual BOOL PreCreateWindow(CREATESTRUCT& cs);
    //}}AFX_VIRTUAL

// Implementation
public:
    virtual ~CMainFrame();
#ifdef _DEBUG
    virtual void AssertValid() const;
    virtual void Dump(CDumpContext& dc) const;
#endif

protected:  // control bar embedded members
    CStatusBar  m_wndStatusBar;
    CToolBar    m_wndToolBar;

// Generated message map functions
protected:
    //{{AFX_MSG(CMainFrame)
    afx_msg int OnCreate(LPCREATESTRUCT lpCreateStruct);
    afx_msg void OnUpdateCaptionNormal(CCmdUI* pCmdUI);
    afx_msg void OnCaptionNormal();
    afx_msg void OnUpdateCaptionColor(CCmdUI* pCmdUI);
    afx_msg void OnCaptionColor();
    afx_msg void OnUpdateCaptionBitmapWood(CCmdUI* pCmdUI);
    afx_msg void OnCaptionBitmapWood();
    afx_msg void OnUpdateCaptionBitmapStars(CCmdUI* pCmdUI);
    afx_msg void OnCaptionBitmapStars();
    afx_msg void OnUpdateCaptionBitmapSpots(CCmdUI* pCmdUI);
```

III

8

```
    afx_msg void OnCaptionBitmapSpots();
    afx_msg void OnUpdateCaptionDialog(CCmdUI* pCmdUI);
    afx_msg void OnCaptionDialog();
    afx_msg void OnUpdateCaptionBitmapBubbles(CCmdUI* pCmdUI);
    afx_msg void OnCaptionBitmapBubbles();
    afx_msg void OnUpdateCaptionBitmapGranite(CCmdUI* pCmdUI);
    afx_msg void OnCaptionBitmapGranite();
    afx_msg void OnUpdateCaptionBitmapRedbrick(CCmdUI* pCmdUI);
    afx_msg void OnCaptionBitmapRedbrick();
  //}}AFX_MSG
  DECLARE_MESSAGE_MAP()
};

/////////////////////////////////////////////////////////////////

//{{AFX_INSERT_LOCATION}}

#endif

// MainFrm.cpp : implementation of the CMainFrame class

#include "stdafx.h"
#include "FrameTest.h"

#include "MainFrm.h"
#include "SelectColors.h"
#include "ErrorDlg.h"

#ifdef _DEBUG
#define new DEBUG_NEW
#undef THIS_FILE
static char THIS_FILE[] = __FILE__;
#endif

/////////////////////////////////////////////////////////////////
// CMainFrame
```

```
IMPLEMENT_DYNAMIC(CMainFrame, CMDIFrameWnd)

BEGIN_MESSAGE_MAP(CMainFrame, CMDIFrameWnd)
    //{{AFX_MSG_MAP(CMainFrame)
    ON_WM_CREATE()
    ON_UPDATE_COMMAND_UI(ID_CAPTION_NORMAL, OnUpdateCaptionNormal)
    ON_COMMAND(ID_CAPTION_NORMAL, OnCaptionNormal)
    ON_UPDATE_COMMAND_UI(ID_CAPTION_COLOR, OnUpdateCaptionColor)
    ON_COMMAND(ID_CAPTION_COLOR, OnCaptionColor)
    ON_UPDATE_COMMAND_UI(ID_CAPTION_BITMAP_WOOD,
        OnUpdateCaptionBitmapWood)
    ON_COMMAND(ID_CAPTION_BITMAP_WOOD, OnCaptionBitmapWood)
    ON_UPDATE_COMMAND_UI(ID_CAPTION_BITMAP_STARS,
        OnUpdateCaptionBitmapStars)
    ON_COMMAND(ID_CAPTION_BITMAP_STARS, OnCaptionBitmapStars)
    ON_UPDATE_COMMAND_UI(ID_CAPTION_BITMAP_SPOTS,
        OnUpdateCaptionBitmapSpots)
    ON_COMMAND(ID_CAPTION_BITMAP_SPOTS, OnCaptionBitmapSpots)
    ON_UPDATE_COMMAND_UI(ID_CAPTION_DIALOG, OnUpdateCaptionDialog)
    ON_COMMAND(ID_CAPTION_DIALOG, OnCaptionDialog)
    ON_UPDATE_COMMAND_UI(ID_CAPTION_BITMAP_BUBBLES,
        OnUpdateCaptionBitmapBubbles)
    ON_COMMAND(ID_CAPTION_BITMAP_BUBBLES, OnCaptionBitmapBubbles)
    ON_UPDATE_COMMAND_UI(ID_CAPTION_BITMAP_GRANITE,
        OnUpdateCaptionBitmapGranite)
    ON_COMMAND(ID_CAPTION_BITMAP_GRANITE, OnCaptionBitmapGranite)
    ON_UPDATE_COMMAND_UI(ID_CAPTION_BITMAP_REDBRICK,
        OnUpdateCaptionBitmapRedbrick)
    ON_COMMAND(ID_CAPTION_BITMAP_REDBRICK, OnCaptionBitmapRedbrick)
    //}}AFX_MSG_MAP
END_MESSAGE_MAP()

static UINT indicators[] =
{
    ID_SEPARATOR,              // status line indicator
    ID_INDICATOR_CAPS,
    ID_INDICATOR_NUM,
```

III

8

```
    ID_INDICATOR_SCRL,
};


/////////////////////////////////////////////////////////////
// CMainFrame construction/destruction

CMainFrame::CMainFrame()
{
    // TODO: add member initialization code here


}

CMainFrame::~CMainFrame()
{
}

int CMainFrame::OnCreate(LPCREATESTRUCT lpCreateStruct)
{
    if (CMDIFrameWnd::OnCreate(lpCreateStruct) == -1)
        return -1;

    if (!m_wndToolBar.Create(this) ||
        !m_wndToolBar.LoadToolBar(IDR_MAINFRAME))
    {
        TRACE0("Failed to create toolbar\n");
        return -1;      // fail to create
    }

    if (!m_wndStatusBar.Create(this) ||
        !m_wndStatusBar.SetIndicators(indicators,
          sizeof(indicators)/sizeof(UINT)))
    {
        TRACE0("Failed to create status bar\n");
        return -1;      // fail to create
    }

    // TODO: Remove this if you don't want tool tips or a resizeable
```

```
    // toolbar
    m_wndToolBar.SetBarStyle(m_wndToolBar.GetBarStyle() |
        CBRS_TOOLTIPS | CBRS_FLYBY | CBRS_SIZE_DYNAMIC);

    // TODO: Delete these three lines if you don't want the toolbar to
    //   be dockable
    m_wndToolBar.EnableDocking(CBRS_ALIGN_ANY);
    EnableDocking(CBRS_ALIGN_ANY);
    DockControlBar(&m_wndToolBar);

    // Subclass the Main window frame
    m_frmCaption.DoInstall(this);

    return 0;
}

BOOL CMainFrame::PreCreateWindow(CREATESTRUCT& cs)
{
    // TODO: Modify the Window class or styles here by modifying
    //   the CREATESTRUCT cs

    return CMDIFrameWnd::PreCreateWindow(cs);
}

////////////////////////////////////////////////////////////////////
// CMainFrame diagnostics

#ifdef _DEBUG
void CMainFrame::AssertValid() const
{
    CMDIFrameWnd::AssertValid();
}

void CMainFrame::Dump(CDumpContext& dc) const
{
    CMDIFrameWnd::Dump(dc);
}
```

III

8

```
#endif //_DEBUG

/////////////////////////////////////////////////////////////
// CMainFrame message handlers

void CMainFrame::OnUpdateCaptionNormal(CCmdUI* pCmdUI)
{
    pCmdUI->Enable();
}

void CMainFrame::OnCaptionNormal()
{
    // Set the Frame back to our "Normal"
    m_frmCaption.SetNormal();
}

void CMainFrame::OnUpdateCaptionColor(CCmdUI* pCmdUI)
{
    pCmdUI->Enable();
}

void CMainFrame::OnCaptionColor()
{
    // Get the colors the User wants
    CSelectColors dlgColors;

    if (IDCANCEL == dlgColors.DoModal())
        return;

    if (dlgColors.GetGradientNum() > 1)
        m_frmCaption.SetGradient(dlgColors.GetActiveColor(),
            dlgColors.GetInactiveColor(), dlgColors.GetGradientNum());
    else
        m_frmCaption.SetColor(dlgColors.GetActiveColor(),
            dlgColors.GetInactiveColor());
}
```

```
void CMainFrame::OnUpdateCaptionBitmapWood(CCmdUI* pCmdUI)
{
    pCmdUI->Enable();
}
```

```
void CMainFrame::OnCaptionBitmapWood()
{
    m_frmCaption.SetBitmaps(AfxGetResourceHandle(),
        IDB_WOOD_ACTIVE, IDB_WOOD_INACTIVE);
}
```

```
void CMainFrame::OnUpdateCaptionBitmapStars(CCmdUI* pCmdUI)
{
    pCmdUI->Enable();
}
```

```
void CMainFrame::OnCaptionBitmapStars()
{
    m_frmCaption.SetBitmaps(AfxGetResourceHandle(),
        IDB_STARS_ACTIVE, IDB_STARS_INACTIVE);
}
```

```
void CMainFrame::OnUpdateCaptionBitmapSpots(CCmdUI* pCmdUI)
{
    pCmdUI->Enable();
}
```

```
void CMainFrame::OnCaptionBitmapSpots()
{
    m_frmCaption.SetBitmaps(AfxGetResourceHandle(),
        IDB_SPOTS_ACTIVE, IDB_SPOTS_INACTIVE);
}
```

```
void CMainFrame::OnUpdateCaptionDialog(CCmdUI* pCmdUI)
{
    pCmdUI->Enable();
}
```

III

8

```
void CMainFrame::OnCaptionDialog()
{
    CErrorDlg errDlg;

    errDlg.DoModal();
}
```

```
void CMainFrame::OnUpdateCaptionBitmapBubbles(CCmdUI* pCmdUI)
{
    pCmdUI->Enable();
}
```

```
void CMainFrame::OnCaptionBitmapBubbles()
{
    m_frmCaption.SetBitmaps(AfxGetResourceHandle(),
        IDB_BUBBLES_ACTIVE, IDB_BUBBLES_INACTIVE);
}
```

```
void CMainFrame::OnUpdateCaptionBitmapGranite(CCmdUI* pCmdUI)
{
    pCmdUI->Enable();
}
```

```
void CMainFrame::OnCaptionBitmapGranite()
{
    m_frmCaption.SetBitmaps(AfxGetResourceHandle(),
        IDB_GRANITE_ACTIVE, IDB_GRANITE_INACTIVE);
}
```

```
void CMainFrame::OnUpdateCaptionBitmapRedbrick(CCmdUI* pCmdUI)
{
    pCmdUI->Enable();
}
```

```
void CMainFrame::OnCaptionBitmapRedbrick()
{
```

```
        m_frmCaption.SetBitmaps(AfxGetResourceHandle(),
            IDB_REDBRICK_ACTIVE, IDB_REDBRICK_INACTIVE);
    }
```

```
// ChildFrm.h : interface of the CChildFrame class
//
///////////////////////////////////////////////////////////////

class CChildFrame : public CMDIChildWnd
{
    DECLARE_DYNCREATE(CChildFrame)
public:
    CChildFrame();

// Attributes
public:
    CXSCaption       m_frmCaption;

// Operations
public:

// Overrides
    // ClassWizard generated virtual function overrides
    //{{AFX_VIRTUAL(CChildFrame)
    virtual BOOL PreCreateWindow(CREATESTRUCT& cs);
    //}}AFX_VIRTUAL

// Implementation
public:
    virtual ~CChildFrame();
#ifdef _DEBUG
    virtual void AssertValid() const;
    virtual void Dump(CDumpContext& dc) const;
#endif

// Generated message map functions
protected:
```

III

8

```
        //{{AFX_MSG(CChildFrame)
        afx_msg int OnCreate(LPCREATESTRUCT lpCreateStruct);
        afx_msg void OnUpdateCaptionNormal(CCmdUI* pCmdUI);
        afx_msg void OnCaptionNormal();
        afx_msg void OnUpdateCaptionColor(CCmdUI* pCmdUI);
        afx_msg void OnCaptionColor();
        afx_msg void OnUpdateCaptionBitmapWood(CCmdUI* pCmdUI);
        afx_msg void OnCaptionBitmapWood();
        afx_msg void OnUpdateCaptionBitmapStars(CCmdUI* pCmdUI);
        afx_msg void OnCaptionBitmapStars();
        afx_msg void OnUpdateCaptionBitmapSpots(CCmdUI* pCmdUI);
        afx_msg void OnCaptionBitmapSpots();
        afx_msg void OnUpdateCaptionBitmapBubbles(CCmdUI* pCmdUI);
        afx_msg void OnCaptionBitmapBubbles();
        afx_msg void OnUpdateCaptionBitmapGranite(CCmdUI* pCmdUI);
        afx_msg void OnCaptionBitmapGranite();
        afx_msg void OnUpdateCaptionBitmapRedbrick(CCmdUI* pCmdUI);
        afx_msg void OnCaptionBitmapRedbrick();
        //}}AFX_MSG
        DECLARE_MESSAGE_MAP()
};


/////////////////////////////////////////////////////////////////


//{{AFX_INSERT_LOCATION}}

#endif

// ChildFrm.cpp : implementation of the CChildFrame class

#include "stdafx.h"
#include "FrameTest.h"

#include "ChildFrm.h"
#include "SelectColors.h"

#ifdef _DEBUG
```

```
#define new DEBUG_NEW
#undef THIS_FILE
static char THIS_FILE[] = __FILE__;
#endif


/////////////////////////////////////////////////////////////////
// CChildFrame


IMPLEMENT_DYNCREATE(CChildFrame, CMDIChildWnd)


BEGIN_MESSAGE_MAP(CChildFrame, CMDIChildWnd)
    //{{AFX_MSG_MAP(CChildFrame)
    ON_WM_CREATE()
    ON_UPDATE_COMMAND_UI(ID_CAPTION_NORMAL, OnUpdateCaptionNormal)
    ON_COMMAND(ID_CAPTION_NORMAL, OnCaptionNormal)
    ON_UPDATE_COMMAND_UI(ID_CAPTION_COLOR, OnUpdateCaptionColor)
    ON_COMMAND(ID_CAPTION_COLOR, OnCaptionColor)
    ON_UPDATE_COMMAND_UI(ID_CAPTION_BITMAP_WOOD,
        OnUpdateCaptionBitmapWood)
    ON_COMMAND(ID_CAPTION_BITMAP_WOOD, OnCaptionBitmapWood)
    ON_UPDATE_COMMAND_UI(ID_CAPTION_BITMAP_STARS,
        OnUpdateCaptionBitmapStars)
    ON_COMMAND(ID_CAPTION_BITMAP_STARS, OnCaptionBitmapStars)
    ON_UPDATE_COMMAND_UI(ID_CAPTION_BITMAP_SPOTS,
        OnUpdateCaptionBitmapSpots)
    ON_COMMAND(ID_CAPTION_BITMAP_SPOTS, OnCaptionBitmapSpots)
    ON_UPDATE_COMMAND_UI(ID_CAPTION_BITMAP_BUBBLES,
        OnUpdateCaptionBitmapBubbles)
    ON_COMMAND(ID_CAPTION_BITMAP_BUBBLES, OnCaptionBitmapBubbles)
    ON_UPDATE_COMMAND_UI(ID_CAPTION_BITMAP_GRANITE,
        OnUpdateCaptionBitmapGranite)
    ON_COMMAND(ID_CAPTION_BITMAP_GRANITE, OnCaptionBitmapGranite)
    ON_UPDATE_COMMAND_UI(ID_CAPTION_BITMAP_REDBRICK,
        OnUpdateCaptionBitmapRedbrick)
    ON_COMMAND(ID_CAPTION_BITMAP_REDBRICK, OnCaptionBitmapRedbrick)
    //}}AFX_MSG_MAP
END_MESSAGE_MAP()
```

III

8

```
///////////////////////////////////////////////////////////
// CChildFrame construction/destruction

CChildFrame::CChildFrame()
{
    // TODO: add member initialization code here

}

CChildFrame::~CChildFrame()
{
}

BOOL CChildFrame::PreCreateWindow(CREATESTRUCT& cs)
{
    // TODO: Modify the Window class or styles here by modifying
    //  the CREATESTRUCT cs

    return CMDIChildWnd::PreCreateWindow(cs);
}

///////////////////////////////////////////////////////////
// CChildFrame diagnostics

#ifdef _DEBUG
void CChildFrame::AssertValid() const
{
    CMDIChildWnd::AssertValid();
}

void CChildFrame::Dump(CDumpContext& dc) const
{
    CMDIChildWnd::Dump(dc);
}

#endif //_DEBUG
```

```
/////////////////////////////////////////////////////////////////////
// CChildFrame message handlers

int CChildFrame::OnCreate(LPCREATESTRUCT lpCreateStruct)
{
    if (CMDIChildWnd::OnCreate(lpCreateStruct) == -1)
        return -1;

    // Subclass the Child window frame
    m_frmCaption.DoInstall(this);

    return 0;
}

void CChildFrame::OnUpdateCaptionNormal(CCmdUI* pCmdUI)
{
    pCmdUI->Enable();
}

void CChildFrame::OnCaptionNormal()
{
    // Set the Frame back to our "Normal"
    m_frmCaption.SetNormal();
}

void CChildFrame::OnUpdateCaptionColor(CCmdUI* pCmdUI)
{
    pCmdUI->Enable();
}

void CChildFrame::OnCaptionColor()
{
    // Get the colors the User wants
    CSelectColors dlgColors;

    if (IDCANCEL == dlgColors.DoModal())
```

```
        return;

    if (dlgColors.GetGradientNum() > 1)
        m_frmCaption.SetGradient(dlgColors.GetActiveColor(),
            dlgColors.GetInactiveColor(), dlgColors.GetGradientNum());
    else
        m_frmCaption.SetColor(dlgColors.GetActiveColor(),
            dlgColors.GetInactiveColor());
}
```

```
void CChildFrame::OnUpdateCaptionBitmapWood(CCmdUI* pCmdUI)
{
    pCmdUI->Enable();
}
```

```
void CChildFrame::OnCaptionBitmapWood()
{
    m_frmCaption.SetBitmaps(AfxGetResourceHandle(),
        IDB_WOOD_ACTIVE, IDB_WOOD_INACTIVE);
}
```

```
void CChildFrame::OnUpdateCaptionBitmapStars(CCmdUI* pCmdUI)
{
    pCmdUI->Enable();
}
```

```
void CChildFrame::OnCaptionBitmapStars()
{
    m_frmCaption.SetBitmaps(AfxGetResourceHandle(),
        IDB_STARS_ACTIVE, IDB_STARS_INACTIVE);
}
```

```
void CChildFrame::OnUpdateCaptionBitmapSpots(CCmdUI* pCmdUI)
{
    pCmdUI->Enable();
}
```

```
void CChildFrame::OnCaptionBitmapSpots()
{
    m_frmCaption.SetBitmaps(AfxGetResourceHandle(),
        IDB_SPOTS_ACTIVE, IDB_SPOTS_INACTIVE);
}
```

```
void CChildFrame::OnUpdateCaptionBitmapBubbles(CCmdUI* pCmdUI)
{
    pCmdUI->Enable();
}
```

```
void CChildFrame::OnCaptionBitmapBubbles()
{
    m_frmCaption.SetBitmaps(AfxGetResourceHandle(),
        IDB_BUBBLES_ACTIVE, IDB_BUBBLES_INACTIVE);
}
```

```
void CChildFrame::OnUpdateCaptionBitmapGranite(CCmdUI* pCmdUI)
{
    pCmdUI->Enable();
}
```

```
void CChildFrame::OnCaptionBitmapGranite()
{
    m_frmCaption.SetBitmaps(AfxGetResourceHandle(),
        IDB_GRANITE_ACTIVE, IDB_GRANITE_INACTIVE);
}
```

III

8

```
void CChildFrame::OnUpdateCaptionBitmapRedbrick(CCmdUI* pCmdUI)
{
    pCmdUI->Enable();
}
```

```
void CChildFrame::OnCaptionBitmapRedbrick()
{
    m_frmCaption.SetBitmaps(AfxGetResourceHandle(),
        IDB_REDBRICK_ACTIVE, IDB_REDBRICK_INACTIVE);
}
```

Summary

In this chapter, we created a caption control, CXSCaption, for handling different variations of backgrounds and text for window caption bars. The class derives heavily on CXSBgCtrl, ourBackground Control created in the previous chapter.

Appendix A — Sample

API and Class Reference

This section includes a *sample* of the HTML appendix included on the CD-ROM — a complete API and Class Reference. The following graphic is used as a navigation tool to move you through the entire Class Hierarchy.

Class Hierarchy

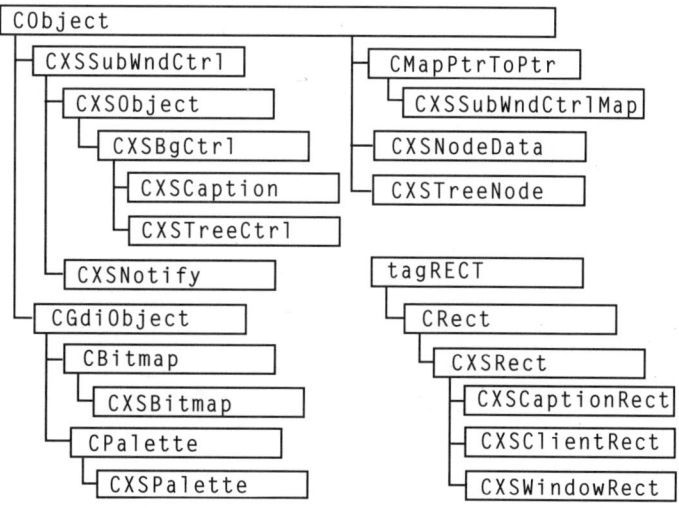

API Functions and Macros

This part of the appendix contains reference information to the API functions and macro declarations used by this extension library. For the sake of clarity, I'll quickly review the naming conventions used with the APIs and macros that was discussed earlier in Chapter 1.

For API functions, the structure of a function name is XS<Ownership>_<FunctionName>. For example, the function that creates a palette from a DIB (Device Independent Bitmap) is named XSDib_CreatePalette. This structure makes the source function calls very readable and identifies ownership. Ownership is the function of type (e.g. XSDib_CreatePalette is owned by the DIB API). The XS stands for the web site my wife and I own called Xendra Software.

Macro names, set up by the #define statement, are usually all upper-case. If macro names are mixed case, they have a mac prefix (i.e. mac<Name>). For instance, the DIB API uses the macro macDibHeaderMarker to verify whether a DIB has the bitmap marker. Macros that are mixed case usually take arguments, whereas macros that are all upper case are used for comparison purposes only.

macDibHeaderMarker

The macDibHeaderMarker macro can be used to fill in the bitmap header marker or test an existing marker for a bitmap type.

```
macDibHeaderMarker
```

Parameters

None.

Returns

Nothing.

Remarks

This macro may be used as in the following examples:

Example 1

```
BITMAPFILEHEADER bmfHdr; // Header for Bitmap file

// Fill in file type
// (first 2 bytes must be "BM" for a bitmap)
bmfHdr.bfType = macDibHeaderMarker; // "BM"
```

Example 2

```
// Verify BITMAP type
if (bmfHdr.bfType != macDibHeaderMarker)
{
    CallErrorFunction();
    return FALSE;
}
```

macDibWidthBytes

The `macDibWidthBytes` macro calculates the bytes per line based on the passed bit count.

```
DWORD
macDibWidthBytes( DWORD dwBits );
```

Parameters

dwBits	Number of bits per scanline

Returns

The number of bytes needed per scanline of a DIB.

Remarks

DIBs are `DWORD` aligned. This macro helps figure out the number of bytes actually needed to fit the `DWORD` boundary imposed by DIBs.

See Also

XSDib_Create | XSDib_CalcBytesPerLine | XSDib_CalcPadding

macIsWinDib

The `macIsWinDib` macro tests for a Windows-style DIB.

```
BOOL
macIsWinDib( LPVOID lpDIB );
```

Parameters

`lpDIB`	Pointer to a packed DIB memory block.

Returns

`TRUE` if the passed pointer represents a true Windows-style DIB. Otherwise, it returns `FALSE`.

Remarks

This macro fails on OS/2-style DIBs.

XSBmp_ChangeFormat

The `XSBmp_ChangeFormat` function converts a DDB to a DIB, while at the same time converting the number of BPP (Bits Per Pixel).

```
HDIB
XSBmp_ChangeFormat( HBITMAP hBitmap, WORD wBitCount, DWORD
dwCompression, HPALETTE hPal );
```

Parameters

hBitmap	(HBITMAP) — Handle to the DDB to convert.
wBitCount	(WORD) — The desired BPP (Bits Per Pixel). May be 0 if you pass BI_RLE4 or BI_RLE8 for dwCompression.
dwCompression	(DWORD) — The desired compression format. Acceptable values are:

Value	Meaning
BI_RLE4	Use with 4 BPP
BI_RLE8	Use with 8 BPP
BI_RGB	Use with 1, 4, 8, 16, 24, or 32 BPP

hPal	(HPALETTE) — Handle to the bitmap's associated palette.

Returns

If the function succeeds, the return value is the handle to the new DIB. If the function fails, the return value is NULL. To get extended error information call XSError_Get.

Remarks

The original HBITMAP is not deleted by this function.

See Also

XSDib_ChangeFormat | XSDib_ToBmp | XSBmp_ToDib | XSError_Get

XSBmp_Load

The XSBmp_Load function loads a bitmap from a specified resource file.

```
HBITMAP
XSBmp_Load( HINSTANCE hInst, UINT nID );
```

Parameters

hInst	Handle to the resource file that contains the bitmap.
nID	ID of the bitmap resource to load.

Returns

If the function succeeds, the return value is the handle to the new DDB. If the function fails, the return value is NULL. To get extended error information call XSError_Get.

See Also

XSDib_Load | XSDib_ReadFile | XSDib_Save | XSDib_WriteFile | CXSBitmap::DoLoad | CXSBitmap::DoSerialize | XSError_Get

XSBmp_ToDib

The XSBmp_ToDib function converts a Device Dependant Bitmap (DDB) to a Device Independant Bitmap (DIB).

```
HDIB
XSBmp_ToDib( HBITMAP hBitmap, HPALETTE hPal );
```

Parameters

hBitmap	Handle to the DDB to convert.
hPal	Handle to the bitmap's associated palette. If NULL is used here, a halftone palette will be created.

Returns

If the function succeeds, the return value is the handle to the new DIB. If the function fails, the return value is NULL. To get extended error information call XSError_Get.

Remarks

The original HBITMAP is not deleted by this function.

See Also

XSDib_ToBmp | XSDib_ChangeFormat | XSBmp_ChangeFormat | XSError_Get

XSCaption_SetText

The XSCaption_SetText function sets the caption text with an option to defer immediate update.

```
BOOL
XSCaption_SetText( HWND hWnd, LPCTSTR lpText, BOOL bRedraw =
TRUE);
```

Parameters

hWnd	Handle to the window for which the caption text is to be changed.
lpText	The text to insert into the caption.
bRedraw	TRUE to redraw the caption text immediately, FALSE to defer the caption text painting. Default = TRUE.

Returns

If the function succeeds, the return value is TRUE. If the function fails, the return value is FALSE.

Remarks

If the window does not have the WS_CAPTION flag set then this function will return FALSE.

XSColor_GetLuminosity

The XSColor_GetLuminosity function returns the luminosity value of the passed COLORREF.

```
int
XSColor_GetLuminosity( COLORREF crColor );
```

Parameters

crColor	The color for which a luminosity value is needed.

Returns

The luminosity value of the passed COLORREF.

XSDib_CalcBytesPerLine

The XSDib_CalcBytesPerLine function calculates the bytes per line required for DWORD alignment.

```
DWORD
XSDib_CalcBytesPerLine( DWORD dwBitsPerPixel, DWORD dwWidth )
```

Parameters

dwBitsPerPixel	Count of bits per pixel (BPP).
dwWidth	Source width.

Returns

The exact number of bytes needed to be DWORD aligned.

Remarks

DIB scanlines are aligned on DWORD boundaries. Therefore, when the actual bits of the DIB are manipulated, it is necessary to determine how many more bytes are required for proper DWORD alignment. Whereas XSDib_CalcPadding determines how many more bytes are needed for DWORD alignment, XSDib_CalcBytesPerLine determines the total number of actual bytes needed for a DWORD aligned boundary.

See Also

XSDib_LastByte | XSDib_CalcPadding

XSDib_CalcPadding

The XSDib_CalcPadding function calculates the number of pad bytes needed for DWORD alignment.

```
DWORD
XSDib_CalcPadding( DWORD dwBitsPerPixel, DWORD dwPixels );
```

Parameters

dwBitsPerPixel	Count of bits per pixel (BPP).
dwPixels	Source width.

Returns

The exact number of pad bytes needed to be DWORD aligned.

Remarks

DIB scanlines are aligned on DWORD boundaries. Therefore, when the actual bits of the DIB are manipulated, it is necessary to determine how many more bytes are required for proper DWORD alignment. Whereas XSDib_CalcBytesPerLine determines the total number of actual bytes needed for a DWORD aligned boundary, XSDib_CalcPadding determines how many more bytes are needed for DWORD alignment.

See Also

XSDib_CalcBytesPerLine | XSDib_LastByte

...

NOTE: For a *complete* listing of the classes contained in Appendix A on the CD-ROM, see the following section, "API and Class Reference Contents," beginning on page 493.

API and Class Reference Contents

CXSObject::OnMButtonUp
CXSObject::OnMdiActivate
CXSObject::OnMdiCascade
CXSObject::OnMdiCreate
CXSObject::OnMdiDestroy
CXSObject::OnMdiGetActive
CXSObject::OnMdiIconArrange
CXSObject::OnMdiMaximize
CXSObject::OnMdiNext
CXSObject::OnMdiRefreshMenu
CXSObject::OnMdiRestore
CXSObject::OnMdiSetMenu
CXSObject::OnMdiTile
CXSObject::OnMeasureItem
CXSObject::OnMenuChar
CXSObject::OnMenuSelect
CXSObject::OnMonCalGetDayState
CXSObject::OnMonCalSelChange
CXSObject::OnMonCalSelect
CXSObject::OnMouseActivate
CXSObject::OnMouseHover
CXSObject::OnMouseLeave
CXSObject::OnMouseMove
CXSObject::OnMouseWheel
CXSObject::OnMove
CXSObject::OnMoving
CXSObject::OnNcActivate
CXSObject::OnNcCalcSize
CXSObject::OnNcCreate
CXSObject::OnNcDestroy
CXSObject::OnNcHitTest
CXSObject::OnNcLButtonDblClk
CXSObject::OnNcLButtonDown
CXSObject::OnNcLButtonUp
CXSObject::OnNcMButtonDblClk
CXSObject::OnNcMButtonDown
CXSObject::OnNcMButtonUp
CXSObject::OnNcMouseHover
CXSObject::OnNcMouseLeave
CXSObject::OnNcMouseMove
CXSObject::OnNcPaint
CXSObject::OnNcRButtonDblClk
CXSObject::OnNcRButtonDown
CXSObject::OnNcRButtonUp
CXSObject::OnNextDlgCtl
CXSObject::OnNextMenu
CXSObject::OnNotify

CXSObject::OnNotifyChar
CXSObject::OnNotifyClick
CXSObject::OnNotifyCustomDraw
CXSObject::OnNotifyDblClk
CXSObject::OnNotifyFormat
CXSObject::OnNotifyHover
CXSObject::OnNotifyKeyDown
CXSObject::OnNotifyKillFocus
CXSObject::OnNotifyNcHitTest
CXSObject::OnNotifyOutOfMemory
CXSObject::OnNotifyRClick
CXSObject::OnNotifyRDblClk
CXSObject::OnNotifyReleasedCapture
CXSObject::OnNotifyReturn
CXSObject::OnNotifySetCursor
CXSObject::OnNotifySetFocus
CXSObject::OnPagerCalcSize
CXSObject::OnPagerScroll
CXSObject::OnPaint
CXSObject::OnPaintClipboard
CXSObject::OnPaintIcon
CXSObject::OnPaletteChanged
CXSObject::OnPaletteIsChanging
CXSObject::OnPaste
CXSObject::OnPopMessageString
CXSObject::OnPower
CXSObject::OnPowerBroadcast
CXSObject::OnPreNcDestroy
CXSObject::OnPrint
CXSObject::OnPrintClient
CXSObject::OnPropSheetApply
CXSObject::OnPropSheetGetObject
CXSObject::OnPropSheetHelp
CXSObject::OnPropSheetKillActive
CXSObject::OnPropSheetQueryCancel
CXSObject::OnPropSheetReset
CXSObject::OnPropSheetSetActive
CXSObject::OnPropSheetWizBack
CXSObject::OnPropSheetWizFinish
CXSObject::OnPropSheetWizNext
CXSObject::OnQuery
CXSObject::OnQueryAfxWndProc
CXSObject::OnQueryCenterWnd
CXSObject::OnQueryDragIcon
CXSObject::OnQueryEndSession

B

Appendix B

Bibliography

Blaszczak, M. *Professional MFC with Visual C++ 5*. Wrox Press,1997.

DiLascia, Paul. "C++ Q&A," *Microsoft Systems Journal* (Jun. 1997).

DiLascia, Paul. "More Fun with MFC: DIBs, Palettes, Subclassing, and a Gamut of Reusable Goodies," *Microsoft Systems Journal* (Jan. 1997).

Gery, Ron. "Bitmaps with Transparency," *Microsoft Developer Network Technology Group* (Jun. 1992).

Gery, Ron. "DIBs and Their Use," *Microsoft Developer Network Technology Group* (Mar. 1992).

Gery, Ron. "Using DIBs with Palettes," *Microsoft Developer Network Technology Group* (Mar. 1992).

Kay, David C., and John R. Levine, *Graphics File Formats, 2nd Edition*. McGraw-Hill, Inc.,1995.

Marsh, Kyle. "Safe Subclassing in Win32," *Microsoft Developer Network Technology Group* (Jan. 1994).

Microsoft Knowledge Base, *Converting Between Device-Dependent Bitmaps and DIBs* Q80080 (Jan. 1995).

Microsoft Knowledge Base, *Converting Colors Between RGB and HLS (HBS)* Q29240 (Nov. 1995).

Microsoft Knowledge Base, *Drawing Transparent Bitmaps* Q79212 (Aug. 1996).

Microsoft Knowledge Base, *GetDeviceCaps(hDC, RASTERCAPS) Description* Q75912 (Nov. 1995).

Microsoft Knowledge Base, *How to Draw a Custom Window Caption* Q99046 (Nov. 1995).

Microsoft Knowledge Base, *How to Draw a Gradient Background* Q128637 (Sep. 1995).

Microsoft Knowledge Base, *How to Use a DIB Stored as a Windows Resource* Q67883 (Nov. 1995).

Microsoft Knowledge Base, *How To Use LoadImage() to Read a BMP File* Q158898 (Nov. 1996).

Microsoft Knowledge Base, *Retrieving Palette Information from a Bitmap Resource* Q124947 (Nov. 1996).

Microsoft Knowledge Base, *SAMPLE: 16 and 32 Bits-Per-Pel Bitmap Formats* Q94326 (Sep. 1996).

Microsoft Knowledge Base, *SAMPLE: DIBs and Their Uses* Q81498 (Aug. 1996).

Microsoft Knowledge Base, *Using SetDIBitsToDevice() with a Memory Device Context* Q66595 (May 1995).

Schroeder, W.; K. Martin; B. Lorensen. *The Visualization Toolkit, 2nd Edition: An Object-Oriented Approach to 3D Graphics*. Prentice Hall PTR,1998.

Index

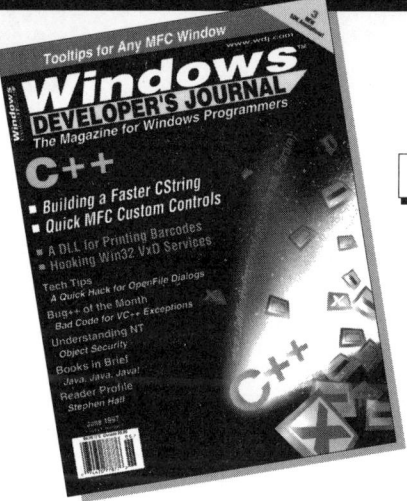

What's on the CD-ROM?

Supercharge MFC is accompanied by the companion CD-ROM which includes much more than just the programming code. It contains example programs that demonstrate the functionality of each class extension. Also included are classes that didn't make it in time to be in the book. You will find that the CD has pre-built libraries and DLLs so you can start using the functionality presented in the book immediately.

Also on the CD-ROM is the HTML file of Appendix A — a complete API and Class Reference. The following diagram is used as an imagemap to guide you through the entire Class Hierarchy.

Class Hierarchy

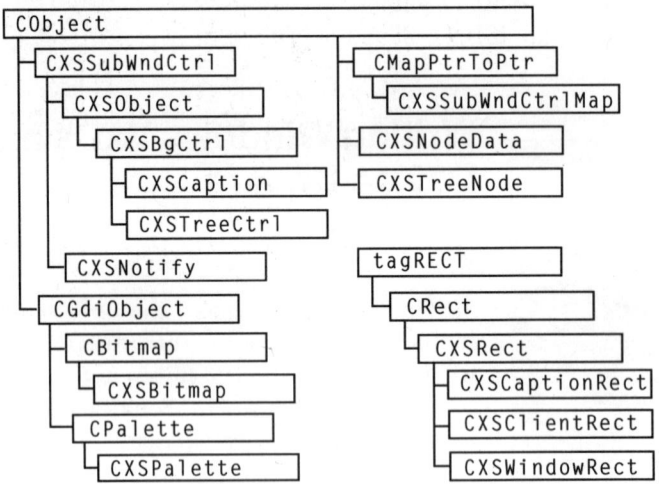

Everything in the book and CD has been written and tested on Windows 95 and Windows NT 4.0, with Visual C++ 5.0 and Visual C++ 6.0. No other platforms or compilers have been thoroughly tested with the code and samples included with this book.

For more information on the CD-ROM's contents and specifications, see the Introduction to **Supercharge MFC**.
